Freedom

T0005796

'Profoundly essential and deeply engaging. If freedom of thought and the very possibility of a free society are to survive the digital century, then we urgently need the rights and laws that will make it so. Thankfully, Alegre stands with us to lead and light the way, beginning with her compelling, powerful and necessary book.'

Shoshana Zuboff, author of
The Age of Surveillance Capitalism

'A brilliant, accessible book by a brilliant lawyer. Freedom of thought is a fundamental human right and Susie Alegre powerfully argues that it needs to be harnessed now.'

Helena Kennedy KC, author of *Eve was Framed*

'Powerful and persuasive. This important, finely written book explains why we must protect that most fundamental of our freedoms at a time when it is in danger of being overborne by profit-making propaganda, fake news and hate-fuelled social media.'

Geoffrey Robertson KC,
founder of Doughty Street Chambers

ABOUT THE AUTHOR

Susie Alegre is a leading human rights barrister and Associate at the internationally renowned Doughty Street Chambers. She has been a legal pioneer in digital human rights, in particular the impact of artificial intelligence on the human rights to freedom of thought and opinion. She is also Senior Research Fellow at the University of Roehampton and Senior Fellow at the Centre for International Governance Innovation. She lives in London.

Freedom to Think

Protecting a Fundamental Human Right in the Digital Age

SUSIE ALEGRE

Atlantic Books
London

First published in Great Britain in 2022 by Atlantic Books, an imprint of Atlantic Books Ltd.

This paperback edition published in 2023.

10 9 8 7 6 5 4 3 2

A CIP catalogue record for this book is available from the British Library.

Paperback ISBN: 978-1-83895-155-9
E-book ISBN: 978-1-83895-154-2

Printed in Great Britain by Clays Ltd, Elcograf S.p.A.

Atlantic Books
An imprint of Atlantic Books Ltd
Ormond House
26–27 Boswell Street
London
WC1N 3JZ

www.atlantic-books.co.uk

MIX
Paper from
responsible sources
FSC
www.fsc.org FSC® C018072

"To the past, to the future,
to a time when thought is free…"

George Orwell, *Nineteen Eighty-Four*

For my parents and my daughter.

CONTENTS

———

INTRODUCTION

—

THE BEST OF ALL POSSIBLE WORLDS

1989 was a year of turmoil, optimism and excitement. It was the year Tim Berners-Lee invented the World Wide Web and the year I turned 18 – one of the last of a generation to live their entire childhood offline. A generation for whom privacy meant trusting your mother not to read your diary and 'thought control' was a Pink Floyd lyric.

As I crammed existential angst from Sartre and Camus and memorised the names and dates of French revolutionaries, Nazi propagandists and English kings, images of resistance from the other side of the world flashed across TV screens as protesters in Tiananmen Square fought for their chance to experience democracy and freedom. Their protest was crushed, but it was only the first act in a year that proved that the eternal fight for human freedom was far from over.

That summer, I joined the crowds on the streets of Paris to celebrate a turning point in that struggle, 200 years earlier, when the French had chosen *liberté, égalité, fraternité* as the foundations of a revolutionary new world order based on democracy and human rights. Thirty years on from the bicentenary, I might have found somewhere to stay through an app, and there would have been a selfie of me smiling by the Eiffel Tower that all my friends could 'like'. But in 1989, there was no accommodation to be had and I didn't feel that I needed any record to show that I was there on the Champs-Elysées, part of the throng of idealists and opportunistic party people celebrating the turbulent history of human freedom. So now I have only the memory of opening myself up to Camus' 'benign indifference of the world' as I slept under a bush by the banks of the Seine, a riverside that was peppered with dog turds but filled with hope and history.

Three months later, the Berlin Wall fell. This time, freedom really had won. The long shadow of twentieth-century totalitarian rule in Germany was erased in a blaze of fireworks. Germany was finally united and could begin to repair its divided soul after almost 60 years of the authoritarian horrors wreaked by both Nazi and communist social control.

While Europe was experiencing the practical rebirth of liberty, I pored over its theoretical foundations in the brutalist atmosphere of Edinburgh University's library. J. S. Mill's *On Liberty* and the Socratic dialogue of Plato's *Republic* taught me to think seriously about what it means to be human, while I revelled in the eternally misplaced optimism of Voltaire's *Candide* and discovered the infinite flavours of the 'water of life' in dark, smoky Edinburgh bars. I read voraciously and eclectically. But struggling to navigate the library index cards and taking notes on pads of A4 ruled paper, my explorations of Jung's dream analysis, virgin birth in the Trobriand Islands and the hidden meanings of French folk tales left no virtual trace of my thought processes for others to track. There was no assessment of my thinking beyond my tutor's notes in the margin of last-minute essays, scribbled through the long, dark Edinburgh winter nights. It was a delight that year finally to be free to think and to drink and to wallow in hopeless unrequited love.

There was a boy. Not the kind I would want my daughter to fall for – he was unreliable and disaster-prone though he was undoubtedly intellectual, anarchic and exciting. He had taken me to Paris, and that Christmas he asked me to lend him money so he could go to the biggest New Year's Eve party ever in a freshly unified Berlin. But in a moment of self-possession, I decided that if I could get the money, I'd rather use it to go myself instead. Always resourceful and persuasive, he found the funds elsewhere and told me he had sorted out accommodation so I didn't need to. We arranged to meet there.

On New Year's Eve 1989, frozen to the bone after twenty-four hours curled in the crushing cold of a midwinter train corridor, I found myself waiting with my friend for a boy in front of a slowly disintegrating Berlin Wall in a crowd that hummed with the collective joy of liberation. The boy never showed up. Ghosting was much, much easier without a mobile phone, and I should have seen it coming. He had already stood me up once late at night on the Côte d'Azur earlier that year. If I'd had a Facebook account, I would no doubt have set my relationship status to 'It's complicated'. But we don't need algorithms to make ridiculous romantic choices. And sometimes, being stood up on a freezing night in a foreign country is what we need to give us a glimpse of the best of all possible worlds.

Abandoned in the biggest freedom party on earth, my friend and I skipped back and forth through the wall all night, dancing, drinking, chipping away pieces of concrete history to carry home in our pockets. The kindness of strangers gave us a warm floor to sleep on when the fireworks died, and a view of the fundamental goodness of the world that we might have missed with the boy. It was much, much better than a bad date; it was a real date with a huge wave of historic hope for freedom and the still weeping sore of what it means for a whole country to lose it.

There are no photos of me at the Berlin Wall either, and the tiny piece of spray-painted concrete I took away as a memento is long gone, lost in the clutter of many house moves. There were no receipts, no card payments, no reservations, no emails, no messages – no proof that I was ever there at all, celebrating the new dawn of freedom and nursing a broken heart. The images are sepia-tinted by the lens of my memory alone. When I messaged my friend to ask what she remembered about the journey, she messaged me back: *There was bratwurst.* I was sure we ate Burger King, but bratwurst would have made an infinitely better Instagram post – had it existed.

I googled the boy to see if he was as I remembered. There's no trace online of the anarchic 18-year-old who fancied himself a modern-day Hemingway. All I found was a photo of a middle-aged doctor smiling out of a tableau of professional respectability. But would he be there now if 1989 had been lived online? Would the algorithms have concluded that medicine should be one of his interests, pushing the idea quietly into his consciousness through online advertising? Or would he have been considered too risky for financial support through his studies, based on a chaotic social media presence and erratic electronic spending patterns? Would the internet echo chamber have left him permanently washed up on the wilder shores of fecklessness? Or would the indelible records of his adolescent thoughts and the impressions he left on others have been held against him in a job interview? We were the last generation who could leave our adolescent thoughts, opinions and feelings behind us. Neither he, nor I, have been punished for our youthful ideas about freedom. Our children may not be so lucky.

Today, children are plugged into the online world from birth, with delightful social media photos, online baby-shower lists and nappy orders. Some children are even tracked before they are born with the help of pregnancy apps. And technology has become an incredible tool to help our children learn. One of my daughter's first 'words' was the tweeting finger sign for a bird she learned from an app, giving her the bridge to connect the noise outside with her internal world. When I travel for work, I can be simultaneously at home and in my hotel room, the beauty of technology keeping me connected to my loved ones across the seas with the power of screens. My daughter misses me, she says, but the screens make it difficult to concentrate, and usually, after 10 minutes of pulling faces at herself on the phone screen, the eternal loop of TV on demand wins and I'm left with a view of the underside of her chin before she disconnects.

The impact of the World Wide Web did not hit us suddenly like the fall of the Berlin wall in 1989. There is no 9 November to celebrate the technological revolution. Rather it has crept up on us like the slow and steady devastation of coastal erosion, each new wave of useful and entertaining tech chipping away at the walls of our consciousness until one day we woke up to discover that our mental geography had been fundamentally altered.

For me, the revelation came while scrolling mindlessly through Facebook on a dark winter night in January 2017. In among the Christmas holiday photos from beaches, mountains and brightly lit cityscapes around the world, I came across an article that made me sit up and think. It was a now infamous story about data, Brexit, Trump and Cambridge Analytica originally published in

German by Swiss investigative journalists on a small online news website.[1]

This article lit a light, a blue light that wouldn't let me sleep. I read and reread. I stepped away from the screen. I remembered the night of the Brexit referendum in June 2016, checking my Facebook account and going to bed early, sure that in the end, the European project that had been built with such hope on the ruins left by the Second World War would win the day. Facebook told me what I wanted to hear – after 20 years of work on human rights in Europe, everyone I knew on Twitter and Facebook agreed with me and I slept soundly. But somehow, in the morning, it was clear that the country did not agree with my Facebook feed. Could it be that my complacency had been curated? Had I been lulled into a false sense of security so that I would not see the need to speak up? Whether this was the case or not, the idea that this could be true – that my smartphone could be used as a portal to manipulate my mind – felt like a personal assault. That this could have been done en masse to manipulate the results of elections that could change our very futures was an existential threat to the democratic society I grew up in, and one that, at the time, worryingly few people were talking about.

Behavioural microtargeting is a technological tool to get inside our minds and rearrange the furniture. The idea that this could be happening, minute by minute, to affect the way we think, feel and behave is unthinkable. But what is even more worrying is that these techniques are not limited to the political sphere. This kind of profiling and targeting is worth billions, because profiling and targeting our minds to influence our thoughts sells things. What's for sale can be banal, like a choice of underwear; or profound, like a belief in the power of national sovereignty. In addition, these algorithmic processes are used to filter us out for opportunities for work, finance and love. And we feed them every time we do anything online. What shook me about the story was how easily our thoughts and opinions can be hacked on such a massive scale, and that little or nothing was being done to stop it.

The decisions we make, the ideas we have and our moods are all influenced by the people we meet. But there are some encounters that shift the dial and change the course of our lives. I had never planned to become a lawyer. At university, poetry, the more esoteric fringes of philosophy and even puppet theatre were the things that inspired me. But in 1995, working for a conflict resolution NGO in the Basque country in the north-west of Spain, I found myself interpreting for the internationally renowned human rights lawyer Professor Kieran McEvoy, doing comparative research on releasing politically motivated prisoners as part of the Northern Ireland peace process. In recently released government documents from around that time,[2] the Northern Ireland Office described him as 'biased and opinionated' and the organisation he worked for as 'fashionably radical rather than sinister'. Bias is a useful criticism of people you disagree with, but being opinionated and fashionably radical are both positives in my book. The influence that Kieran had on me, however, was much more profound than a passing fashion. Interpreting for him as he talked about human rights cases and raising community grievances in courts, it dawned on me that the law could be just as potent a force to change the world as the anger and burning buses I saw in the protests that choked the streets around me. It was a revelation that it could be exciting. For me, that was a turning point. Instead of my planned life of poetry in the Pyrenees, that summer I moved back to London and started studying for a life in the law, discovering in the process that, just like poetry, public international law is a distillation of the human condition.

I studied philosophy and languages at university because I wanted to understand how the world works and how we explain it in different ways. I hoped that reason and art would fill the void and explain humanity. But while I found the arguments of Mill, Locke and Hume interesting in an abstract way, philosophy left me empty. And though I loved French literature with a passion, particularly the exuberant excesses of Rabelais and Voltaire, I couldn't quite see how I could use it to put my own mark on the world. I became a human rights lawyer because it seemed to me that it was a way to work at the heart of what it means to be human, to make sense of the world and to create the kind of world I wanted to live in.

Over the past 25 years since qualifying, I have not been disappointed with my choice. I have prosecuted crimes that ruined victims' lives and represented people whose liberty hangs in the balance in criminal courts. I have challenged governments on heavy-handed responses to terrorism and advised diplomats on ways to stem corruption. It doesn't matter what the topic, human rights law lights the way for humane responses to the world's problems, big or small. For me, it made the ethics I studied in Edinburgh tangible. But when I started to look specifically at the right to freedom of thought, I finally found what I had been looking for when I chose to study philosophy – the key to what it means to be human.

The rights to freedom of thought, conscience, religion and belief and freedom of opinion are absolute rights protected in international law. Without freedom of thought or opinion, we have no humanity, and we have no democracy. Making these rights real requires three things:

1. the ability to keep your thoughts private;
2. freedom from manipulation of your thoughts;
3. that no one can be penalised for their thoughts alone.[3]

The right to freedom of thought is a cornerstone of all our other rights. And its profound importance for humanity means it is protected in the strongest possible way in human rights law. Yet somehow we have allowed ourselves to be lulled into the false assumption that we don't need to worry about it because no one can actually get inside our heads. The Cambridge Analytica scandal is just one piece of evidence that this assumption is no longer true, if it ever was. The scale and range of interferences with our ability to think and feel freely that technology can and might facilitate is in many ways beyond our imagination. But it is happening now. We have forgotten that rights need protections to be real and effective.

Voltaire's Candide declared proudly that 'I read only to please myself and enjoy only what suits my taste.' In the twenty-first century, it is increasingly difficult for any of us to do otherwise. Algorithms dictate the news stories we are presented with, giving different windows on the world to different people on the same site in order to 'improve our experience'. Spotify will even stream music for you tailored to your DNA, if you have ever shared your saliva with AncestryDNA.[4] The adverts we see for jobs, homes, finance and social opportunities are all targeted at the people Facebook, Google and the data brokers think us or want us to be. Our opportunities and actions are guided by invisible actors.

The economist Shoshana Zuboff describes this problem in her seminal book *The Age of Surveillance Capitalism*. However, most of the discussion so far about the solutions has focused on privacy and data protection. But the fundamental problem with techniques like behavioural microtargeting and the 'surveillance capitalism' model is not the data; it's how it is used as a key to our minds.

What could be more human and intimate than thought? People feel they have nothing to hide when you talk about privacy. But if you talk about freedom of thought, how many of us are really prepared to admit 'I have nothing to think'?

While the idea of privacy feels closed, introspective and exclusive, designed to constrain and obscure the self, keeping others out, the idea of freedom of thought is expansive, exploratory and open. It is the space to discover new ideas, try on new viewpoints, be scurrilous, irreverent and naughty, profound and pompous, in order to understand our place in the world around us. Freedom of thought is a voyage of discovery and privacy is the tollbooth.

Tim Berners-Lee did not invent the World Wide Web to enslave our minds. But over the past three decades, a Panglossian optimism combined with cynical self-interest has allowed the scale of our dependence and the reach of technology into our minds to expand unchecked. Big tech has dodged regulation by scaring policymakers with the threat that regulation would stifle innovation – no one wants to be branded a Luddite. Now that we have begun to wake up to the reality, we are told that it is a done deal, something so complex and all-pervasive that we must just learn to live with it. But we do not have to learn to live with a system that denies our dignity. We must remember the revolutionary spirit of Paris and Berlin that characterised the year the internet was born. And we need to learn how to change the internet into a system that contributes to our individual and collective liberty. In his open letter in 2019 celebrating 30 years of his invention, Tim Berners-Lee wrote:

Against the backdrop of news stories about how the web is misused, it's understandable that many people feel afraid and unsure if the web is really a force for good. But given how much the web has changed in the past 30 years, it would be defeatist and unimaginative to assume that the web as we know it can't be changed for the better in the next 30. If we give up on building a better web now, then the web will not have failed us. We will have failed the web.[5]

At the start of 1989, the Berlin Wall seemed like a solid and immutable fact of life – the embodiment of a world split by ideology for decades. And then Berliners started to pick up hammers to chip away at the concrete facade, and by Christmas it was history.

In 2020, the global pandemic that ended so many lives and locked us up in our houses made the use of the word 'unprecedented' banal. But it did provide an unprecedented opportunity for reflection. Now that we understand what it means to lose our physical liberty and to live our lives online, we need to focus on what freedom, including mental freedom, should mean for our future in the digital age.

The lockdown gave me an opportunity to reread the classics of twentieth-century dystopian fiction with a fresh eye. George Orwell's *Nineteen Eighty-Four*, Aldous Huxley's *Brave New World*, Philip K. Dick's *The Minority Report* and Margaret Atwood's *The Handmaid's Tale*, with its recent sequel *The Testaments*. And I make no apology for the references to them scattered liberally through this book. Their visions have become so deeply carved in our collective consciousness that we regularly use their terminology as an easy way of describing the tidal wave of surveillance, consumerism and injustice that we see around us. But we do not really engage with the detailed accuracy of their futuristic vision. Rather than taking their visions as a warning, it sometimes seems as though we have adopted them as a template for our world.

For Orwell's hero, Winston Smith, the original thoughtcrime was to buy a notebook, a pen and some ink. It did not matter what he wrote; the mere fact of writing outside the sphere of surveillance of the telescreen or the speakwrite was punishable by death, or at least 25 years of forced labour. But as humans, we cannot help ourselves. Our need for inner freedom will always drive us, ultimately, to put pen to paper, to speak out, or to make a tiny rebellion to challenge oppression no matter what the cost. This book too started out in royal-blue ink on smooth lined paper away from the ubiquitous screens of lockdown. Writing so much by hand may have given me tennis elbow, but it also gave me a different way to think and to get my ideas in order before committing them to the eternal cloud.

In Part 1 of the book, I explore the historical groundings of the right to freedom of thought, the way it connects to other human rights and the battles over millennia to achieve the freedom to think for ourselves. If we look back through history, we can see what it means for individuals and societies to not have freedom of thought. The philosophers I studied – Mill, Socrates, Voltaire and Spinoza – knew only too well what it was to be deprived of freedom of thought and opinion, whether through the threat of torture, imprisonment or even death as a penalty for heretical or treasonous thought, or through the heavy weight of social control. Scientists and doctors from ancient Greece to Silicon Valley have tried to understand what makes us tick, and have developed imaginative and intrusive methods to infer what we might be thinking and to manipulate our minds as individuals and groups. And the histories of war, propaganda and marketing illuminate the ways our societies have been manipulated through the ages and the potentially deadly consequences of mind control whether political or commercial. All of these had impacts on both collective and individual mental freedom in the time before freedom of thought was established as a legal right.

Part 2 looks at the new threats to freedom of thought that we now face, by exploring how technology is increasingly engaging directly with our minds and questioning the effectiveness of current legal approaches to protecting the right. From the criminal law to the ways we vote, find love, stay healthy and educate our children, science and technology are used to try to understand what we think and feel and how that can be changed without us noticing, for the benefit of others. The examples given do not necessarily amount to a legal breach of the right (though several may yet prove to be), but they all illustrate the rapidly growing incursions on our inner freedom that affect us all, directly or indirectly.

In Part 3, I offer potential avenues to a future where our right to freedom of thought is secure along with all our other human rights. It is a call to reflect on what we need for freedom and how we all have a part to play in building a future that recognises and respects human rights for all.

This is not a book about technology; it is a book about human rights and why they matter. Almost three quarters of a century has passed since humanity came together as one to recognise the rights set out in the Universal Declaration of Human Rights. But what felt like a definitive period of peace and prosperity, at least in Europe and North America, has allowed people to forget why human rights matter for all our lives. Even worse, rights and freedoms have been weaponised (quite literally in the United States, with the right to bear arms), with a fundamental lack of understanding about what they mean and how they work. I have a right to freedom of expression, but it does not give me the right to provoke hatred and discrimination against you and people like you. I have a right to privacy, including the right to keep my health status private and to engage in intimate activity with other people, but it does not give me a right to intentionally or recklessly infect others with a deadly virus. The idea of freedom has been harnessed and corrupted to represent a selfish individualism that has little to do with the ideal of liberty that set us on the road to legally enforceable human rights.

We are at a defining point in our history. If, like me, you want a future of peace and prosperity for generations to come, it is time to think very seriously about what human rights and fundamental freedoms mean, how they work and how they can be protected. They are universal, indivisible and inalienable. Freedom of thought sits alongside and operates with many other rights. But it has been largely overlooked, with a misplaced complacency. If we lose our ability to think and form opinions freely, we will be powerless to defend any of our human rights. Once we have lost our rights, we may never get them back. Before we throw them away, we should remember where they came from, why they matter and how they can save us in the future.

It is time to take a step towards defining what the rights to freedom of thought and opinion mean in practice, so that we can draw a protective ring around them and find the mental space to think, feel and understand freely. We need freedom of thought to combat climate change, racism and global poverty, and to fall in love, laugh and dream. The right to freedom of thought is an individual right, but it is crucial to the cultural, scientific, political and emotional life of our societies. Freedom of thought gives us the chance to think ugly thoughts and push them away before we act on them or let them take root; it allows us to choose how we behave to others, to moderate our speech according to the context and the audience, and to be ourselves. Freedom of thought lets us imagine new futures without having to prove them first. It keeps us dynamic and adventurous; it keeps us safe; and above all, it keeps us human.

I have no desire to stop technology in its tracks. This book is not a Luddite manifesto for the end of modernity. But it is an urgent call to think about what we want from technology in the future, and what we need to preserve our humanity and our autonomy – these should be the guiding principles of our relationship with technology and the future development of the tech industry. Our future should not be built on the best way to monetise the global population and obtain world domination for the few. It must be grounded in what it means to be human, and for that, we must have the freedom to think.

Part 1

—

THE ANALOGUE

CHAPTER 1

———

INNER FREEDOM

All human beings are born free and equal in dignity and
rights. They are endowed with reason and conscience and
should act towards one another in a spirit of brotherhood.

Article 1, Universal Declaration of Human Rights

In a dusty Ivy League law library, the walls lined with leather-bound books written by men who looked a lot like him, Zechariah Chafee came to understand, viscerally, that there was a gulf between the ideal of human freedom expounded by the Founding Fathers and what that freedom meant in practice in the United States in the early twentieth century. As he contemplated the dust motes dancing in the shafts of late-afternoon sunlight that penetrated the tall windows, waiting for the illustrious legal minds poring over his opinions to decide his fate, Chafee's absolute dedication to making freedom of opinion a reality in law and in life crystallised around him.

An upper-middle-class East Coast lawyer who had specialised in contract law, and a professor of law at Harvard, Chafee could have chosen a comfortable and easy life in the ivory towers of the American establishment. But he had views. And he had very

3

strong views on the right of everyone to hold and express their opinions, no matter how unpalatable those opinions might be. The First Amendment now seems like such a fundamental part of the American approach to civil liberties, but before 1919, the US courts had not even looked at it. In the aftermath of the First World War, as the American government used the 1917 Espionage Act and the 1918 Sedition Act to crack down on critics of its war effort and to combat the first 'Red Scare', provoked by the Bolshevik Revolution in Russia, Chafee's was a rare voice speaking out for freedom of speech. But his voice had global reach and impact.

Chafee's scholarship and activism around the First Amendment were said to have informed the first Supreme Court declaration on free speech, in Justice Oliver Wendell Holmes Jr's dissenting judgment in the case of *Abrams v. United States*,[1] in which immigrants were convicted for distributing leaflets condemning American intervention in Russia. While Chafee did not share their opinions, he could not step back from defending their rights both to hold and to share their views.

Academic freedom is fundamental to the development of human knowledge and wisdom. But far from finding a haven in academia, Chafee's stance on freedom of opinion and expression threatened to undermine his academic career. He was effectively put on trial when Harvard Law School carried out an extraordinary investigation and hearings to determine whether his writing on free speech made him 'unfit as a law school professor'.[2] Although he ultimately survived this challenge and stayed on at Harvard, his opinions saw him dragged before the House Committee on Un-American Activities and listed by Senator Joe McCarthy as a person who was 'dangerous to America'.[3] Chafee knew only too well that 'the inclination of men who obtain the power to govern is to use that power for the purpose of controlling not only the actions but the thoughts of men'.[4]

He understood the need to protect the right to hold opinions without interference, not because of an innate American respect for the principles enshrined in the First Amendment, but rather because he had direct experience of state suppression of unpopular opinions and the pressure of conformity of thought, even in the intellectual palace of Harvard. For Chafee, it was clear that freedom of opinion was not just an idea or a value; it was a necessity for human society, and one that was in urgent need of protection, in law and in practice, in the United States and around the world.

The right to freedom of thought, religion, conscience and belief along with the closely related right to freedom of opinion are fundamental but often overlooked pieces in the universal human rights jigsaw. They are the inner freedoms that allow scientific progress, artistic inspiration, emotional fulfilment, political engagement and spiritual enlightenment. For democratic elections to function, each of us needs to be able to freely form an opinion so we can contribute to decisions on the direction of our country. Without this freedom, democracy is meaningless. And these are freedoms that underpin our personhood and the way we see ourselves as human beings.

Ideas and values can help shift the way we approach and view our lives, but it is the translation of ideas and values into laws that really moulds our societies and gives ethics weight. Laws regulate human relationships. They set the limits on the way we interact and how we treat each other. And human rights laws have provided humanity with a moral compass after periods of turmoil when it became clear that we had lost our way. They are nuanced, profound, principled and fundamental to our individual and collective humanity, dignity and autonomy. We all need them, and if we want to keep them, we need to think about what our rights mean and defend them. To do that, we need freedom of thought.

The fight for rights

Human rights are not new. Over the centuries, human rights and fundamental freedoms were developed primarily to rein in state powers. The international human rights laws that emerged in the twentieth century were a response to the atrocities of the Holocaust and were designed to prevent our governments from harming us, but they also put obligations on states to protect us from each other and from the actions of private businesses. In recent years, as the line between the public and private spheres of life has blurred, the importance of human rights to restrain corporate reach into our lives has become increasingly important. They provide a bulwark against governmental or societal excess and a crucial foundation for democracy. Without human rights, democracy runs the risk of becoming a 'tyranny of the masses', as philosopher J. S. Mill once feared.

Understanding how the philosophical ideas of the Enlightenment were transformed into universal laws requires a brief introduction to where human rights come from and why they matter. Human rights are universal, indivisible, inviolable and interdependent, but, perhaps inevitably, there is some debate about who discovered them as legally recognised rights. In ancient Babylon, Hammurabi's code, one of the earliest-known examples of a written legal code, recognised civil rights such as the presumption of innocence in criminal trials and economic rights including a minimum wage almost 4,000 years before such a radical law was passed in the United States in the 1930s. But alongside these progressive ideas, the ancient code included a litany of barbaric punishments and grisly ways to be put to death should anyone transgress. It is a far cry from the kind of human rights template we want to live by in the twenty-first century.

England, France and the United States scrap, rather predictably, over their relative importance in the origin story of modern human rights. The Magna Carta of 1215 is often cited (at least by the English) as evidence that Runnymede, a green field just outside London, was the true birthplace of human rights. But while the Magna Carta did serve to curtail the powers of the deeply unpopular King John by introducing important rights, such as access to due legal process, it was designed to protect the interests of the Church and the barons rather than those of ordinary people, who barely had any rights in law. For the serf in his field, it would have made very little difference, except perhaps to reduce the likelihood of being sent to war. In 1215, the idea that all men were born equal would have been not only ridiculous, but also a huge threat to the status quo – even expressing the idea would have been to risk serious punishment or death. No doubt that is why Robin Hood, King John's legendary nemesis, who stole from the rich to give to the poor, has such an enduring appeal. The 1689 English Bill of Rights, which took a further step down the path to codifying civil and political rights, particularly freedom of elections and freedom of speech in Parliament, also did little to advance human rights or freedom for the average man or woman on the street or country lane. Most of them did not have a vote anyway. Civil and political rights, in England at least, were for the rich and powerful; they were not for the people.

Ironically, perhaps Britain's most important contribution to the explosion of rights onto the eighteenth-century legal and political landscape was its oppressive rule in the Americas, which would go on to provoke one of the greatest leaps forward in the history of human rights as we know them today. Tired of the tyranny of the British Crown, the drafters of the American Declaration of Independence put the well-being of people as a primary purpose of governments (alongside a long list of complaints about the king) and set a template for the future of American democracy: 'We hold these truths to be self-evident, that all men are created equal, that they are endowed by their Creator with certain unalienable Rights, that among these are Life, Liberty and the pursuit of Happiness. That to secure these rights, Governments are instituted among Men, deriving their just powers from the consent of the governed.'[5]

The first amendment to the American Bill of Rights from 1787 develops the theme of individual freedom as protected from state excess: 'Congress shall make no law respecting an establishment of religion, or prohibiting the free exercise thereof; or abridging the freedom of speech, or of the press; or the right of the people peaceably to assemble, and to petition the government for a redress of grievances.'[6]

Finally, the governed had the right to take a view on their government. The focus on civil liberties reflected the history of the United States as a refuge for those escaping religious and ideological persecution in Europe. The primary place of freedom in the US constitution has made it a defining feature of the American approach to human rights, with a stronger focus on freedom of expression without limitation by the state than in many other countries, particularly in continental Europe. The American Founding Fathers, such as Benjamin Franklin, knew that 'without freedom of thought, there can be no such thing as wisdom',[7] but they stopped short of setting down that freedom explicitly in law. However, the interpretation of the constitution, in particular the First Amendment, by the courts has underlined the fundamental importance of both freedom of thought and freedom of expression to the American model of democracy in the twentieth century. Justice Brandeis explained the importance of free thought in his concurring opinion in the 1927 US Supreme Court case of *Whitney v. California*, a case involving a woman who was convicted for her part in helping to establish the Communist Labor Party of America:

> Those who won our independence believed that the final end of the State was to make men free to develop their faculties, and that, in its government, the deliberative forces should prevail over the arbitrary. They valued liberty both as an end, and as a means. They believed liberty to be the secret of happiness, and courage to be the secret of liberty. They believed that freedom to think as you will and to speak as you think are means indispensable to the discovery and spread of political truth ... They recognized the risks to which all human institutions are subject. But they knew that order cannot be secured merely through fear of punishment for its infraction; that it is hazardous to discourage thought, hope and imagination; that fear breeds repression; that repression breeds hate; that hate menaces stable government; that the path of safety lies in the opportunity to discuss freely supposed grievances and proposed remedies, and that the fitting remedy for evil counsels is good ones. Believing in the power of reason as applied through public discussion, they eschewed silence coerced by law ... the argument of force in its worst form.[8]

How far the Founding Fathers could have predicted the ways that their ideas about freedom would be developed in law is debatable. But it is clear that their work on the US constitution had a profound effect on the future of human rights far beyond their borders.

Liberté

The last two decades of the eighteenth century were a time of upheaval on both sides of the Atlantic, with radical ideas fuelling a desire to create a new world order that would overthrow the abusive privilege of monarchy and aristocracy. The radical thinkers of the time cross-pollinated their ideas as they swept away physical and intellectual borders, with the likes of Thomas Paine, Mary Wollstonecraft, Thomas Jefferson and Benjamin Franklin riding the waves across the Atlantic and the English Channel to share their ideas as effectively, if not as efficiently, as an undersea data cable. The revolutionary spirit of eighteenth-century France, inspired by the philosophers of the Enlightenment, saw the first comprehensive legal proclamation of human rights and democratic principles as we know them today. Unlike its British precursors, there was no doubt that the Declaration of the Rights of Man and of the Citizen, drafted by the French National Constituent Assembly in 1789, was for the people, not the ruling classes. It was the legal embodiment of the Enlightenment ideals of natural and civil rights.

In 17 clauses, it set out the principles that prescribe the way in which the sacred rights of men must be protected and respected to ensure the happiness of all. These were sweeping and basic principles that described the fundamental freedom and equality of all men (women still had a while to wait) and established the preservation of the natural rights of liberty, property, security and resistance to oppression as the necessary aim of all political associations. As a precursor to modern human rights laws, these clauses placed the rule of law at the heart of government, ensuring that any limitations on freedom must be set down in law and could only be justified to protect the good of others or to prohibit actions that were harmful to society. The rules of due process, including the right to be considered innocent until proven guilty, the principle of no punishment without law, and humane treatment for detainees, were also codified in the Declaration. Principles governing the military, taxation, representation, the separation of powers and the accountability of the administration, which form the bedrock of modern liberal democracy, had their place too. But as well as these principles of governance and law, the Declaration codified the rights to have and express one's own ideas, opinions and beliefs, clearly setting out both an internal and an external aspect of those rights:

> 10. No one shall be disquieted on account of his opinions, including his religious views, provided their manifestation does not disturb the public order established by law.
> 11. The free communication of ideas and opinions is one of the most precious of the rights of man. Every citizen may, accordingly, speak, write, and print with freedom, but shall be responsible for such abuses of this freedom as shall be defined by law.[9]

These clauses, with their recognition of the need to limit some external freedoms when required to protect others, and the responsibilities associated with freedom of speech, formed the basis of the rights and freedoms that we know in the twentieth-century international human rights texts as the right to freedom of thought, religion and belief and the right to freedom of opinion and expression. Both rights go to the heart of human autonomy and identity, as we experience them internally and live them externally in our daily lives.

This represented a fundamental shift. As the political theorist Hannah Arendt noted in *The Origins of Totalitarianism*: '[The Declaration of the Rights of Man] ... meant nothing more nor less than that from then on Man, and not God's command or the customs of history, should be the source of Law ... The proclamation of human rights was also meant to be a much-needed protection in the new era where individuals were no longer secure in the estates to which they were born or sure of their equality before God as Christians.'[10]

In the new world order, we needed new ways to protect ourselves – God might save our souls from Satan, but he could not protect us from each other. Human rights were designed to protect us from the perils of the future.

Equality?

The Declaration of the Rights of Man was a first step to recognising that we all have the right to think for ourselves, and that this is a right that needs protection. It was radical but, in line with the social mores of the day, its egalitarian principles did not, in practice, extend beyond the idea that only free white men had such rights. Even those who proclaimed themselves committed to the idea of freedom of thought as a natural right were unwilling to consider that women, or non-white men, might also be entitled to such things.

In 1791, the French feminist activist, philosopher and writer Olympe de Gouges, recognising the limitations in male political Enlightenment thinking, penned the Declaration of the Rights of Woman and the Female Citizen,[11] demanding equality between the sexes and expanding the provisions in the Declaration of the Rights of Man to include women. Rather than being supported in expanding the concept of freedom, she was convicted of treason based on her political writing, and executed.

In a democracy, it is the vote that gives you the key to civil and political rights and marks the value society puts on your opinion. Historically, the right to vote has been very much dependent on your wealth, sex, age, religion and the colour of your skin. In the United States, 'all men' were theoretically given the vote in 1870, regardless of race, but women had to wait until 1920 to vote across the country, and it was only in 1924 that all Native Americans were given suffrage. The way the law treats women and their opinions is often a good indicator of the real state of human rights and equality in a particular country. In nineteenth-century Britain, there was only one woman wealthy enough to have an opinion on the way the country was governed – Queen Victoria – and she had been appointed by God so her right was not open to question. When my homeland, the Isle of Man – a small semi-autonomous British territory in the Irish Sea – decided to give all women the vote in 1881, it was the quiet result of a genteel suffragist lecture tour.[12] Her Majesty's governor, deeply disturbed by the proposal, managed to limit the damage of such a radical move by restricting suffrage to women of property over a certain age. Similar women in the UK had to wait until 1918 for the vote, after a violent struggle and the social upheaval of the First World War. Universal suffrage for men and women over 21 was finally introduced in the UK in 1928. In

France, equality in terms of voting did not extend to women until 1944, following the liberation of France towards the end of the Second World War.

Throughout much of human history, large swathes of humanity had no rights at all in law. Slavery is so appalling because it is the antithesis of human freedom. The idea that a person can be owned by another undermines the most basic idea of what it means to be human. It is a negation of human dignity and autonomy. Subjugating a person to slavery denies their right to think. And despite the historical declarations on human rights, it has been a lived reality for millions around the world, thanks, historically, to a global commercial imperative driven by the very powers that were at the forefront of the philosophical and legal development of human rights.

In Britain, it was only with the Slavery Abolition Act of 1833 that the practice was ended in most of the British Empire (and India had to wait until 1843). The French, for all their liberty and equality, wavered in and out of tolerating slavery in their colonies until it was finally abolished in 1848. And in the United States, 'the land of the free', many of the Founding Fathers, including Benjamin Franklin, continued to own slaves while they thrashed out the foundations of the US constitution. It was not until 19 June 1865 that slavery in the United States was finally ended, and formally abolished with the Thirteenth Amendment that December. Its deep scars are still apparent today, and 'Juneteenth' was only finally recognised by President Biden as an official federal holiday in 2021. In many parts of the world, slavery continued in law until over a century later. Sadly, we are still dealing with its legacy and its continued practice in the twenty-first century. The swathe of protests in the Black Lives Matter movement following the murder of George Floyd in the

United States in 2020 is a clear sign that there is still a long way to go to make true freedom and equality a reality on the ground. And the continued existence of modern forms of slavery around the world proves that making laws is not enough to protect our rights; those laws need to be respected and enforced and we can never afford to be complacent about the rights we enjoy.

The early history of human rights was predominantly a history of wealthy white men's rights. It wasn't until the middle of the twentieth century, with the birth of a truly international human rights movement, that the rest of us were really deemed to be deserving of rights and capable of being trusted to exercise our minds freely at all. And some of the visionaries who brought us universal rights had first-hand experience of what it means to lose them.

The truth will set you free

Charles Malik kept himself close to the walls of the building as he skirted the University of Freiburg on his way home. His winter hat was pulled down tight in the hope that his thick, wavy dark hair would not draw any unwanted attention. This was his last day. He just needed to get back to his room one last time and pack his suitcase, and he would be on his way. His hands bunched in his pockets against the cold and his head down, he was trying to make himself as small as he could, hoping that neither the bitter cold nor the SS would pick him out from the crowd. He walked briskly, like a man with a purpose, but not so quickly as to arouse suspicion.

As he turned the corner down the west side of the building, he looked up briefly at the golden words inscribed over the entrance, '*Die Wahrheit wird euch frei machen*' ('The truth will set you free'), which had so inspired him when he had first arrived several months earlier to learn how to think. But his time in Germany in 1936 had not given him the truth, or the freedom, he had been looking for. Now the inscription spoke to him of the urgency of his imminent departure. The truth, he had discovered in Nazi Germany, was the inescapable march of the totalitarian state through every single layer of society. The truth was the SS officer who had beaten him in a fit of anti-Semitic rage, mistaking his dark, chiselled Arab features for the caricature of Jewishness so reviled by the Nazis. The truth was that the man he had come to learn from, Martin Heidegger, espoused Nazi ideology as a defence against the dangers of freedom of thought and expression. And it was this truth that no amount of philosophy could ever cure. Tackling the horrors Malik saw in Nazi Germany would need law, international law that would override the power of the state and protect the people no matter who was in power.

Charles Malik, Lebanese mathematician, philosopher, Christian and Arab, saw the writing on the wall in Europe in the 1930s and set sail to finish his studies in America, the land of the free. But the brutal truth of fascism that he carried with him for many years in the pain in his legs from the SS attack was a key driver for his desire for freedom and plurality of thought across the world. The tolerance he knew in the diverse traditions of his native Lebanon were the ideals that he hoped would take root everywhere, even in Europe. And he was one of the drafters of perhaps the most ambitious global project for humanity of all time, the document that would make this dream real.

The Universal Declaration of Human Rights (UDHR), proclaimed in 1948 in a brief window of time between the atrocities of the Second World War and the ideological entrenchment of the

Cold War, established, for the first time, a common understanding of what fundamental human rights must mean for everyone in the world. It was the moment we all became human in the eyes of the law. The UDHR was a truly international project, designed to create a road map that would guarantee the rights of all people, everywhere, regardless of status, sex, race or religion. It was both visionary and pragmatic, building bridges between cultures and making philosophical principles concrete without compromising the values that are intrinsic to our humanity. And its inclusive aims were reflected in the make-up of its main drafting committee. Chaired by a woman, the wide range of geographical, political, philosophical and cultural perspectives of its members was designed to ensure that it would reflect universal principles that would be acceptable to all.

Each of the committee members had a role in the drafting, bringing their own individual and cultural perspectives to the Declaration. Eleanor Roosevelt, the American chair of the committee, a committed social justice activist and former First Lady, was a driving force for ensuring that the days of freedom and rights being only for men were over. She was joined by Malik and seven other committee members. René Cassin, a French Jewish lawyer and judge, had been a member of the Free French government in exile during the war. His contribution to the drafting of the UDHR was rooted in his personal response to the horrors of the Holocaust. Peng Chun Chang, a Chinese philosopher, educator, playwright and musician, who had brought *Mulan* to the Broadway stage in the 1920s, was also a consummate diplomat. Chang used Confucianism as a tool to find a path across seemingly intractable ideological chasms, and insisted on the removal of all references to nature and God in the text to make it truly universal. Alexandre Bogomolov, a diplomat from the USSR, brought the Soviet perspective to the drafting table, while Charles Dukes, a British trade unionist and Labour politician, brought a practical approach on labour rights. William Hodgson, a veteran of the First World War and an Australian diplomat, was a vociferous proponent of the need for a legally binding international convention on human rights with a court to enforce it. And Hernán Santa Cruz, an educator and judge from Chile, was dogged in his insistence that socio-economic rights must be included in the Declaration, despite resistance from the north. The final member, John P. Humphrey, a bilingual Canadian international lawyer working for the United Nations Secretariat, provided a bridge between francophone and anglophone cultural perspectives, bringing together and analysing the background documents that informed the United Nations Commission on Human Rights' work. Together, the nine committee members sought to find a text that would distil the essence of human rights in a way that would suit the infinite variety of ideological tastes across the world.[13]

The drafting of the UDHR required complex manoeuvring around different cultural and political understandings of the building blocks of humanity and human societies. French and Anglo-American ideas about rights had historically diverged significantly, with French models focusing on the responsibilities of the state and social and economic rights, while Anglo-American models focused on individual civil liberties and political rights. In the new republics of Latin America, constitutions had developed hybrids of the approaches taken in Europe and North America, while the relationship between the individual and the state in the USSR was built on economic and social rights, with little regard for the idea of individual human autonomy; likewise, the teetering structures of colonialism were revealing new relationships and power dynamics between the global north and south. A good deal of diplomacy was needed to pass the final text in a UN General Assembly that was increasingly fractious with the deepening ideological divides that characterised global politics in the second half of the twentieth century.

Man's proper nature

Negotiating the UDHR meant grappling with foundational questions of ideology that would set a framework for humanity's future. It was not simply the animal existence of humanity that needed protection through basic economic rights. Charles Malik insisted that 'unless man's proper nature, unless his mind and spirit are brought out, set apart, protected, and promoted, the struggle for human rights is a sham and a mockery'.[14] Malik was passionate about the spiritual aspect of humanity and fought hard for the 'human person' against the communist push for societal over individual rights.[15] In response to pressure from the Yugoslav delegation in favour of collective rights reflecting socialist ideals, he suggested a new draft to resist social and state pressure on the individual, and asserted that 'the human person's most sacred and inviolable possessions are his mind and his conscience, enabling him to perceive the truth, to choose freely, and to exist'.[16]

Although others disagreed vociferously with his ideas that the human person should take precedence over the state and society in this new world order, this focus on inner freedom and the essential spiritual nature of mankind was supported by many in religious communities, and René Cassin agreed that 'it was this right to the freedom of conscience which gave the human person his worth and dignity'.[17] While his explicit drafting did not survive, Malik's views on the nature of personhood and humanity won out in the final draft of Article 1 of the UDHR. Reason and conscience are a defining feature of the human person protected by international human rights law against both the materialist threat of the West and the potential for tyranny of the masses that he perceived from communism.

Malik brought metaphysics, spirituality and the relative tolerance of his homeland to the table, but Chang, the Chinese delegate, brought poetry and the Chinese tradition of Confucianism. While Malik had driven 'reason' as the key component of what it means to be human, Chang felt that this was not the whole picture. Struggling to translate the Confucian idea represented by the Chinese character '*ren*', he described the missing piece of humanity as 'plurality of mind'. To him, it was something so obviously and fundamentally human, yet it did not really exist in any of the other official UN languages. Chang's idea was finally translated into the English word 'conscience', but that perhaps fails to grasp the complexity of the Chinese concept of *ren*. *Ren* is a fundamental principle of Confucianism, and has been translated variously as 'humaneness', 'benevolence', 'empathy' and 'co-humanity'. It could be described as the virtuous quality of altruism. Rather than referring to an individual state of mind, it deals with the way an individual interacts with others. It is the inner quality that allows us to reach out and touch others.[18] And it is also connected to the idea of *fraternité* that the French revolutionaries espoused, and which is reflected in the statement that 'All men are brothers'[19] in the preamble to the UDHR. It is relevant to the sphere of personal relationships, where it may reflect a form of love, but it is also relevant to the global political sphere. When the mayor of Hiroshima called for a regional ban on nuclear weapons on the fiftieth anniversary of the horrific bombing of his city, it was the idea of *ren* that he appealed to as a justification for this step to guarantee a humane future.[20] *Ren* is the inner quality we need as humans to live together in dignity and humanity.

The UDHR is the international statement on human rights that has achieved the greatest level of international consensus, being adopted unanimously in the General Assembly with only eight abstentions.[21] It is recognised as having the status of *jus cogens*, meaning that its contents have international legal force that cannot be set aside, regardless of whether a country signs up to it. But it is declaratory, and it lacks the detail needed to apply law effectively in practice. Making the rights in the UDHR real meant translating them into more detailed and binding international treaties. This took the form of the International Covenant on Civil and Political Rights (ICCPR) and the International Covenant on Economic, Social and Cultural Rights (ICESCR), adopted in 1966, two treaties that taken together with the UDHR form what is known as the International Bill of Rights.

The discussions around drafting the two Covenants started at the same time as the UDHR, but dragged on for over 20 years as the international mood began to shift and countries baulked at the idea of signing up to commitments they might actually be held to.[22] But the debates and arguments over the drafting of clauses that protect our inner freedoms in both the UDHR and the ICCPR give useful insights into the way states thought about them at the time. Both instruments contain articles on freedom of thought, conscience, religion and belief (Articles 18) and on freedom of opinion (Articles 19), and although the final text of the provisions is slightly different in each document, the drafting processes illuminate the heart of what the drafters were trying to do in their different ways.

The right to think for ourselves

Malik's drive was to capture the human soul in human rights law. The Soviet Union wanted to protect the space for scientific innovation. Confucianism identifies reflection as the noblest route to wisdom. And one of the strongest arguments for freedom of political opinion came from Zechariah Chafee, who knew personally what it meant to have that freedom curtailed. When he was appointed to the Sub-Commission on Freedom of Information and the Press charged with drafting Article 19 of the UDHR, he was adamant that the right to hold opinions without interference had to be ring-fenced explicitly at the heart of it.

The rights to freedom of thought, conscience and religion in Articles 18 and the right to freedom of opinion and expression in Articles 19 of the UDHR and the ICCPR build on the idea of the human being as a conscious, spiritual and reasoning person. They seek to protect the mental space that we need in order to use the reason and conscience with which we are endowed. Drafting these articles in a way that would be acceptable to all the different interests sitting around the table was not a simple task. The practical meaning of religious freedom and freedom of conscience provoked extremely divergent reactions worldwide, but freedom of thought had general support for very different reasons.

During the drafting process of the UDHR, the Soviet Union submitted an alternative version of Article 18, with no reference to conscience and religion but with a strong focus on freedom of thought. The Soviets considered this crucial for 'the development of modern sciences' and for the 'existence of free-thinkers whose reasoning had led them to discard old-fashioned beliefs and religious fanaticism. The times when scientists were condemned to be burnt at the stake were past, and science occupied a most important place in human life.'[23] Malik saw the UDHR with its rights to freedom of thought and opinion as a 'faint echo, on the international plane', of the spiritual quality of humanity against the backdrop of a rising tide of materialism that he believed denied the human soul. But it is clear that the Soviet acceptance of the final draft was based on a very different perspective on the text.

The debates between national delegations in the negotiations of the ICCPR reveal differences in both national priorities and their perceptions of our inner lives. Some felt that including references to both 'thought' and 'opinion' created a duplication in the text. Others argued that 'thought' should be understood in the context of religious belief, while 'opinion' belonged to the realm of politics. At the suggestion that 'thought' was superfluous and should be removed from the text of Article 18, the Soviet delegation objected that 'science had a right to protection on the same terms as religion. Out of respect for the heroes and martyrs of science, those words should not be deleted.'[24]

Some delegates argued that it was impossible to interfere with freedom of opinion so no protection was needed.[25] But the British, with their intimate knowledge of the power of propaganda, insisted that 'in totalitarian countries, opinions were definitely controlled by careful restriction of the sources of information',[26] stressing that interference could happen even before an opinion was formed.[27] The ultimate decision to keep freedom of thought and freedom of opinion as two discrete provisions with absolute protection in both the UDHR and the ICCPR perhaps reveals what Professor Evelyn Aswad, an American law professor, member of the Facebook Oversight Board and former US government adviser, has described as 'the broadness of the right to control the inner sanctum of one's mind'.[28] And Finnish international law professor Martin Scheinin, a former UN Special Rapporteur on human rights and counter-terrorism and former member of the UN Human Rights Committee, in his commentary on the UDHR, suggests that freedom of thought, conscience and religion taken together cover all possible attitudes towards the world and society, protecting the 'absolute character of the freedom of an inner state of mind'.[29]

The inner sanctum

So, what do these rights to inner freedom mean in practice? The right to freedom of thought has been described by the European Court of Human Rights as 'the foundation of democratic society',[30] and René Cassin called it 'the basis and origin of all other rights'.[31] It is intrinsically connected to the corresponding right to freedom of expression and opinion, which provides the social backdrop and access to information crucial to developing critical and intellectual thought. It doesn't really matter how you distinguish between them – thought, conscience, belief and opinion mesh together to create the inner state that gives us our humanity.[32]

Our inner lives are complex and diverse. We have fleeting feelings and transient thoughts and we have serious opinions about political or philosophical issues that colour our world views. We may have absurd opinions about trivia or carefully crafted ideas about the pointlessness of war. Deeply held beliefs about deities that we can't see or an absolute conviction that the world is flat because that is what our eyes (and YouTube) tell us. Our thoughts may be right, or wrong, or arguably a bit of both. Should everything that goes on inside our heads be protected?

So far, there is little case law on freedom of thought or the freedom to hold opinions, but what there is indicates a 'comprehensiveness of the concept of thought' that the European Commission of Human Rights has found to be broad enough to include a parent's wish to name their child in a particular way.[33]

The UN Human Rights Committee, which ensures the full implementation of the ICCPR, explains the scope and absolute nature of the right to freedom of thought as 'far-reaching and profound; it encompasses freedom of thoughts on all matters, personal conviction and the commitment to religion or belief, whether manifested individually or in community with others'.[34] And it has made it clear that the right to hold opinions without interference covers all forms of opinion, including those of a 'political, scientific, historic, moral or religious nature', as well as the right to change your opinion.[35]

The rights that protect our freedoms to think for ourselves have a dual aspect: the internal practice of thinking and the external aspect of sharing our thoughts. There is a clear distinction between what goes on inside my head and the way my thoughts, beliefs and opinions are manifested in the outside world. Human rights law treats those inner and outer freedoms quite differently. Essentially, you can think what you like without limits, but you can say what you like only up to a certain point. What happens inside your mind is not subjected to any moral or value judgement to assess whether a particular idea or emotion should be protected. But as soon as your thoughts are translated into words or behaviour that affect other people in the outside world, you will only be free to express them as long as they do not destroy the rights of others.

The rights to freedom of expression, private and family life and the freedom to manifest religion or belief or associate with others are all qualified rights. This means that they can be limited by the state for a prescribed set of reasons, such as protecting the rights of others or ensuring public order. They are rights that are universal, but their exercise entails responsibility to others. 'Sticks and stones may break my bones, but words will never hurt me' is no truer in the real world than it is in the playground. There is a long trail of historical evidence to justify suppressing hate speech – without propaganda, the real-life impact of Nazi ideology would have been very different indeed. Therefore, human rights law recognises that people need protection from both physical and mental harm. Expression that destroys the rights of others loses its legal protection. And propaganda for war or inciting national, racial or religious hatred is explicitly banned by international human rights law.[36]

Absolute rights are deemed so essential to our dignity and our humanity that there can be no balancing act in deciding whether to protect them, and there are very few rights that are given this level of protection. There can never be a justification for torturing someone or treating them in a way that is inhuman and degrading. No one can enslave another person for any reason. Torture and slavery are prohibited absolutely, as they are anathema to human dignity and an affront to humanity. So too is anything that interferes with our right to inner freedom.

The space inside my head is the place where I can practise being human, apply my reason and morality (or lack of it) to problems, work through the bad ideas and let off steam without any consequences for anyone but myself. I can think unspeakable things so long as they remain unspoken. It is not about my rights against the world; it is about the individual finding their place in society. Freedom of thought and freedom of opinion give us the space to decide whether to shut up or speak out. And this inner freedom of thought and opinion can never be restricted or interfered with for any reason.

Protecting freedom

Human rights law guarantees freedom of thought, conscience, belief and opinion in three basic ways:

1. We must be able to keep our thoughts and opinions private.
2. We must be able to form our thoughts and opinions free from manipulation.
3. We must never be penalised for our thoughts or opinions.

The right to keep our thoughts private connects to several other human rights. Mental privacy is in some ways the absolutely protected core of the right to private life. And the right not to be coerced to reveal your thoughts is also a protection against the centuries-old practice of torture as a way to get people to confess their beliefs. It doesn't matter whether what you confess to is true, torture and the threat of it has been used to condemn people for socially unacceptable ideas for millennia. And the prohibition on torture is itself an absolutely protected right. But there have been other ways through the years that people have sought to get inside the mind to understand what and how people are thinking, by reading faces and bodies for signs of evil intent. Today, these techniques are increasingly being adapted and used by artificial intelligence (AI) to try to understand when people are thinking dangerous thoughts and to neutralise them before they can act.

Influence over our thoughts can happen in many different ways, and there is a sliding scale between lawful persuasion and unlawful manipulation. Professor Manfred Nowak, an Austrian international human rights lawyer and former UN Special Rapporteur on torture, has explained that the right to freedom of opinion includes the right to form and develop opinions by reasoning, so it would seem that persuasion that supports the reasoning process would not violate the right. Nowak is clear that the right to hold opinions without interference 'requires States parties to refrain from any interference with freedom of opinion (by indoctrination, "brainwashing", influencing the conscious or subconscious mind with psychoactive drugs or other means of manipulation)'. [37] And while he recognises that it is often difficult to draw the line between legitimate and illegitimate influence, he does suggest some pointers. Methods that use 'coercion, threat or similarly unauthorised means' to influence someone's thoughts or opinions would clearly be unacceptable. Influence against the person's will or without their consent and methods that try to bypass a person's rational faculties to influence them are likely to be manipulative. In the digital world, the tools of technological influence are increasingly shaping our minds without us realising it. The modern-day threat to our freedom of thought comes from global business as much as it comes from totalitarian states.

We should never be punished for our thoughts alone, and as the French delegates pointed out in the drafting process of the ICCPR,[38] the danger relates not only to our actual thoughts, but also to inferences about our thoughts or opinions. The UN Human Rights Committee reaffirmed that 'no person may be subject to the impairment of any rights under the Covenant on the basis of his or her actual, perceived or supposed opinions'.[39] If we are to be penalised, punished or judged, it should be for what we do, not what we think, and certainly not for what other people think we think. Criminalising the holding of an opinion (as opposed to the expression of it) would be a breach of the right, as would 'the harassment, intimidation or stigmatization of a person, including arrest, detention, trial or imprisonment for reasons of the opinions they may hold'.[40] Through history, people have been persecuted and put to death for opinions that society, often driven by a dominant religion, found disturbing. And for some, a woman having a black cat was enough to make an inference about heretical beliefs. In the modern context, profiling people based on inferences about their criminal thoughts derived from big data about the wider populace or the metadata on their personal phone could well fall on the wrong side of the line.

These three elements of the rights to freedom of thought, conscience, belief and opinion are key to understanding what an interference with our inner freedoms looks like in practice. Given the absolute nature of the rights to freedom of thought and opinion, once an interference or limitation is established, it can never be justified. This means that governments must not do anything that interferes with our inner freedoms and that they also have a duty to protect us from others, including private companies, who seek to interfere with that inner space. And businesses should be obliged to respect these rights.

These rights do not exist in a vacuum; they are part of a comprehensive system of human rights recognised in international law that together build up a protective fence around our humanity and our dignity. Privacy guards against people wanting to know our thoughts; freedom of expression allows us to share, develop and change our opinions; the prohibition on propaganda for hatred or war protects us not just as individuals, but as societies from psychological manipulation; and the prohibition on torture, inhuman and degrading treatment or punishment protects our minds (as well as our bodies) from excessive pressure. All of these rights support our inner freedom, and they are all part of the legal armoury to protect our dignity and humanity.

If you live in a modern liberal democracy, you may be tempted to take these rights for granted. But for much of history, our ancestors knew what it meant to be deprived of human rights and freedoms. Scientific discovery of philosophical exploration that challenged established religious thinking could lead to a death sentence in Renaissance Europe. And science itself could be used as a tool to get inside and disrupt or destroy the mind through the unscrupulous practices that paved the road to modern psychiatry. The power of propaganda in the twentieth century led to the unimaginable horrors of the Second World War that inspired the international human rights project itself. And since then, in many parts of the world, political dissidents have still felt the harsh consequences of exercising their freedom of opinion in places where human rights are not respected. We can learn from the experiences of the past how vital it is for us to protect our rights as we face new threats. In the digital age, our freedom is not owned by kings and cardinals; increasingly, access to our minds is controlled by corporations and states. We need to own our rights to freedom of thought and opinion and take action to defend them before it is too late.

CHAPTER 2

——

OF GODS AND MEN

The notion that there exist dangerous thoughts is mistaken for the simple reason that thinking itself is dangerous to all creeds, convictions, and opinions.

Hannah Arendt

399 BC: an old man sits in the baking heat of the town square in Athens drinking a cup of thick, dark brew. His feet are bare and calloused, his beard white and unkempt. Socrates knows that he will die. We will all die, but he will die soon; the cup in his hand gives him a matter of minutes. He swirls the substance around and drains it, swallowing decisively. He does not know if he will be remembered. There are no writings that he will leave for posterity, curled up in parchment or carved in stone. He does not approve of the modern technology of writing because he believes it rots the mind, robbing man of his capacity for memory and mental reflection.[1] He came to the city to sting it awake, attaching himself to the cradle of democracy to provoke it. His job is done: 501 of his fellow citizens were so enraged by his ideas and their effect on the precious young minds of Athens that he

has been sentenced to death by drinking the hemlock he holds in his hands.

What was it about this scruffy, rotund old man that so provoked his countrymen? He didn't kill or even hurt anyone. Rather, it was his radical thoughts and the way he used them to twist the minds of others that upset his fellow Athenians. Socrates was clearly charismatic and popular with the Athenian youth, who, just like the youth of today, were hungry for change and keen to overthrow all their parents stood for. Every generation has a Socrates – a figure who challenges the wisdom of society's morals and questions parental authority; someone whose ideas are so deliciously edgy that they light up the chemistry of the adolescent brain with fireworks. Sometimes those ideas provoke change, for good or ill. In the fourth century BC, Socrates' ideas threatened democracy, and the good people of Athens did not approve.

Martyrs to thought

Socrates did not really 'do' anything to deserve this punishment. His crimes – impiety and corruption of young minds – were crimes of thought, not action. But killing him did not soothe the sting. It did not make his ideas go away. Two and a half thousand years later, Socrates, with his scurrilous ideas and dangerous demagogic rhetoric, is still revered as the father of Western thought, and the arguments about him and his trial and punishment rage on. As the nineteenth-century British philosopher J. S. Mill put it, 'Socrates was put to death, but the Socratic philosophy rose like the sun in heaven and spread its illumination over the whole intellectual firmament.'[2]

He did not leave us his teachings in writing; we have them only second hand, burned into the minds of his followers, in particular through the Socratic dialogues of Plato. But they have endured through the dusty libraries of time to make him the go-to philosopher for internet memes[3] and Trump family Twitter feeds. In 2018, Ivanka Trump famously tweeted him as saying, 'The secret of change is to focus all your energy not on fighting the old but on building the new.'[4] The overwhelming mockery of her attempt at motivational philosophy revealed pretty quickly that she had mixed him up with a fictional gas attendant with the same name.[5] But that didn't stop her brother, Eric Trump, having another go the following year, incorrectly ascribing the quote 'When debate is lost, slander becomes the tool of the losers' to Socrates.[6] But while the Trumps may have shared Socrates' desire to shake things up, the Greek, famed for his logical prowess, may have been unimpressed by their debating skills.

Whatever you may think of Socrates' ideas, it is clear that his trial was essentially one for crimes of thought or opinion. His first crime – *asbeia*, or impiety – was a challenge to the Athenian gods; the outrageous idea that perhaps the gods could be questioned. In the Athens of antiquity, Socrates had no *right* to think those thoughts, let alone share them. His thoughts were a threat to the foundations of society and Athenians believed that his heretical ideas provoked the wrath of Zeus, leading to the turbulent decade that Athens had suffered in the years before his trial.

Perhaps if he had kept his thoughts to himself, he could have escaped the hemlock. But then perhaps without the hemlock his ideas would not have achieved immortality. We have all met a bloke in the pub with some challenging opinions, but mostly we do not remember his name or his beliefs the next morning, let alone after two millennia. But Socrates was not a man for silence, and perhaps, even more than his impiety, what disturbed the people of Athens so profoundly was his capacity to argue *without* conviction, and his penchant for teaching others the trick. It was his ability to divorce what went on in his head from what came out of his mouth to touch and twist the minds of others that made him such a threat to society. Socrates could argue that black was white until his audience was blue in the face. And he taught his students how to construct a sophisticated argument that would justify murdering their own fathers. There was no morality at the heart of the argument, just the appeal of using reason to justify the unreasonable. He may have argued that this was a tool to provoke the labour pains needed for the birth of new ideas. But the Athenians didn't see it that way. They just heard toxic ideas delivered as irrefutable common sense.

Socrates was the original ancient 'influencer', and his followers led two coups that overthrew democracy in the city for brief periods before the status quo was re-established. So it is perhaps unsurprising that Athenians blamed him for the devastating fallout of the political upheaval, divine or otherwise. The potential physical consequences of dangerous ideas once they are shared is the reason why human rights law makes a distinction between the absolute protection of thought inside your head and the limited protection of free speech and the sharing of thoughts and opinions.

Was the trial and punishment of Socrates an early attempt by democracy to protect itself from the threat of autocratic propaganda and fake news? If so, it illustrates how durable the legacy of a martyr to free speech can be, no matter what their message. Socrates' fate has been variously portrayed as a lesson in the dangers of mob rule[7] or the rightful application of Athenian law, which reflected the needs of Athenian society to protect itself from tyranny.[8] Whatever your views on the teachings or ideas of

Socrates, one thing is clear: the democracy of antiquity did not respect the right not to be penalised for your thoughts or beliefs, and if sharing your thoughts upset the status quo, you could be made to pay for your audacity with your life.

Socrates is just one of many martyrs to inner freedom whose ideas and beliefs have been amplified by the brutal attempts to silence them. And their ideas have changed the world far beyond their own lifetime. Jesus Christ was perhaps one of the most influential martyrs to freedom of thought and belief of all time, as J. S. Mill pointed out.[9] And Voltaire, in his essay on freedom of thought, quipped: 'If the first Christians had not had the freedom to think, is it not true that Christianity itself would never have come into being?'[10] But that history did not prevent Christians themselves from attacking others who thought outside the box. Take Hypatia of Alexandria, in ancient Egypt, a mathematician, astrologer, scientist and philosopher. One of the few female thinkers of antiquity whose life and work are relatively well documented, she was a Neoplatonist pagan with her own school and was tolerant of other faiths. She taught Christians and pagans alike while establishing herself as a person of significant political influence. But tolerance was no protection against religious violence, and Hypatia met her death in 415 AD at the hands of a mob of Christians who felt that her paganism and scientific beliefs were a threat to their religious institutions. Her murder transformed her into a philosophical martyr, ensuring that her legacy would last through the millennia, her reputation shifting, ironically, from a legend of Christian sainthood in the Middle Ages to feminist intellectual icon in the twentieth century. All of these martyrs discovered how deadly it could be to live without the right to freedom of thought and belief.

Did the earth move?

Deep suspicion of radical thought and the dangers of opinions that questioned the status quo were not simply a quirk of antiquity, and Hypatia was not the only scientist to clash with Christian dogma. Over 2,000 years after Socrates' death, across the Aegean Sea, another bearded septuagenarian, the astronomer and 'father of modern science',[11] Galileo, found himself facing the wrath of the Roman Inquisition for his scientific and philosophical ideas about the nature of the universe. His views about heliocentrism, the idea that the earth moved around the sun and was not a fixed point at the centre of the universe, were controversial at the time, both scientifically and, more importantly, theologically. In 1616, on the orders of Pope Paul V, Cardinal Bellarmine ordered Galileo 'to abandon completely ... the opinion that the sun stands still at the center of the world and the Earth moves, and henceforth not to hold, teach, or defend it in any way whatever, either orally or in writing'.[12] It wasn't just spreading or sharing the opinion that the Church was concerned about; holding the opinion was enough to breach the papal edict – but how could anyone actually tell whether or not Galileo really held an opinion?

Fortunately for science, but not for him, Galileo just couldn't help himself. After more than a decade outside of the searing glare of religious controversy, he published *Dialogue Concerning the Two Chief World Systems*, a book that explored arguments for heliocentrism alongside the Aristotelian ideas of geocentrism supported by the Church. Pope Urban VIII had allowed him to write the book on the agreement that he would include the Pope's words so that it would be a balanced discourse rather than a treatise in favour of heliocentrism. But the Pope's ideas were expressed by a character called 'Simplicio', and despite Galileo's protestations in the preface that this was a reference to the Aristotelian philosopher Simplicius, it seems Pope Urban just couldn't get past the possibility that the author had lent his ideas to a character known by the Italian word for 'simpleton'.

Galileo was tried in 1633 for 'holding as true the false doctrine taught by some that the sun is the centre of the world and the view that one may hold and defend an opinion as probable after it has been declared contrary to Holy Scripture'. It was holding the opinion that was the transgression, though it was its defence that got him caught. Having cast the Pope's view as that of a simpleton, the book was taken to be an advocacy tool for heliocentrism rather than a neutral exposé of two schools of thought that might just have got past the censors. Yet Galileo maintained the position throughout his trial that he had not held any of the banned opinions since 1616. In the seventeenth century, the technology for extracting people's thoughts was fairly rudimentary, but the tools of torture had always been a reliable method for gathering irrefutable proof of heretical ideas when more obvious evidence was not readily available. In his final interrogation, Galileo was threatened with torture if he didn't speak the truth.[13] Still he maintained that the heresy had not crossed his mind since 1616, though he did eventually admit that someone else could read those ideas into the *Dialogue* if they were so inclined.

His protestations of innocent thought did not save him, though. He was found to be 'vehemently suspect of heresy', required to 'abjure, curse and detest'[14] those opinions and sentenced to indefinite imprisonment.[15] Not having been found guilty of heresy itself, he narrowly avoided a sentence of torture or even capital punishment. But he was held under house arrest for the rest of his life and died nine years later knowing that he was right. In a famous portrait attributed to the seventeenth-century Spanish painter Murillo, an exhausted Galileo holds a nail and looks wistfully at the words he has carved into the wall of his prison cell, '*E pur si muove*' ('And yet it moves') – the rebellious barb he is said to have muttered after renouncing his opinions before the court.[16] Galileo would no doubt have approved of George Orwell's assertion: 'Freedom is the freedom to say that two plus two make four. If that is granted, all else follows.'[17]

Most people now accept Galileo's theories as a true picture of the universe. But the rights to freedom of thought and opinion mean that those who question scientific received wisdom today, at least in countries where human rights are respected, do not find themselves imprisoned for that, whether or not they voice their opinions. If you want to believe that the earth is flat, you can go ahead, but you might need to be prepared to be called a simpleton if you choose to share the thought with others, especially online. In 2019, YouTube influencer Logan Paul produced a mockumentary, *FLAT EARTH: To the Edge and Back*,[18] in which he documented his experiences speaking at a flat-earth conference. At the time of writing, the movie has had over 7.6 million views. Luckily for Paul, despite the alleged biblical foundations of their beliefs, flat-earthers are in no position to condemn him to house arrest for laughing at their views, even if they did not appreciate the joke. But where questioning received scientific wisdom might put others' lives at risk, like the social media influencers spreading disinformation on vaccinations, human rights law does allow, and even require, the state to take action to protect the rights of others. Individual freedom does not include the freedom to cause harm to other people.

Back in seventeenth-century Europe, it was not only the Catholic Church that frowned upon dissent. While Galileo was trying to hold his tongue in Catholic Italy about his scientific discoveries, further north, others were struggling to align their religious views with those of mainstream Protestant institutions. Times of turbulence like the Reformation blurred the lines between political and religious belief. No doubt millions of people took the political decision to hold their religious beliefs quietly inside their heads while paying lip service to whatever religion was flavour of the month for the monarchy. But there were also thousands of martyrs who chose death or exile over denying or changing their beliefs. The strength of inner conviction would simply not allow them to renounce their faith or act in a way that went contrary to it.

When the Pilgrim Fathers set sail on the *Mayflower*, it may have been the external manifestation of their beliefs that got them into trouble in England, but it was their inner convictions, their fervent beliefs that made it intolerable for them to stay where they were and adapt to the status quo. For most of us, it is hard to imagine the kind of inner conviction that could drive you to board a ship with no clear idea of a destination, and a remote chance of survival. But the twin drivers of passionate belief and fear of persecution have been behind the migration of millions over millennia. And religious freedom, the siren call of America, ranks for many above the pursuit of happiness and the economic lure of the American dream. But even relative religious freedom does not protect you from the kind of inferences about your inner world that could make you a threat to society. For many people, whether or not they actually held the beliefs ascribed to them or ever expressed a controversial idea did not matter. The mere suspicion of moral corruption could be enough to be burned at the stake, if not in the eternal fires of hell.

Bewitched

When I was about 12, one of my sisters came home from school concerned about a rumour going around that I had joined a coven. As it happened, at that time I might have done so if I had had the benefit of the internet to find out how to go about it. But in fact the rumour was totally groundless, put about by a girl from school who I didn't much like and it seems did not like me. By the 1980s in the Isle of Man, being accused of witchcraft no longer carried the risk of being rolled down the witches' hill in a spiked barrel to check whether you were evil enough to survive, but it was clearly still enough of a taint to be worth gossiping about. The famous witchcraft trials of Salem may have taken place in the relative freedom of the New World, but they had their roots in a European hostility to thinking outside of the religious box, particularly if you were a woman, that was not shaken off by crossing the Atlantic.

Today in Europe it is hard to imagine the true horror of being accused of witchcraft that many still experience around the world. But the Basque village of Zugarramurdi, in the mountainous region near the border between France and Spain, carries deep scars of what a witch hunt really meant in seventeenth-century Europe. On a sunny summer day, the scene is idyllic: rolling pastures, deep green from the regular rains sweeping in from the Atlantic, the heavy white walls and red shutters of slumbering *basseri* farmhouses dotting a landscape peppered with idle livestock. It is a picture postcard of rural calm, not how you expect the epicentre of mass persecution and the torture of thousands of men, women and children to look. But this was 'ground zero' for one of the most devastating witch hunts in history. It was triggered by one young woman, Maria de Ximildegui, who, returning from France to the area in 1608, felt the sudden, urgent need to confess to the local priest about her participation in black masses, or *akelarre*. Who knows what prompted her to confess to involvement in witchcraft – did she really want to save her own soul, or was she looking for a way to exact revenge on Maria de Jureteguia, who she implicated with her? Either way, she could not have imagined the scale of the trauma that she would bring down on her whole community.[19]

The Basque country, with its deep, impenetrable valleys, incomprehensibly archaic language and hints of matriarchal history, has always felt very different to the rest of Spain, and being different can be dangerous. The Spanish Inquisition launched the biggest witch hunt ever seen in Spain from Logroño in 1609. It resulted in around 7,000 cases being examined, the largest number of any witch hunt in history.

Alonso de Salazar Frías was tasked with looking into the problem in the region of Zugarramurdi. His investigations included the promise of pardon to all those who handed themselves in voluntarily or reported on their accomplices. When he returned from his travels, he had confessions from around 2,000 people, 1,384 of whom were children aged between seven and fourteen. But only six ultimately stood by their confessions, the others claiming that their statements had been extracted through torture. Despite Salazar's own concerns about the credibility of the confessions, the *auto-da-fé*, an elaborate public ceremony where sentences for witchcraft were read and carried out, went ahead in November 1610, with thirteen people condemned as witches, six of whom were sentenced to death by burning at the stake because they refused to confess and repent. They took with them five wax effigies of others who had died during their imprisonment and torture without confessing, but whose likeness would be burnt again just to be sure. Maria de Jureteguia, who had wisely confessed her sins, was fined and sentenced to prison but ultimately pardoned.[20]

The world may have been poorer without their ideas, but Galileo and Socrates would probably have led long and peaceful lives if they had just kept their thoughts to themselves. It was, ultimately, the expression of their ideas and arguments, rather than the holding of them, that meant they were perceived as a threat to their respective societies. But keeping quiet is not necessarily a protection from persecution for thoughts, opinions and beliefs, regardless of whether you even hold them. The policing of ideas and beliefs has rarely been restricted to the suppression of ideas actually expressed. Inferring 'bad' thoughts, whatever form they may take, is not just a phenomenon of the digital age. It has a long and brutal history. And if you were not prepared to admit to your thoughts, tools of torture were developed to make you confess to pretty much anything.

The ideas of women and children were not generally given much weight in medieval and early modern society in western Europe. But the need to control and dominate thought and belief, ignited by the economic, religious and political fault lines emerging out of the Reformation,[21] pushed the authorities to imagine and impute dangerous beliefs and thoughts wherever they looked. Whole swathes of the population who didn't quite fit in were targeted and destroyed. Rooting out witchcraft was a deadly business. Across Europe, of the 80,000[22] people prosecuted in the wave of witchcraft trials that accompanied the Reformation, over 80 per cent were women; 40,000 were executed following trial. In most cases, the processes of the trial and punishment left little opportunity to prove the innocence of your thoughts or change your mind. The internal truth of the belief in and practice of witchcraft was inferred from external signs that could be construed from almost anything – moles, skin tags, warts and scars reinterpreted as witches' teats; cats, birds and other animal companions clearly suspect as witches' familiars.

Witch hunts and witchcraft trials were common fixtures in Britain and northern Europe too, and spread across the Atlantic with Protestant emigrants to North America, where the witch trials of Salem have captured the imagination of generations. This scale of persecution, torturing women and children to get them to report on the supposed spiritual deviance of their friends, neighbours and families, may seem like a blip in history. But it was as recently as 1944 in Britain that Helen Duncan, a Scottish medium, became the last woman convicted under the Witchcraft Act of 1735,[23] the jury having failed to convict her on the less esoteric charges of fraud or breach of national security. And across the world, literal witch hunts continue. The prosecution of witches, whenever or wherever it happens, is perhaps one of the clearest examples of the way inferences about a person's inner state, their beliefs, intentions and mental powers, can be an extremely powerful and dangerous tool for authorities to stamp out anyone they perceive as different or difficult.

Thinking about freedom

Believing the wrong thing in the wrong place at the wrong time in the seventeenth century was viewed as a potentially fatal character flaw. In a world without freedom of thought, thinking itself was dangerous, but thinking about freedom of thought was particularly risky. Despite the inherent dangers, the human urge for freedom was irrepressible, and the nascent shoots of ideas around inner freedom could be found if you knew where to look. Socrates' philosophy may have aimed to provoke, shaking up the status quo, but other philosophers developed ideas of freedom of thought itself that were grounded in tolerance and the concept of mental and spiritual liberty as a natural right. The philosophers who developed the ideas that formed the basis of the right to freedom of thought understood from their own experience how pressing the human urge for freedom was, even in the face of religious, political or social barriers. And freedom is not a uniquely European concept.

Born in 1599 on an Ethiopian farm, Zera Yacob showed such intellectual promise as a child that he was sent at an early age to study rhetoric, poetry and critical thinking before learning the Christian teachings of the Catholic, Coptic and Orthodox churches at Bible school. As a philosopher and teacher in the 1620s, Yacob taught that no religion could be considered as 'right' over any other,[24] a view that the Ethiopian king, having been converted to Catholicism by a visiting Portuguese Jesuit, could simply not permit. The purge of free thinkers in Ethiopia in 1630 led Yacob to hide out in a remote cave for two years, protecting his ideas from the imported intolerance and developing the rationalist philosophy he went on to transcribe in his *Hatata*, a collection of philosophical investigations into the nature of knowledge and of God. Yacob believed that reason was supreme, that all religions and doctrines could be open to critique, but that the existence of a creator god was the most rational explanation for our existence.

In an extremely unequal world, Yacob's ideas were radical: 'All men are equal in the presence of God; and all are intelligent, since they are his creatures; he did not assign one people for life, another for death, one for mercy, another for judgment.'[25] His belief in the equality of all humans did not allow for exceptions – men and women were created equal and slavery could not be justified.[26] Freedom is not a uniquely European ideal; it is fundamental to our humanity, no matter where you are. The scope and scale of Yacob's ideas about freedom developed in the sanctity of his Ethiopian cave almost 200 years before the French Revolution have been overlooked by history.[27] But it would be three centuries before his European or American counterparts, prompted by their Chinese and Lebanese colleagues, could conceive of such an unequivocal and far-reaching notion of human equality and inner freedom in the Universal Declaration of Human Rights.

In seventeenth-century Holland, a relatively tolerant society at the time and no longer governed by the might of the Catholic Church, it was still dangerous to be raising questions about the nature of faith. In 1610, a Dutch religious group known as the Arminians wrote a 'Remonstrance' explaining the ways in which their beliefs differed from the orthodox Calvinism of the state. They argued for religious tolerance on the basis that faith was a matter of individual conscience and so should not be subjected to the power of the state. Unfortunately for them, in 1618, the national synod took a different view, finding that their tolerant opinions could simply not be tolerated. As a result, they were purged from political and intellectual positions of influence while their leader was put to death.

This was the world that Baruch (also known as Benedict) Spinoza, a Dutch philosopher from a Sephardic Jewish family was born into in 1620.[28] Spinoza's philosophical vision was as clear and far-reaching as the telescopic lenses he ground to earn his living. He may have led the life of a 'secular saint'[29] by stepping outside religious boundaries and living according to his teaching, but he had no time for miracles and his reason was unclouded by spiritual or emotional concerns. Spinoza's courage in actually publishing a treatise on freedom of thought and expressing avowedly atheist views despite his own direct experience of the existential battles between politics and theology is a testament to the strength of his convictions.

The Jewish community of Amsterdam was well aware of the risks of being found on the wrong side of discussions on religion and faith. Spinoza's family had made Amsterdam their home after being hounded out of Portugal for their religious beliefs. So when Spinoza was excommunicated in 1656 for his 'evil opinions' and 'abominable heresies', it may be that the community was trying to protect itself from the taint of irreligious views expressed in his correspondence. Accusing organised religions like the 'Catholic and Mahomedan Churches' of being both 'politic and lucrative to many' while 'suited to deceive the people and to constrain the minds of men'[30] was a risky business. Spinoza, perhaps unsurprisingly, though at the time daringly, did not seek to replace his Jewish faith community by joining another church. Instead, he chose to keep his mind for himself, even as he watched his close friend and fellow philosopher Adriaan Koerbagh rot in jail for publishing heretical ideas that he himself essentially agreed with. But despite, or perhaps because of, his deep and personal understanding of what it could mean to live without freedom of thought, Spinoza's *Tractatus Theologico-Politicus* is one of the first clear treatises on freedom of thought as we understand it today.

He argued that 'in a free state every man may think what he likes, and say what he thinks'.[31] In doing so, he put freedom of thought and expression at the heart of political freedom, and made clear the foundational importance of the internal aspect of freedom of thought as a bulwark against tyranny. As he put it, 'If men's minds were as easily controlled as their tongues, every king would sit safely on his throne ... for every subject would shape his life according to the intentions of his rulers, and would esteem a thing true or false, good or evil, just or unjust, in obedience to their dictates.'[32]

Spinoza defined freedom of thought as a deeply personal and natural right. And he argued that no one could transfer their right of free reason or judgement to another, either by consent or by compulsion. This helps to explain why inner freedoms should not be subjected to the limitations of state interpretation in the way that other liberties may be. Free thinking, even on religion, was, for Spinoza, the supreme right and a question solely for the individual. Only those rights that could be considered public rights should be subjected to the interpretation of the law rather than the individual.[33]

Although Spinoza's concern was primarily with freedom of philosophical thought rather than freedom of religion, he recognised that there was a fundamental difference between the practice of religion and the holding of religious belief, remarking that 'Inward worship of God and piety in itself are within the sphere of everyone's private rights, and cannot be alienated.' So while he advocated for the state having priority over the Church, his approach to faith is grounded in the concept of inner freedom rather than organised religion: 'Simplicity and truth of character are not produced by the constraint of laws, nor by the authority of the state, no one the whole world over can be forced or legislated into a state of blessedness.'[34]

Spinoza's description of the inner aspects of the right to freedom of thought, conscience, religion and belief, and its inalienable and inviolable nature, are remarkably prescient of the rights we see encoded in twentieth-century international human rights law. His ideas about individual liberty were radical and potentially dangerous in his time. But while they ran through the eighteenth-century Age of Enlightenment like a clandestine undercurrent, like Yacob in

Ethiopia his influence is hard to track. Contemporaries and later thinkers distanced themselves from him, and his ideas carried the still toxic taint of atheism. Reasoning without God was still not a reasonable thing to do in a world where believing the wrong thing carried a potential death sentence.

On Liberty

If Spinoza and Yacob were the unattributable midwives of inner freedom, Enlightenment thinkers like Voltaire, Rousseau, Wollstonecraft and Paine brought liberty to political maturity in the eighteenth century, laying the groundwork for a political movement that would make freedom a reality. But thinking was still a risky business. Even Voltaire, the French satirist, writer and philosopher, spent several years of his life either locked up in the Bastille or in exile for his scurrilous ideas about freedom in the decades before *liberté* became a cornerstone of what it meant to be French. Voltaire was not around to see the bicentenary party of the French Revolution on the Champs-Elysées in 1989. Sometimes it can take a while for society to catch up.

But it was J. S. Mill, the nineteenth-century British utilitarian philosopher who built on the Enlightenment ideas about freedom and outlined the bare bones of a right to freedom of thought as we might recognise it today. By Mill's time, although religion was still the backbone of society, in Britain at least there was little threat of torture or a death sentence for exploring philosophical or scientific ideas. But Mill felt that the weight of social stigma in Victorian England was a more effective suppressor of individual thought than the harsher penalties enshrined in other countries' laws for thinking, or saying, the wrong thing.

When I first read Mill's 1859 essay *On Liberty*[35] under the fluorescent strip lights of the student cafeteria on a dark January afternoon in Edinburgh, I approached it with a distinctly utilitarian mindset. Mill was just another Victorian man whose words I had to process in order to pass my exams. It lacked the revolutionary glamour of the Bastille and the Berlin Wall that had forged my ideas on freedom the year before, and most importantly, where was the party? Freedom without fireworks just wasn't freedom. But if I had understood then that the genesis of *On Liberty* was an epic, tragic love story comparable to the tale of Tristan and Isolde that I was entranced with on my medieval French course, I might have paid more attention at the time to the emotional and intellectual truth in the pages. Mill's life, like his work, was an exploration of the ways in which we must strive for inner freedom, even through the heavy bars of social constraints.

London Zoo may not be the first place you would go to think about freedom. But for Mill and Harriet Taylor, the zoo offered an escape from the cage of Victorian middle-class society they found themselves trapped in and judged by. It is not only laws and political or religious institutions that can limit our freedom; the threat of social ostracisation can be enough for most people to limit what they allow themselves to think or feel. But for Mill, inner freedom was not something he could give up.

When they first met in 1830, Harriet was stuck in a stultifying marriage to a rather dull man with whom she had two small children. The depth of her dark eyes in the picture of her in the National Portrait Gallery gives an idea of how Mill was entranced by the windows to her soul. Mill himself was recovering from a profound period of depression after an intensely intellectual upbringing. His serious, bony face and flinty eyes give away nothing of the soft, romantic heart and openness of spirit that Harriet found in him. They were both so enthralled with each other that they managed to spend time together despite their impossible predicament, and it was the rhinoceros enclosure at London Zoo that provided the backdrop to their budding romance. Despite its inauspicious start, their relationship survived through a test run living together in Paris and an interlude of sharing social and marital space, until finally, following the death of her first husband in 1849, they were married in 1851. Sadly, Harriet only survived another seven years, dying of a wasting disease the year before Mill finally published *On Liberty*, which was dedicated to the woman who had shared his intellectual love of freedom and driven his belief in true equality of the sexes. For Mill and Taylor, freedom of thought included the freedom to love no matter what anyone else thought of them. It was their experience of the pressures of social constraints that drove their understanding of what liberty means in practice.

On Liberty was a testament to the wilful unpredictability and force of human love. In defining the scope of human liberty, Mill recognised its expansive and comprehensive inner aspect, including 'liberty of thought and feeling; absolute freedom of opinion and sentiment on all subjects, practical or speculative, scientific, moral or theological'. While he distinguished this inner realm from the liberty of expressing or publishing opinions, he was clear that these two aspects were 'practically inseparable'. He was particularly concerned with the interaction between personal thought and society, noting the crushing effect that public opinion could have on individual freedom of thought.

Mill and Taylor had managed to maintain their own freedom regardless of what others thought of them, and throughout his essay he explores how freedom can be maintained and protected from the stifling influence of society. He was particularly scathing of English society, which he said 'practises a social tyranny more formidable than many kinds of political oppression, since, though not usually upheld by such extreme penalties, it leaves fewer means of escape, penetrating much more deeply into the details of life, and enslaving the soul itself'. Even in our modern global, connected world, where we all feel that we can reach out across the ether and find people who think like us, the threat of a Twitter pile-on and the constant sharing of idealised lives can have a corrosive impact on genuine freedom to think and feel about the world and about ourselves. Social disapproval may not be as harsh a punishment for thought as death by hemlock, and in some countries, even today, Mill and Taylor could have faced the death penalty for their adulterous love. But for many, the threat of social opprobrium is enough to put them off thinking too freely. And this chilling effect is a death knell for human development and innovation. Freedom of thought is not only vital for the individual, but it is also the beating heart of a dynamic and prosperous society. As Mill noted, 'there have been, and may again be, great individual thinkers, in a general atmosphere of mental slavery. But there never has been, nor ever will be, in that atmosphere, an intellectually active people.' For him, the protection of individuality was the ultimate bulwark against political despotism.[36]

Freedom implies the possibility of change, and Mill recognised explicitly that opinions change and become redundant and absurd as time moves on. His analysis of freedom of thought was open-minded and modern. He had very little time for xenophobia and had a deep love for Europe, splitting his time between London and Avignon as he appreciated the 'free and genial atmosphere of Continental life', despite the devastating failure of 1789's revolutionary promise of liberty, equality and fraternity. But notwithstanding his wide-ranging commitment to freedom of thought in the Victorian era, a twenty-first-century assessment must certainly reject his assertion that freedom should not be extended to those he considered 'immature in their faculties', including children and 'those backward states of society in which the race itself may be considered as in its nonage'.[37] Mill had clearly not read the work of Yacob, whose ideas on freedom of belief, the power of reason and human equality had been so much more fully developed in his cave in Ethiopia 200 years earlier. But he would always have been open to being proved wrong and to changing his mind.

Three quarters of a century on from the development of the right to freedom of thought in the UDHR, in many parts of the world, thinking freely in ways that challenge the status quo can still land you in jail. In 2020, 69 countries around the world still had criminal blasphemy laws, with Pakistan, Iran and Russia leading the scoreboard on the numbers of people prosecuted under laws that still carry penalties, including in some cases the death penalty, for daring to believe beyond the official religious doctrine.[38] Even in the UK, blasphemy laws dating back to the Middle Ages were only formally abolished in Scotland in 2021 and remained on the statute books of Northern Ireland at the time of writing. For most people in history, following the right church services and saying the right things might have saved their skins, if not their souls, during times of political and religious unrest. But in the twenty-first century, we are no longer in control of the outward signs we leave of our inner worlds in the infinite constellations of our data trails. In the digital world, heretical thoughts may be inferred not only from what you say online, but also from what you search for and who you know. As the Taliban took over in Afghanistan in the summer of 2021, many of my friends who had lived and worked in the country on human rights projects removed their Afghan contacts from social media friend lists for fear that any connection to the West would put them in danger as a signal of heretical thought. The challenge of erasing the traces of your thoughts and beliefs online in a world where they can still land you in jail has a chilling effect on both spiritual and intellectual exploration that has consequences not only for the individuals who may be silenced, but for humanity as a whole.

Without freedom of thought, we would all be sitting on a flat earth worried that if we strayed too far, we might fall off the edge. So we must be thankful for those thinkers, from Socrates to Mill and beyond, who were prepared to take the severe risk of thinking about freedom of thought, no matter what the consequences, so that we now can enjoy it. But true inner freedom requires protection. Just as Yacob found his inspiration in the safety of a mountain cave, we need to carve out our own space to allow our inner freedom to flourish, away from the constraints and pressures of the modern world. To protect us from the risk of judgement or penalty for our thoughts and to allow them to flourish, we need to be able to keep our thoughts to ourselves. But while freedom of thought is a prerequisite for scientific discovery, as we will see in the next chapter, it may also be a casualty of science.

CHAPTER 3

———

INSIDE YOUR HEAD

Freedom to think is absolute of its own nature, the most tyrannical government is powerless to control the inward workings of the mind.

US Supreme Court 1942[1]

Ballamona, the old psychiatric hospital in the Isle of Man, took up a mythical space in my childhood mind alongside the witches' hill. It was a place of 'otherness', a Victorian edifice originally built as a lunatic asylum and ringed by wind-weathered trees full of the kind of crows that will peck your eyes out if you show any sign of weakness. It was also the backdrop of my mother's short-lived professional life as a psychiatrist, before I was born, and before small-town sex discrimination put an end to her medical career.

From her short time there, one woman's story affected her deeply. The woman, originally from North Africa, had married a Manxman and come home with him sometime in the first half of the twentieth century. When things started to go wrong and love soured, this woman's response – a dramatic, foreign response with an unfamiliar accent – was cast by her husband and his family as evidence of a dangerous mental condition that led to her being sectioned and losing her freedom for life. She was left to rot away in the dark Victorian corridors without a chance of reprieve or understanding. By the time my mother met her, decades later, she was so institutionalised, so far from herself, that there was no way out. The story of this woman's institutional ossification is a particularly familiar female story through history. When the attempts to understand oddness gave way, there were two choices for the diagnosis of problematic women – witchcraft or lunacy. If you can't blame the devil, you can always medicalise the issue.

In previous centuries, religion was the key to controlling and penalising wayward thoughts. But science and medicine, in particular psychiatry, have also played a pivotal role in the quest to understand what we are thinking and to fix it, or shut it down when it does not conform. They have offered up both the tools and the justifications for getting into our minds and rearranging the furniture, whether we want it or not. Millions of people have had their mental and physical liberty stolen away from them either to fix the way they think or to keep thoughts perceived as dangerous away from the rest of society. The field of psychiatry epitomises the interconnection between the three aspects of freedom of thought: the right to keep your thoughts to yourself, the right not to have your thoughts manipulated and the right not to be penalised for your thoughts.

When the US Supreme Court referred to the absolute character of freedom of thought in the lofty terms of natural rights,[2] they had clearly underestimated the ingenuity of scientists and doctors to get inside and control the inner workings of our minds, and the drive of governments to harness that. What the Supreme Court justices assumed to be a safe inner space was already embattled by the progress of scientific study. The shift from religion to science as the dominant driver of mind control in the twentieth century meant that, even at the time of their judgment in 1942, their assumptions about freedom of thought were already out of date.

Reason and unreason

The judgements we make of each other, when they are systematised, can change the course of people's lives and the collective psyche of whole communities. How societies have treated people who think differently has evolved over time. As we have seen, as well as the draconian responses to thinkers whose ideas threatened the theological or political status quo, societies have struggled to find an approach to managing people whose thoughts or passions do not fit comfortably within societal or cultural norms. Michel Foucault, in his *History of Madness*, describes the almost mystical exclusion of people considered mad in the Middle Ages, with boatmen carrying those categorised as insane in exile down Europe's waterways on boats like the *Ship of Fools* depicted by Hieronymus Bosch in the fifteenth century. Later, in 'the confinement' of seventeenth-century France, when those considered insane were locked away, the borders between reason and unreason were drawn up to exclude a broad swathe of unorthodox thoughts and feelings from polite society. Unreason and madness became a moral question. Foucault mentions the Marquis de Sade and a woman who refused to love her husband as examples of 'the venereal, the debauched, the dissolute, blasphemers, homosexuals, alchemists and libertines [who] found themselves on the wrong side of a dividing line, and were thrown together as recluses in asylums destined, in a century or two, to become the exclusive preserve of madness'.[3]

With the European Enlightenment in the eighteenth century there came a move towards a more compassionate approach to mental health, with the ideas of philosophers like Descartes, Hobbes and Hume informing the development of psychology. And through the nineteenth and twentieth centuries, psychology evolved both through the soul-searching psychoanalysis techniques exemplified in the work of Freud and Jung and through empirical studies on human and animal behaviour alongside direct explorations of the functioning of the brain. This was a shift towards understanding what was going on inside the mind and changing it, rather than simply locking people up who thought, or seemed to think, outside the norm. The range of psychological study since that time has informed education, medicine, politics, advertising, warfare, love and almost every other aspect of our lives.

Understanding and changing the workings of the human mind through the brain has taken over from religious control of the soul as the key to managing the future of humanity. But despite its medicalisation, as Foucault explains, the 'scientific' knowledge of mental illness today is still based on the way religious and sexual prohibitions and the freedom of thought and of emotion were lumped together with madness in the domain of unreason in the classical age.[4] The term 'psychiatry' was first coined in 1808, by the German physician Johann Christian Reil, from the Greek words *psyche* (the mind or soul) and *iatros* (healer). And through the nineteenth and twentieth centuries, psychiatry explored the biological causes and potential cures of mental states. In Nazi Germany, psychiatrists and other doctors and mental health professionals played a crucial role in the identification, sterilisation, torture and murder of thousands of people with mental disabilities and illness, or, as Canadian psychiatrist Mary V. Seeman put it, 'the socially and spiritually unworthy – persons with mental illness, the socially wayward, criminals, Gypsies, homosexuals, and Jews'.[5] Seeman studies psychiatrists' involvement in Nazi atrocities not simply as a historical curiosity, but to shine a light on the risks of a profession that has such a unique ability to interfere with what it means to be human – as a warning for the future. The horrors of many of the psychiatric interventions of the early twentieth century are hard to square with the idea of 'therapy'. Treatments like deep sleep therapy used drugs to induce profound sleep for days or weeks, while other drugs induced daily comas or convulsions. Electroconvulsive therapy, which puts massive voltages of electricity through a patient's brain, causing seizures, was portrayed in the movie *One Flew Over the Cuckoo's Nest*, shocking audiences with its apparent inhumanity.

Perhaps the most horrifyingly invasive form of treatment aimed at getting inside the mind is the use of psychosurgical procedures like the lobotomy or leucotomy. This kind of treatment may not try to read what is going on inside the head, but it would certainly change it. And in some cases, it was used as a kind of punishment, to neutralise people who were deemed to be problematic. Its originator, the Portuguese neurologist António Egas Moniz, controversially won the Nobel Prize for Physiology or Medicine in 1949 for his invention, which was, by 1950, banned in the Soviet Union for its extreme inhumanity. Surgery designed to cut connections in the brain as a treatment for mental disorders like schizophrenia and depression was carried out on tens of thousands of people in Europe and North America in the decades after the Second World War, in particular in the UK and the US. But far from being a panacea, the effects of such dramatic psychosurgery were mind-numbing and dehumanising. Quite apart from the 5 per cent death rate for these procedures in the 1940s, many who underwent them went on to commit suicide. Others were left infantilised, unable to function in society and denuded of their emotions and personality. Walter Freeman, an American physician who practised lobotomies, described the results as 'surgically induced childhood'. Of one woman post-lobotomy, he said she was a 'smiling, lazy and satisfactory patient with the personality of an oyster'.[6] The British psychiatrist Maurice Partridge described the effects as 'reducing the complexity of psychic life'.[7] It is hard to imagine a more potent limitation on freedom of thought.

It was not just a last-resort therapy in a handful of severe cases, and the majority of lobotomies were carried out on women.[8] The New Zealand author Janet Frame was famously scheduled for a frontal lobotomy, which was cancelled when she won a national literary prize the day before the operation was due to take place. Children as young as 12 and people who did not fit well into society's mould were subjected to this soul-destroying practice. Psychiatry, with some extreme forms of cruel, inhuman and degrading treatment, was used in the twentieth century to manage unorthodox minds as well as to treat mental illness.

These treatments are not only concerning from a medical ethics perspective. They raise serious concerns about the violation of the rights to physical and mental integrity as well as absolute rights, including the prohibition on torture, inhuman and degrading treatment and the right not to have your thoughts manipulated or be punished for your thoughts alone. Scientific interferences with freedom of thought touch all three aspects of the right. In order to manipulate or penalise thought, the first step is to find out or at least to guess what someone is thinking and what makes them tick. And scientists through the ages have devised a range of ingenious ways to try to read our minds and to identify those of us who do not conform.

What's in a face?

Things may have accelerated in the twentieth and twenty-first centuries, but scientists have been looking for ways to get into our heads, to read, change and constrain our minds, for as long as there have been scientists. What goes on inside our heads is physically protected by our skulls and the skin stretched over them. We all know that we shouldn't judge a book by its cover, but at the same time, we seem to be programmed to do just that. We have to rely on external clues to try to understand what is going on inside other people, so we can decide how we should respond to them. We try to read their expressions when we are talking to them or walking past them on the street to gauge if they are friendly or might be a threat. And we may make an even more basic assessment about their physical features. The problem is when we go too far. We may instinctively judge each other on sight, but most of us recognise that we need to rein in our first impressions to respond to what people say and do, not just what they look like. Relying on your gut in your day-to-day interactions is one thing. Justifying your prejudice with science is quite another.

The institutionally biased assumptions about criminality and race that minorities suffer at the hands of the police, authorities and wider society are still tragically commonplace and potentially deadly, as the Black Lives Matter movement has recently underlined. But at least in Europe, we have laws that prohibit discrimination based on race, gender, disability and other grounds, which aim to stop our propensity for prejudice. These biases are a flaw in the observer, not the observed. But over millennia, from ancient Mesopotamia to Silicon Valley in the present day, some people have sought to justify such prejudice through the veil of 'scientific truth' – to get at our character or our thoughts and feelings through the supposedly scientific analysis of what we look like.

The word 'physiognomy' has its roots in two Greek words: *physis* (nature) and *gnomon* (one who knows), and it is the claim that someone can know our minds through the map of our faces. The first written work on the art, *Physiognomonics*, dates from the time of Aristotle and gives three keys to reading the mind through the face. The first indication of a person's character is the animal they most resemble; next, their race should be taken into account; and finally, the interpretation of their facial expressions would cement the analysis. In short, according to the principles of physiognomy, if you look like an angry dark shrew, you probably are one. *Physiognomonics* gave the person judging you the intellectual reassurance of a carefully argued cod theory to back up whatever lazy prejudice already informed their view of you.

The traces of misogyny were also laid thick in the pseudoscience of mind-reading in the ancient world. Male faces were assessed as being strong or generous, while women's faces displayed the well-known feminine characteristics of fear, envy or greed. Such biases pervade the modern world too. In 2019, an art installation created by Google PAIR called *Waterfall of Meaning*[9] at the 'AI: More Than Human' exhibition at the Barbican in London was designed as 'a poetic glimpse into the interior of an AI, showing how a machine absorbs human associations between words'. Chosen words descended the screen through machine-learning analysis that would tell you how they ranked through a set of associations, including 'he' or 'she' and 'good' or 'bad'. As I selected random words and watched their trajectory, I noticed, perhaps unsurprisingly, that words with a high correlation with 'she' tended to also have a high correlation with 'bad' as they made their way down the screen. 'Fluff' was 83 per cent 'she' and 73 per cent 'bad'; while 'safe' was 64 per cent 'he' and 90 per cent 'good'. Words that are commonly associated with femininity are also commonly viewed as negative. Masculine words, by contrast, are generally positive. These correlations reflect the way people see things when asked to categorise them. The machine, it is clear, was not immune to the disease of human prejudice; it was fed on it.

For the Greeks, physiognomy was not only a way of diagnosing illness and character flaws; it was also a window into the future, with face-reading providing insights into a person's fate alongside other divination methods like astrology or palmistry. The lines on your face would not only reveal the rigours of your past; they would also help plot the path of your future. And it was this reach into the esoteric that eventually brought the practice into disrepute, rather than its potential for justifying discrimination against whole swathes of the population. In sixteenth-century England, physiognomy was outlawed not because of its prejudicial impact on the people subjected to it, but because of its association with the fortune-telling of Romani people and vagrants, who were themselves viewed as suspect and antisocial by the authorities. But in the Italian Renaissance period, physiognomy was resurrected and rebranded as 'natural science', thanks to the illustrated *De Humana Physiognomonia* of Giambattista della Porta, published in 1585. And it was the *Essays on Physiognomy* by the eighteenth-century Swiss physiognomist and Protestant pastor Johann Kaspar Lavater that propelled physiognomy into its Victorian heyday.

Of course, physiognomy was not the only scientific exploration of character analysis from the physical. The development of the 'science' of phrenology by the German physician Franz Joseph Gall in the eighteenth century was based on his observation that people with bulgy eyes seemed to have very good memories. Bringing his personal experience together with the idea that the brain was the physical organ of the mind, he concluded that brains of different shapes and sizes indicated characters and mental qualities of different types. Phrenology claimed to analyse a person's personality or talents by mapping the shape of their skull. If the mind is manifest in the brain, and variations in the size of different parts of the brain are indications of the relative strength of different characteristics, Gall believed that reading the contours of bumps and plateaus on the head could give a clear insight into the workings of the mind. The craze for phrenology spread from Germany via Edinburgh to Britain and the United States during the nineteenth century, turning from a serious attempt by men of science to understand the human mind to a quick way to make money by capitalising on the human need to understand ourselves and each other.

Consultations with physiognomists or phrenologists sat alongside other fads for psychics and mesmerism in the Victorian era. The veneer of dubious science lent a degree of credibility to their claims to give insight into our innermost thoughts. Physiognomists could advise you on the true character of a potential spouse based on a photograph. And at the height of phrenology's popularity in the nineteenth century, prospective employers could ask for character references based on phrenological analysis of candidates.[10] Recruitment today continues to be fertile ground for selling scientific and psychological assessments that claim to reveal the inner workings of a candidate's mind, whether through AI interpreting their data trails or facial expressions, or through the science of psychometric testing to check if they will be a good fit.

Phrenological assessments were also sold to doting parents as a scientific confirmation that their darling children would achieve great things and would grow up to be both kind and brilliant. A 1912 report by a Professor W. Hatfield, a graduate of the American Institute of Phrenology, on the mental qualities of a Miss M. J. A. Percival,[11] a pre-schooler, must have reassured her parents with the conclusion:

> In reference to a vocation, she will be in her element as a lady doctor or science teacher. She is a remarkable child, & with suitable management & training her mental qualities will evolve, & she will develop into a capable & superior woman – earnest, resolute, aspiring, positive, & independent. Her intellectual & social powers are so blended that she will be persuasive & magnetic. When her strong qualities are reversed, she will desire to argue the point, & exhibit temper, wilfulness, & sarcasm. She must be treated in a gentle, considerate manner, & her parents should appeal to her intelligence, pride, & affection, then she is easily managed.

It would be interesting to see how these predictions compared with her astrological chart, and whether her parents could get a refund if she turned out to be dull and lazy. And it would also be good to know how this early character analysis affected her future life chances.

Phrenology and physiognomy may have started out with serious thinkers who, however misguided, rooted their theories in the science and philosophy of their times. But their potential for money-making and social control meant they were soon adopted by charlatans, selling spurious insights into the future and finding business opportunities for lazy prejudice that could have very serious implications for job or marriage prospects. If the physiognomist your true love hired to analyse your face did not like the look of you, you might have found yourself swiftly dumped without ever knowing why. A bad phrenological assessment could cost you the chance of a job. Even Charles Darwin's career narrowly missed being derailed when the captain of the *Beagle*, a keen amateur physiognomist, felt that his nose did not show the necessary energy and determination for such a challenging mission.[12] These are the kind of risks we all face today as artificial intelligence is trained to parse data, including biometric data like our photographs, to see if our face fits. From border controls to banks, the automated descendants of Victorian physiognomists are everywhere.

The Enlightenment ideals of liberty, fraternity and equality, while not perfectly executed, had at least opened up the potential for true equality in humanity. But theories of racial superiority based on supposedly scientific ideas also gained ground in the nineteenth century. While Darwin himself believed that the human species was basically the same, his *Origin of Species* fed into the sinister debates about fundamental genetic differences between the races. These discussions fed into the judgements of phrenologists and physiognomists based on the slant of our brows or the cut of our jaws.[13] And the inferences about a person's inner life from their outer appearance risk penalising people for assumptions about the workings of their mind, regardless of their actual thoughts or character. John Beddoe, who went on to be president of the Royal Anthropological Institute, wrote in his *Races of Britain* (1862) that men of genius were all endowed with less prominent jaws. By contrast, the Irish and Welsh with their Celtic origins had prominent jaws that indicated a close relationship to cavemen, whom Beddoe linked to the 'Arficanoid' type.[14] Against this backdrop, J. S. Mill's dubious views that the scope of liberty could not be extended to all races are perhaps less surprising, if no less wrong. The journalist Angela Saini's 2019 book *Superior: The Return of Race Science*[15] explains how in the twenty-first century these kinds of theory about race are again being justified by dubious science, this time using machine learning and artificial intelligence to categorise people's minds according to their race. Saini's book is a stark warning about the enduring appeal of racism dressed up as science. We should never discount the very real threat of men like Beddoe and their ideas for our humanity.

That threat is perhaps at its most acute when applied to crime. The nineteenth-century Italian criminologist and psychiatrist Cesare Lombroso made the link between the study of phrenology and physiognomy and the criminal mind, shifting the understanding and management of crime from the legal field to the scientific. His work *L'uomo Delinquente* (1876)[16] described how the criminal was essentially an evolutionary throwback who could be identified by his physical characteristics from a young age. Clear signs of criminality for Lombroso included a failure to blush, a large jaw, large orbits, large incisors and a thin upper lip. Epilepsy was another clear sign of innate criminality. In Lombroso's study of female criminality and prostitution (*La Donna Delinquente: La Prostituta e la Donna Normale, 1893*), he set photographs of Russian female convicts alongside pictures of Russian prostitutes, concluding that the convicts' faces displayed a coarser physiognomy, thereby revealing their corrupted minds. Looking at the tragic photographs today, the main thing that stands out is how hard the convicts' lives must have been. As Jodie Jenkinson, assistant professor of biomedical communication at the University of Toronto, points out in her study on the history of physiognomy, 'to look at the photographs you might think that these are "before and after" shots featured in many fashion magazines'.[17] The convicts, with their hair brutally parted down the middle, their white prison clothes and their grim expressions, just look exhausted, while the prostitutes, with their curled hair and flamboyant clothes, no doubt had a more 'feminine' look about them despite their hard stares. But that was probably more to do with their circumstances and their clothes than any fundamental inner distinction. Take any of the women pictured and put them in prison and you'd be hard pushed to see the difference.

Lombroso's ideas were widely discredited in the twentieth century. His analysis was a lesson in the pointlessness and dangers of stereotyping. But it is a lesson it seems we are yet to learn. Now we train machines to do it for us automatically, with emotion analysis and face-reading artificial intelligence instead, without really understanding why the machines make the assumptions they do about extremely personal issues like sexual or political orientation.[18] And disturbingly, there are still researchers in the twenty-first century trying to prove that you can see whether a child will turn into a criminal just by looking at their face.[19]

People have always been searching for external clues to the inner lives of those around us. Judging people's character by their outward appearance has bolstered racism, xenophobia, classism, misogyny, homophobia and prejudice against people with disabilities or disfigurement throughout the ages. If inferences can be drawn about your inner world based on your appearance, it does not matter what you actually think or feel. Your freedom to be who you are is curtailed by society's judgement of you. Scientific, or pseudo-scientific, justifications for this type of inference have always helped people to feel more comfortable in the superior skin of their own prejudice. Such reasoning holds that our personalities, propensities, thoughts and feelings are stamped through our bodies like the writing in a stick of rock for anyone to read and judge us as they see fit. The idea that we have the freedom to change our minds, our feelings or our characters has no place in such a theory.

The trajectory of phrenology and physiognomy from the men of science to the snake-oil salesmen of the nineteenth century and on to the darkest corners of the history of criminology and eugenics in the twentieth century should serve as a precautionary tale. But the behavioural scientists of the twenty-first century who claim that machines can read our faces to see if we are a terrorist, a Democrat or a woman are just not listening. And reading our faces for signs of our character is not the only way that scientists have sought to find out what we might be thinking. Aside from our immutable inner natures, scientists have looked at the ways our bodies might reveal our thoughts at any given time, and in particular, whether or not what we say is a true reflection of what is in our minds.

The lasso of truth

Lynda Carter's 1970s incarnation of Wonder Woman was a weekly fixture for me and my childhood best friend. As we crammed our faces with Monster Munch, glued to the screens in her cosy sitting room behind the village shop for our Saturday fix of girl power, we had no idea that the inspiration for Wonder Woman and her Lasso of Truth was a woman born just down the road from us almost a century earlier. Elizabeth Holloway Marston, a Manx-born American lawyer and psychologist, lived with her husband, psychologist William Moulton Marston, and Olive Byrne, his lover, in what was undoubtedly an unusual arrangement in its time. When William was asked to design a new type of comic-book hero for DC Comics, it was apparently Elizabeth who insisted that the superhero must be a woman. And William drew inspiration from the two women in his life, Elizabeth and Olive, for the incarnation of Diana Prince, Wonder Woman's alter ego.

While Wonder Woman and her creators may have had the freedom to think outside the strictures of their society and to live unconventional lives, their ground-breaking scientific enquiries created something that would be a serious threat to the freedom of thought of others. Elizabeth and William were pioneers of the systolic blood pressure test in the early twentieth century, a key part of the modern polygraph (or lie detector), designed to identify the physiological signs of lying. Inspired by Elizabeth's observation that 'when she got mad or excited, her blood pressure started to climb',[20] the couple developed technology to measure emotional states through changes in blood pressure. By contrast, the Lasso of Truth, instead of detecting when someone was lying, forced them to speak the truth. Wonder Woman's lasso worked more like a 'truth serum' than the lie detector developed by her real-life inspiration. But whether the goal is to force someone to speak the truth or to reveal their deceit, techniques that coerce someone into exposing what is in their minds interfere directly with their right to keep their thoughts private. Whether Wonder Woman's Lasso of Truth was inspired by their work on lie detector tests or by William's belief in the persuasive powers of women to extract the truth is, like many aspects of their unconventional life, hotly debated. But what is clear is that both Wonder Woman and the lie detector test have had an impact on the collective psyche and on freedom of thought well beyond their creators' lifetimes.

As much as trust is a crucial part of human interaction, so too is the ability to know when someone is lying. We know people lie because we do it ourselves, or we know people who do,[21] and yet lying is one of the things we find morally reprehensible. We teach our children that it is better to be honest and admit a mistake than to try to cover it over with lies. When my daughter says 'You lied!' because I forgot a casual promise to play a game the day before, the passionate disappointment in her voice reflects the gravity of the crime. In the deep pain of sexual infidelity, it is often not the sex but the lies that really, really hurt.

Honesty is the basis for human interaction at individual and societal levels. As politicians have regularly discovered, perjury is viewed as 'one of the most serious offences on the criminal calendar because it wholly undermines the whole basis of the administration of justice'.[22] It doesn't matter whether the lie under oath might have felt like a small white lie, or a massive 'porky'; if you are convicted of perjury in England and Wales, you are highly likely to go to prison for quite some time. The British politician Jonathan Aitken famously announced his intention to sue the British press for libel 'with the simple sword of truth and the trusty shield of British fair play ... The fight against falsehood and those who peddle it.'[23] However, he clearly did not expect that the sword would be turned on him. Pleading guilty to perjury after evidence he had given during the libel trial was shown to be untrue, Aitken was given a custodial sentence of 18 months as the trusty shield of British fair play showed itself to be rather down on peddling falsehood in the courtroom.

Aitken was caught out in his lie when investigative journalists pieced together the evidence to prove that neither his wife nor his daughter had been where he said they were at the relevant time. In most cases, it is not so easy to prove whether someone is lying or not. But there is a very big difference between collecting objective evidence to show what really happened in order to catch someone in a lie and trying to prove a subjective state of deceit inside their mind. Criminal justice systems in many countries include the right to remain silent. This is also known as the right against self-incrimination and is fundamental to the presumption of innocence, a cornerstone of the right to a fair trial in international human rights law. If the prosecution can't prove a case against you, you cannot be forced to help them prove it by your own evidence. You may be prosecuted for telling a lie, but you can never be forced to reveal what is on your mind.

The human propensity for lying combined with our natural revulsion at being lied to has driven attempts to get inside our minds and identify our deceptions at source. In ancient China, one lie detection test involved filling a person's mouth with bread; if the bread was still dry after questioning, it was a sign that they were lying. The polygraph tests of more recent times, like those developed by the Marstons, have relied on other physiological signs of stress or discomfort that are believed to accompany our attempts to deceive. But scientific techniques designed to make inferences about a person's inner state based on their physical responses pose significant problems for the right to freedom of thought, particularly in cases where those inferences may be relied on in court. They are, in effect, methods designed to coerce a person into revealing their thoughts. And this can never be allowed, for good reason.

Once your thoughts are revealed, or even inferred, it is always possible that someone will try to punish you for them. The spectre of Orwell's Thought Police may seem far-fetched, but you can never tell when your thoughts – political, philosophical, social, religious or sexual – may become something the rest of society, or at least those in power, find dangerous or disgusting enough to criminalise. In many countries around the world, as we have seen, serious penalties, including the death penalty, can be imposed for thought crimes like apostasy and blasphemy, or crimes against the moral order like adultery. In Saudi Arabia, the crime of adultery carries the penalty of death by stoning.[24] It is rarely carried out because it is recognised as difficult to prove, and allegations of adultery are not made lightly when the stakes are so high. Confessions may be rare in such circumstances, but what if adulterers could be subjected to lie detector tests as part of the evidence against them?

Science can liberate us, but it needs some constraints. Freedom of thought is crucial for the genesis of innovative ideas, but the related right of freedom of expression is vital to test those ideas. If you want to put your ideas out into the world, you need to make sure there is someone who can tell you if your idea is terrible before it's too late.

The desperate desire to extract the truth is evidenced in the devices for crushing fingers, chairs designed to rip people apart excruciatingly slowly, stretching racks and barrels with spikes on the inside that line museum walls. Torture may not have been eradicated in the world, but at least as a matter of international law it is absolutely prohibited. And surely a lie detector test is better than torture as a means of getting to the truth? Torture may induce someone to say what their torturer wants them to, but that does not necessarily equate with the truth. But the legal prohibition on torture is not about reliability, it is about the inhumanity of torture and the way it destroys human dignity. Torture is an unacceptable way of getting to the truth, not because it does not work, but because it is something we cannot tolerate in human society. It can never be justified to coerce someone into revealing their thoughts or opinions, no matter what and no matter how. But people still try.

Knowing the truth on a person's mind is one thing, but changing that truth can be just as valuable, and sometimes we can persuade ourselves that the ends really do justify the means.

Mind control

The Tavistock Clinic in London was founded in 1920 with the goal of treating the thousands of victims of 'battle shock' who had been devastated and sent home broken by their experiences in the Great War. During the Second World War, the use of injections of mind-altering drugs as a therapy for shell shock was widespread.[25] Soldiers traumatised by the horrors of war often developed amnesia, withdrawal and paralysis in response to the experiences they had been through. Psychiatrists used sedative drugs firstly to gain an insight into the source of the disturbance, and then to get the patient into a mental state where they were able to talk about and process their trauma. The drugs were seen as a way to unlock and heal the mind. But in the post-war period, the drive to use drugs and other techniques as a skeleton key to the mind took a much more sinister turn, as the allies who had worked together to destroy fascism started to learn from Nazi experimentation in mind control in their rush to win the Cold War arms race on brainwashing.

In the United States, the MK-Ultra programme, otherwise known as the CIA mind control programme, ran from 1953 to 1973.[26] It was wide-ranging and ambitious. Drugs that could extract the truth from Cold War spies under interrogation were the holy grail. But other techniques that would lead to memory loss, provoke incoherence, shock and confusion or allow control of the minds of foreign leaders, from west African witchcraft to electric shocks, were also explored in the 20 years of the programme's existence. One of the most controversial aspects of the research programme was its experimentation without consent on American and Canadian subjects.

To understand the true impact of drugs on the mind, they needed to get out of the labs and test it in the wild. LSD was a big focus of the MK-Ultra research, but the key to understanding how it worked on the mind was to watch its effects on people who didn't know they were taking it. Having your coffee or drink spiked with LSD or other mind-altering drugs and finding your working day transformed into a hallucinatory horror show was an occupational hazard as a CIA employee in the 1950s and 60s, one that in some cases had deadly consequences.[27] Drugging people unawares is obviously not conducive to informed consent, even if the people working on the programme could arguably have had some idea of what they were getting into. But the programme did not limit itself to internal experimentation on government employees. Instead, it sought out vulnerable civilian guinea pigs who would never be able to fight back, even if they wanted to.

Operation Midnight Climax[28] operated like the tightening of Wonder Woman's Lasso of Truth, with the additional use of feminine persuasion. Sex workers on the CIA payroll lured unsuspecting clients into CIA safe houses in San Francisco and New York, where they were drugged and monitored through one-way mirrors to see how they responded to different drugs. The men who were snared in the operation would have been so ashamed of what had happened to them that there was no way they would speak out about their ordeals. Unwitting American punters were mentally dismembered by the CIA's desire to understand the human mind and deploy psychological warfare on their enemies. The experiments were in clear breach of the requirement for informed consent and the need for experimentation to be carried out for the good of society in the

Nuremberg Code on medical ethics established following the Second World War. But if nobody talked about their experiences, who cared?

The experimentation was not restricted to the insalubrious corridors of sexual impropriety, drug addicts and convicts in the United States. Anyone who could be coerced and controlled, inside or outside the country, was fair game. Bob Logie was an 18-year-old boy admitted for treatment for psychosomatic leg pain to the Allen Memorial Hospital in Canada. Repeatedly dosed up with LSD, subjected to massive electrical shock therapy and kept asleep for weeks at a time while tapes were played on a loop, he found himself subjected, without consent, to processes known as 'depatterning' and 'psychic driving' designed to deconstruct the individual's consciousness so that it could be replaced with something else. The man behind the experimentation in Montreal was distinguished Scottish psychiatrist Ewen Cameron,[29] one-time president of the Canadian, American and World Psychiatric Associations and, ironically, one of the psychiatrists asked to assess the mental state of Rudolf Hess during the Nuremberg Trials. Depatterning was designed to leave the victim's head like a hollow gourd, ready to be reanimated by Cameron as a crudely carved Halloween lantern. The first part of the process, the complete obliteration of the self, was relatively successful, with some victims left unable to remember their own names. The reanimation, or supposed therapeutic goal of the treatment, however, never really materialised.

The idea of washing away one mental state through induced sleep and the repeated playing of recorded messages is a horror reminiscent of Aldous Huxley's 'hypnopaedia' in *Brave New World* or the forced treatment of the delinquent Alex in Anthony Burgess's *A Clockwork Orange*. But this was not futuristic fiction; it was happening to real people at the most respected psychiatric institution in Canada, for almost 20 years. Speaking of his experience in a documentary in 1980, Bill Logie said, 'I feel like I've been completely used. I feel like my mind has been completely invaded. I suppose if guinea pigs have feelings, they'd feel like I do.'[30] Logie was one of hundreds of patients at the Allen Memorial Hospital who were experimented on in this way with funding from the Canadian government and the Human Ecology Fund, a front for the CIA.[31]

The impact on lives and families was absolutely devastating. For vulnerable people like Jean Steel, admitted to the hospital with post-partum depression, their hope for help was turned into an experience that destroyed their souls.[32] Many of those experimented on were left in what one psychiatrist described as 'an animal state',[33] unable to remember the names of their children or to control their own bowel movements, their conscious life scraped clean. Unlike the victims of Operation Midnight Climax, as news about the experimentation in Montreal came out, many of the victims tried to get justice, suing both the CIA and the Canadian government. But while several have had out-of-court settlements, the use of non-disclosure agreements and tactics to prevent class action has meant that the true scale of the horror meted out on unsuspecting innocent people remains unknown.

Psychiatry gave the experimentation the scientific veneer of propriety. The Nobel Committee had made it clear in 1949, when it commended Moniz for inventing the lobotomy, that messing with people's minds, no matter how gruesome it might be, was a route to professional glory. While Cameron was appalled by the atrocities that had been committed by the Nazis during the Second World War, blaming the German people as a whole for what had happened, he was apparently unable to see that his psychiatric experiments on patients in his own care were brutal, dehumanising mental torture.

Whatever his motive for conducting these experiments, the CIA's interest in them was for their potential to extract information during interrogations. And the use of techniques designed to break a person's mind did not stop with Cameron's death in 1967 and the closure of the MK-Ultra programme in the 1970s. The techniques that had been born in the atmosphere of paranoia around the Cold War have been used to inform government responses to the new threat of terrorism ever since.

In the 1942 judgment in the case of *Jones v. City of Opelika*, US Supreme Court Justice Black opined that you could not get inside someone's mind, but he was considering the question from a philosophical perspective in relation to licensing laws and their impact on the ability of Jehovah's Witnesses to distribute leaflets, while it is clear that in practice, the scientists of the twentieth century disagreed with him. Then, like now, it seems as though the scientists and the lawyers were barely speaking to each other. Religion, famously described as 'the opium of the people' by Karl Marx, may have had a strong influence on thought and belief for millennia, and it certainly penalised thoughts and beliefs that did not fit with the orthodox world view, but science has offered new ways of reading, interpreting and manipulating thoughts, feelings, opinions and beliefs. And it is the new opportunities provided by science and technology to get inside our minds that pose the greatest threat to our right to freedom of thought in the twenty-first century. But while the impact of psychiatric treatments would be felt most acutely at the individual level, psychological research provided the platform for mind control of the masses, with new ways to understand, influence and control whole populations with deadly effect.

CHAPTER 4

THE POLITICS OF PERSUASION

*Evil comes from a failure to think. It defies thought for as soon
as thought tries to engage itself with evil and examine the
premises and principles from which it originates, it is frustrated
because it finds nothing there. That is the banality of evil.*

Hannah Arendt

Controlling the minds, or souls, of whole populations had been a
particularly religious activity for centuries. The term 'propaganda'
itself comes from Pope Gregory XV's creation in 1622 of the
Congregatio de Propaganda Fide to propagate the Catholic faith
in non-Catholic countries. It was this brand of seventeenth-century
Catholic propaganda that landed Zera Yacob in his Abyssinian
cave, although the tactics were widespread well before that – the
ancient Greeks and Romans and the medieval Church were all adept
propagandists. Propaganda is a way of managing the information we
receive as individuals to mould the opinions of whole societies. It
may be used to fire us up or dampen us down according to the needs
of those pulling the strings. While early propagandists may have
understood the levers needed to control their populations' minds

intuitively, in the twentieth century propaganda took a huge leap forward with the unholy marriage of some of the greatest minds in the arts, science and politics bringing thought control of the masses to a whole new level of technical excellence. And it was the British who were among the first to industrialise propaganda for the secular, political dimension, though they also understood when to call on the earlier, spiritual power of propaganda to make a political point.

At the turn of the twentieth century, the British Empire had effective control over huge swathes of territory around the globe, and its colonial ambition remained unrivalled. In Kenya, the endless lush green vistas of the Rift Valley held an overwhelming appeal for the business-minded colonists, who saw a prosperous future for themselves and their descendants in the fertile soil that seemed to have been sent from God to grow tea. The only drawback was that the land they coveted already belonged to someone else: the Kalenjin, and in particular the Talai clan, who did not want to hand it over to the British. Not easily deterred, the colonists dealt with resistance in various ways, trying exile of the Talai leaders and detention of the whole community, but despite their best efforts, the Talai were not cowed. A less direct approach was required.

'Divide and conquer' has been the go-to tactic of empire builders for as long as humans have been invading each other's space. For the British to establish their rule over Kalenjin land in the Rift Valley, they needed to turn the opinion of the majority against their dogged opponents. The Talai clan held a position of respect and leadership in the area, but colonisation of land went hand in hand with Christian colonisation of the soul in the British Empire, and it was the conversion of hearts and minds that offered the British the key to shutting down opposition. Christian converts were primed and sent back into the community to spread the word that the Talai were evil wizards possessed of supernatural powers. If the British could not break the Talai's spirit, they would tarnish it with allegations of witchcraft spread via that timeless analogue system of disinformation – gossip and rumour. And in this case, it was not difficult individuals but the entire clan who would be damned for witchcraft.

Religion and belief are always a useful underpinning to political propaganda. Even today, the conspiracy theory that Barack Obama is a secret Muslim is apparently believed by almost a third of the American electorate[1] and was effectively used to discredit him. While detention and exile did not curb the influence of the Talai, spiritual suspicion demolished them in the eyes of Kenyan society to such a degree that their descendants are still suffering stigma to this day.[2] The slur of witchcraft, an accusation that is impossible to disprove, is a devastatingly effective way to neutralise opposition without lifting a finger. But it was not only in the colonies that the British deployed their technical efficiency in information warfare, although at home they needed a more positive hook than straightforward suspicion of sorcery.

As the God-given omnipotence of kings and queens gave way to the necessary pragmatism of democracy at the turn of the last century, you had to bring the people with you on your journey if you wanted to win in war or politics. In 1914, the British government had made a bold move when it declared war on Germany. As Lord Kitchener put it, 'They have no army and they declared war on the mightiest military nation in the world.' Waging a war on Germany was going to need a lot of men. Conscription had not been used for over a century, so the only way to get soldiers was to make joining up seem like a good idea. As historian Philip M. Taylor noted,[3] before the First World War, the idea that the state would advertise itself had occurred to very few people, and if state self-promotion had been drawn to the attention of the public at large, they would have found it repellent.

But signing up for an unwinnable war focused the minds at the head of the British state. The only way to get men to sign up voluntarily was to effectively sell the war to an unenthusiastic populace. And so the British Great War marketing machine was born. In October 1914, *London Opinion* magazine ran with a cover that has been burned onto the collective subconscious ever since. The instantly recognisable moustachioed face of Lord Kitchener, eyes locked on the reader, stared out of the picture, finger pointed, with the words 'Your country needs YOU'. It was sent out to the magazine's 300,000 readers, and similar posters, cards and leaflets spread the message across the country. The power of the image and its message resonated so strongly in the cultural psyche that, over a hundred years later, copies, parodies and echoes of that picture still appear on mugs, tea towels and advertising campaigns in Britain and beyond. In the 1990s, the British Army even used the same framing for a recruitment drive, featuring a Black soldier in Kitchener's famous pose. You may not know who Lord Kitchener is, but at least if you are British you will know this iconic image.

The durability of that picture is a testament to its persuasive power at the time. In August 1914, Britain had a professional fighting force of around 80,000 men. Within a month of the launch of Kitchener's advertising campaign, 30,000 men a day were joining up, and within two months the army had swollen to almost 10 times its original size.[4] But this was just the start of the wide-ranging and sustained information campaign that was required to meet the continuous need for new blood in what would prove to be a long and brutal war.

To form opinions based on reason, we need information we can rely on. We may take a view on whether something is hot or cold based on information we receive through our senses. But deciding rationally on whether a politician is good or bad for our interests or whether we should be sending our children into war requires a complex analysis of information from a variety of sources. Only then can we begin to understand the actions and motives of all the actors so we can form an independent opinion. In the past, sources of information for most people were limited to their immediate friends and family or what they heard from the pulpit. But the public education, widespread literacy and mass communications that were the hallmarks of the twentieth century had an explosive impact. Information and access to the public mind were suddenly all around us. Freedom of information is key to freedom of opinion, because if you can control the information, you can control public opinion. As propaganda expert Emma Briant explains:

> It's helpful to think of propaganda as a spectrum of
> manipulation – spanning from more ethical efforts
> to persuade us in our interests, to the truly dark
> arts of deception. Those manipulative 'dark' arts
> suppress or organize out available alternatives, may
> use data asymmetry against an unwitting audience's
> psychological weaknesses, aim to dehumanize a group,
> mislead or destabilize, and above all try to hide the
> fact they are propaganda at all – obscuring actors and
> intentions to undermine choice and secure a monopoly
> we may never become aware of.[5]

This is why the dawn of the internet, accessible to all, appeared to hold such promise for freedom, but also why the concentration of control over the internet, whether in state or corporate hands, is such a threat to freedom of opinion today. At the turn of the last century, the British, just as they took the lead in colonising the physical world, were at the forefront of the global campaign to conquer the public psyche, at home and abroad.

Fake news

'Fake news' may feel like a peculiarly twenty-first-century phenomenon, but as a tool for controlling the opinions, thoughts and emotions of whole populations, it has a long pedigree.[6] In ancient Rome, Octavian launched a campaign of slurs against Antony, characterising him as Cleopatra's lapdog via catchy slogans stamped on coins. And my daughter's confident assertion that unicorns exist because Google says so would have been bolstered in the nineteenth century by the 'Great Moon Hoax of 1835', when *The New York Sun* published a series of articles claiming to prove the existence of life on the moon, including pictures of bearded blue unicorns just to prove it was true. But it was in wartime that the utility of fake news as a means of gaining public support for the unjustifiable really came into its own.

In 1917, *The Times* and the *Daily Mail* in London ran a story that horrified their readers while confirming their worst fears about the enemy they had been fighting for three long years. The articles described how the Germans had built 'corpse factories' to dispose of the bodies of their fallen soldiers by boiling them down and turning them into pigswill and other by-products.[7] The first-hand description of the stench of the factory added to the horror, bringing the inhumane depravity of it to life as if the fumes had just wafted in your window. In 1917, many people would have been familiar with the smell of slow-boiled bones and the all-permeating stench of processes that turned animals into household products. The smell in the story made it visceral and real. And if you could smell that corpse factory in your head, with all the inhumanity that entailed, it would be hard to break bread with the kind of person who could do such a thing. If you had lost your son, or your husband, or your father to the war, you would think that anyone who could do this to their own must be a monster. Once you had thought it, could you ever really unthink it? Even if it turned out to be untrue? Who, after all, could doubt their senses? If you could smell it, you just had to believe it.

The articles that ran in the British press were not only vivid and appealing to the public's need to believe in the depravity of 'the Hun', but they were also carefully referenced for the avoidance of doubt. This was not the work of a maverick journalist. The story was corroborated by its connections to other sources. It had apparently first appeared in a Belgian newspaper, the *Independence Belge*, which in turn cited another newspaper source, *La Belgique*, which was supposedly printed in Leiden in the Netherlands. The article also made reference to a German newspaper story with a first-hand account of a *Kadaververwertungsanstalt*, which the British press translated as 'corpse exploitation establishment'. But the credibility given by the sources did not stand up to scrutiny. The Belgian newspaper, rather than being a foreign source, was printed in London, while the original source in Leiden appears never to have existed. This layering of information sources is similar to what Facebook calls 'coordinated inauthentic behaviour', where multiple social media accounts work together to amplify and corroborate disinformation.

Variations on the story of the corpse factory had done the rounds in various forms from London via Shanghai, Madrid, Jerusalem and Belgium, with layers of coincidence, speculation, misinterpretation and convenient juxtaposition building up to a story that was so horrifically believable that it would damn the entire German nation for a generation. It did not matter that it was not true.

The grains of truth that carried the tale were that the Germans were boiling up the carcasses of dead warhorses to make glue and other products, and that they were cremating their dead. You might feel sad about the horses, but it is hardly a war crime. The story mattered because it demonised the enemy, giving a gut-level justification for a brutal war that was otherwise difficult to justify. If people could be united in their horror at the enemy, they could more easily feel fired up to fight. This is the effect of Orwell's Hate Week in *Nineteen Eighty-Four*, or of the kind of coordinated online propaganda that led to the storming of the US Capitol in January 2021. If our information flows are controlled, so are our minds.

The corpse factory story was just one part of an extremely slick British propaganda operation, the first of its kind in terms of scale and ambition. In 1914, as Kitchener's face was being splashed across the country, the British established the Wellington House Propaganda Bureau in response to reports that the Germans had their own propaganda machine. The Bureau was headed by the writer and Liberal MP Charles Masterman, who brought together some of the most persuasive writers of the time, including the novelists Hall Caine, Arthur Conan Doyle, H. G. Wells and Thomas Hardy, to inform its efforts to promote British interests. Their talents for animating the public with gripping tales of morality, crime and futuristic vision were employed, in secret, in the interests of the state, with over 1,000 pamphlets being produced throughout the war to build vivid pictures of German monstrosity and British pluck. Writing, illustration, posters and cinema were all harnessed to win hearts and minds, in Britain and beyond. By 1918, the green shoots of organised propaganda had been transformed into a behemoth of mind control – the Ministry of Information – which managed three types of propaganda: domestic, foreign and military. It would go on to provide a model for state propaganda machines all over the world to this day.

The impact of the corpse factory story went far beyond the war years and is a lesson in the unintended consequences of information control. When the British military establishment claimed the propaganda coup of the fake corpse factory in a speech in New York in 1925, it did nothing to reduce the public image of the Germans as monsters, but it did undermine faith in the media. When stories started to come out of Germany in the 1930s about Nazi death camps and the horrific human experimentation that was being carried out, the public were reluctant to believe it. They might still hate Germans, but they did not want to be taken for credulous fools twice. Fake news not only makes you believe, it also makes you doubt everything. Questioning is good for freedom of opinion, but deep mistrust can be as corrosive of our freedom to think for ourselves as blind faith.

The British had shown what information management and advertising on a grand scale could achieve to control a population at war, but the success of the propaganda effort was seen by some as an own goal for the burgeoning ideal of democracy in peacetime. The ability to sway public opinion so thoroughly and effectively brought into question the idea that people should choose their representatives, their values and the way they were governed. If people could be so easily manipulated, could you ever have a free and fair election? But others, like advertising guru Edward Bernays, the Austrian-American nephew of Sigmund Freud, thought that 'the conscious and intelligent manipulation of the masses is an important element in a democratic society'.[8] Without manipulation, there was no way to ensure that the masses would vote for the right thing. But this approach falls into the same trap as the idea of benevolent dictatorship. You may have good intentions for your use of mind control to make the world a better place. But what about the next person who uses your carefully honed techniques? They may not have such benevolent motives. Political campaigning always involves persuasion, but it should never tip over into manipulation. A truly democratic system needs genuine freedom delivered through legal and institutional checks and balances and a population capable of critical thinking, not mind control.[9]

Torches of freedom

While the British were playing politics with propaganda, across the Atlantic it was the immense commercial opportunity of marketing to the masses that struck a chord. Aside from its political potential, what Edward Bernays saw above all was a huge opportunity to make money by harnessing the developing science of mind control and mass persuasion to serve commercial interests. His 1928 book *Propaganda* was ground-breaking in its time, extolling the potential of the propagandist's psychological toolbox for the enterprising and highly profitable art of sales. This power to infer and control our thoughts and feelings was turned to a purely commercial purpose with the advent of mass-marketing and advertising.[10] And it was clear that 'freedom' could sell pretty much anything.

Smoking is essentially an utterly pointless, addictive, dangerous and expensive activity. It stinks, it kills you and it doesn't even give you much of a buzz in the process. Few people today would disagree with King James I's assessment that it is 'a custome loathsome to the eye, hatefull to the nose, harmefull to the braine, daungerous to the Lungs, and in the blacke stinking fume thereof, nearest resembling the horrible Stigian smoke of the pit that is bottomlesse'.[11] Even smokers who may cling to their habit through addiction dressed up in the clothes of individual liberty would not suggest that smoking was any good for them. What started out as a ritual activity in the Americas became an international fashionable fad, supported by the horrors of plantation slavery, which would go on to become a global industry worth billions of dollars with the social, economic and political clout to change, and end, the lives of millions of people around the world. Its success was not down to the quality of the product, the innate appeal of tobacco or even the addictive hook of nicotine. Getting so many people to start smoking in the first place was ultimately down to the marketing, which sold not just a product, but a whole new cultural mindset.

In 1920s America, it was frowned upon for women to be seen smoking outside. Smoking was not considered ladylike. This social restriction meant that the number of cigarettes a woman could smoke in a day was limited by the amount of time she was in a place where she could reasonably consider reaching for one. For George Hill, the owner of the Lucky Strike cigarette brand, this meant a large shortfall in his potential profits. It was not that women were legally prohibited from smoking outside;[12] it was just not done. So it was not simply a question of getting women to buy Lucky Strike over another brand of cigarette, or of lobbying for changes in the law to let women do what they wanted. What was needed was a change in the individual and societal attitudes to outdoor smoking. It was about making women *want* to smoke outside. And who better to find the key to a woman's mind than Edward Bernays? Inspired by the success of his book, and with his familial Freudian pedigree for understanding the female psyche, Bernays grasped the concept that marketing was not just about getting an individual to buy a particular product in the moment. It was a much more holistic process, which involved creating the cultural space to drive consumer demand.

There was a period of great societal change in the wake of the Great War, with fundamental shifts in the role and status of women in society. The Nineteenth Amendment gave women across the United States the right to vote in elections. Pioneers like the aviator Amelia Earhart were rebranding women as independent, daring and free – Earhart summed up the feelings of the new generation when she said, 'I believe that a girl should not do what she thinks she should do, but should find out through experience what she wants to do.' This buzz and excitement offered up a whole new marketing angle to Bernays and his colleagues.[13] Getting women to smoke outside would be about liberating them from the strictures of society and allowing them to know their own minds.

Smoking was freedom – not the bra-burning appeal of later eras of political feminism, but the glossy, lipsticked version of consumer feminism. To push the point, a group of attractive young women were hired to join the New York City Easter parade in 1929, brandishing Lucky Strikes as 'torches of freedom', while prominent feminists were paid to sign a letter inspiring women to join them on the march with the rallying cry 'Light another torch of freedom! Fight another sex taboo!' Freedom – what more could a woman want? There was one more thing that the advertisers knew women sought: health, otherwise known as weight loss. And Lucky Strike had that covered too, with their campaign of adverts exhorting women to 'Reach for a Lucky instead of a sweet'. Cigarettes would not only liberate you politically and sexually; they would also help you live that freedom to the full by suppressing the deadly urge to stuff your face with sweets. Sixty years after the 'torches of freedom' campaign, having cast off the chains of school and my Boost bar habit, Lucky Strike was the cigarette my friends and I celebrated with on the banks of the Seine in 1989 – our newly won freedom tainted by the aftertaste of tobacco. In the 2020s, weight loss is still a key to women's minds and wallets in the lucrative game of targeted online advertising. The cultural shifts caused by advertising have consequences for generations.

Commercial advertising is not necessarily any more benign than its political sibling. Kitchener's war left around 20 million dead, but the death toll of tobacco has been even greater.[14] A century on from the Lucky 'freedom' campaign, the tobacco epidemic is considered by the World Health Organization (WHO) to be 'one of the biggest public health threats the world has ever faced'. Despite bans on advertising and smoking in public driving down numbers of smokers in many wealthier countries around the world, in 2020 the WHO estimated that eight million deaths a year are still caused by tobacco. Now that the wealthy have been protected from the publicity of big tobacco through effective law and regulation, 80 per cent of the world's 1.3 billion tobacco users[15] come from poor and middle-income countries, where the fraudulent promise of freedom and glamour is still for sale.

Herd poisoning

In the 1930s, it was not only big tobacco and the ad men who recognised that for marketing to be really effective it must distort not only our rational thoughts, but also our feelings. It doesn't matter what you are selling, the principles and the tools are the same. If you cannot get people to agree with you by following their heads, you can always go for the gut. Aldous Huxley's dystopian classic *Brave New World*, published in 1932, showed a vision of the future where it was the soft hand of consumerism and marketing that effectively controlled the minds of the masses through comfort and distraction for political ends, rather than the hard boot of Orwell's post-war Thought Police. A key commentator and observer of the power of propaganda over the war years and beyond, in his 1958 book of essays *Brave New World Revisited*, Huxley, with the benefit of hindsight, noted that advertisers get us to buy a toothpaste, a brand of cigarettes or a political candidate by manipulating hidden forces. And it was by 'appealing to the same hidden forces – and to others too dangerous for Madison Avenue to meddle with – that Hitler induced the German masses to buy themselves a Fuehrer, an insane philosophy and the Second World War'.[16]

Adolf Hitler, musing in a prison cell after the Great War, admired the British propaganda effort for its clear approach, which left no space for grey areas where doubt could be sown. But he realised that informational propaganda was only a part of the puzzle; you also needed the right atmosphere. It's not about the content, it's about the feel. If it strikes an emotional chord somewhere below our powers of reason, it doesn't really matter if it's true or not.[17]

Understanding how to deliver the thrill of hatred, to set those subhuman, primitive chords vibrating, was the key to the Nazi's overwhelming hate machine. The British may have learned how to colonise information to control reason, but Hitler's empire was built on the mass orchestration of emotion. He understood that if you want to conquer the minds of the people, you have to bring them together to be sculpted. It does not work quite so well when you chip away at an individual sitting reading quietly in an armchair with a cup of tea. The British approach to managing information built pictures in the mind to help justify loathing the enemy and supporting the war effort. They had gone for the slow but steady approach of a river manipulating the landscape. But the Nazis wanted nothing less than an emotional tsunami, leaving the crowd devastated, spiritually homeless and clamouring for the new ideological world they promised to provide.

Finding the German lower middle classes destroyed by war, inflation and depression through the 1920s, Hitler harnessed their collective frustration and anxiety by assembling them in tens of thousands in vast halls and arenas. Emotional manipulation is all about context. Hitler understood the importance of scale and timing, pitch and performance in the art and science of persuasion. How we behave and feel in a crowd is quite different to how we behave and feel pottering about on our own in a private garden. The social psychologist Jonathan Haidt[18] calls it 'the hive switch', the collective psychology that takes over when we gather together for a joint purpose. It is what Aldous Huxley called 'herd poisoning', which makes the individual escape 'from responsibility, intelligence and morality into a kind of frantic, animal mindlessness'.[19] Huxley believed that people lose their capacity for reason and moral choice in a crowd, so that 'a man in a crowd behaves as though he had swallowed a large dose of some powerful intoxicant'.[20] We lose elements of our personal identity as we meld into the pulsing heat of the mass.

Religions have long been adept at harnessing the power of the crowd with sensory overwhelm: the power of organ music and celestial choirs in the epic grandeur of a cathedral; the collective spiritual ecstasy of the hajj; or the fired-up frenzy of an evangelical rally. Hitler had great admiration for the Catholic Church's ability to exact complete devotion from its adherents. He himself used ritual – the repetitive brain-numbing marching, the gestures and the chanting – to get below the rational resistance to his political ideas, and like some religions, the Nazi ideology was built on absolute adherence to social norms. Religions have historically turned their congregations against each other on the slimmest of doctrinal differences to murderous effect, but the Nazis used race and culture as the drivers for their domination of the public psyche.

With '*Ein Volk, ein Reich, ein Führer*' ('One People, One Country, One Führer'), there was no space for dissent or difference. Nazi ideology was everywhere, in every nook and cranny of German life: at work, at home and in the regimented childcare of the Hitler Youth. And a real community needed a real and undeniable common enemy. Restoring German self-confidence was reliant on hatred of the 'other', and German hatred was directed in particular against the Jewish population through a process of steady dehumanisation and demonisation against a backdrop of wider, deep-rooted international anti-Semitism. Once you have identified your enemy and removed their humanity, the Final Solution becomes a possibility. Nazi propaganda was inescapable, overwhelming the national psyche, already dented by economic depression, with a new racial pride and a target for murderous hate.

While the Gutenberg press had made it possible to spread the written word faster than ever before, the Nazis recognised the emotional power of oratory. But speech-making in person, even with mass rallies, still had a naturally limited audience: Hitler could only be in one place at one time. The wonders of modern technology, however, meant that while the Führer himself was limited by his physical reality, the Führer's voice could be everywhere. In the early 1930s, the radio, still a relatively new invention, was out of the price range of the average German family, but as Joseph Goebbels, the Nazi's chief propagandist, recognised the potential power of piping Hitler's voice into every home around the country, he launched the *Volksempfänger*, or 'people's radio', a new, cheap version made of Bakelite, cardboard and cloth, adorned on either side with the unmistakable Nazi symbols of the eagle and the swastika. Similar budget items like the 'people's refrigerator' and the 'people's car' were also manufactured, the lure of consumerism bringing the German people together and distracting them from the hardships and horrors being conducted in their name. Industrialists profited from massive sales, low-income consumers got access to new media and the Nazis got direct access to 'the Volk'.[21] Everyone was a winner. With total control over national radio broadcasts and programming, and criminal penalties for listening to foreign media like the BBC, the distribution of the 'people's radio' to an estimated 65 per cent of German households by 1941 ensured overwhelming Nazi domination of German information channels and entertainment.

The inescapable presence of Nazi ideology throughout society was one of the keys to the success of their propaganda. Hannah Arendt, in *The Origins of Totalitarianism*, explains how, for members of the movement, Nazi ideology became:

> ... as real and untouchable an element in their lives
> as the rules of arithmetic ... In Nazi Germany,
> questioning the validity of racism and anti-Semitism

when nothing mattered but race origin, when a
career depended upon an 'Aryan' physiognomy
(Himmler used to select the applicants for the SS
from photographs) and the amount of food upon
the number of one's Jewish grandparents, was like
questioning the existence of the world.[22]

For the Nazis, propaganda transcended personal opinion and
transformed their views into unquestionable fact. When messages
and ideas infiltrate every part of your life and your future chances,
they can feel inescapable and true, even if they are neither.

Albert Speer, Hitler's former Minister for Armaments, spoke at
length about the techniques and power of Nazi propaganda when
he faced trial at Nuremberg. Speer was convicted of war crimes and
crimes against humanity for his part in the wartime slave labour
programmes. But the tribunal noted in mitigation that 'in the
closing stages of the war he was one of the few men who had the
courage to tell Hitler that the war was lost'.[23] Speer's observations at
his trial offer not only direct insight into the Nazi propaganda effort,
but also highlight the risks posed by technological advances that
have only become more acute in the past 70 years. He explained how
Hitler's dictatorship, the first in that period of modern technical
development, harnessed technology to dominate the nation:

Through technical devices such as radio and
loudspeaker 80 million people were deprived of
independent thought. It was thereby possible to subject
them to the will of one man ... Today the danger of
being terrorized by technocracy threatens every country
in the world. In modern dictatorship this appears to

me inevitable. Therefore, the more technical the world becomes, the more necessary is the promotion of individual freedom and the individual's awareness of himself as a counterbalance.[24]

When propaganda deprives 80 million people of independent thought, it undermines their right to freedom of thought and opinion. And it is not only a threat to the rights of those who are manipulated. As the world saw with Nazi Germany, it becomes a threat to all our rights. When propaganda can be automated and targeted to reach billions worldwide, it is an existential threat to humanity and one that none of us can afford to ignore.

But as Speer also pointed out, it was the absolute control of thought and opinion that ultimately prevented the Nazis from reaching their full, devastating technological potential. Without questioning and freedom of thought, technological advancement will stall. The Nazis were defeated. Hitler and Goebbels, unable to face that defeat, took their own lives along with their loved ones. But their almost complete domination of the German psyche remains perhaps the most successful example to date of the potential for propaganda to poison the minds of an entire population if left unchecked.

Prolefeed

Propaganda comes in many forms. The twentieth century saw the rise of British information control, Nazi propaganda and the iron fist of communist social control alongside the commercial drive of mass marketing in the battle to conquer our minds. And writers were not only involved in creating propaganda, they were also at the heart of critiques and warnings about the way in which information and societal control was developing. Two of the most iconic dystopian novels of the mid-twentieth century, Huxley's *Brave New World* and Orwell's *Nineteen Eighty-Four*, explore one of the less obvious, but no less iniquitous ways in which propaganda and information control can influence our minds. Propaganda doesn't necessarily push or pull in one political direction or another. It can be equally effective when it is used to distract people from what really matters.

If people are distracted or amused, they are less likely to notice the urgent realities of their situation. Distraction is not necessarily sinister – wartime entertainers like Dame Vera Lynn were flown around the world to raise troop morale by giving soldiers a chance to briefly forget their dreadful daily experience. But Huxley identified 'man's almost infinite appetite for distractions' – or, as professor of law Tim Wu puts it, our 'incredible, magnificent power to ignore'[25] – as one of the biggest threats to human freedom. Propagandists and politicians are astute at harnessing that power to their own ends. In *Nineteen Eighty-Four*, Orwell identifies 'prolefeed' as 'the rubbishy entertainment and spurious news which the Party handed out to the masses'. And in *Brave New World*, Huxley uses the ever-present sensory distractions of the 'feelies', 'orgy-porgy' and 'centrifugal bumble-puppy' as political tools to stop people thinking too much about their social or political realities.

Huxley's 1958 essays *Brave New World Revisited* re-explored the themes of his famous early novel, in particular the devastating potential of propaganda and brainwashing in the hands of both the state and the new breed of slick, commercial marketing men.[26] His observations on the threats to freedom of thought and opinion offer a preview to the challenges we face in the twenty-first century. He recognised the techniques of the twentieth-century dictator using 'the repetition of catchwords which they wish to be accepted as true, the suppression of facts which they wish to be ignored, the arousal and rationalisation of passions which may be used in the interests of the Party or the State'. These were the precursors to the memes, viral clips and fake news of the twenty-first-century authoritarian. And he warned that the dictators of the future would combine these techniques with the non-stop distractions that in the West were already drowning out rational discussions about liberty and democracy in a sea of irrelevance. He saw that 'a society, most of whose members spend a great part of their time, not on the spot, not here and now and in the calculable future, but somewhere else, in the irrelevant other worlds of sport and soap opera, of mythology and metaphysical fantasy, will find it hard to resist the encroachments of those who would manipulate and control it',[27] and predicted that in the future, the 'punitive methods of *1984*' would 'give place to the reinforcements and manipulations of *Brave New World*'. Both works are remarkably prescient about the challenges our minds and societies face today, but it is difficult to know whether Orwell and Huxley would have laughed or cried at the election of an authoritarian reality TV host to the White House. After 30 years of reality TV and social media, the accuracy of Huxley's vision has never felt more acute.

Distraction, advertising and entertainment may seem harmless, but they are a part of our information ecosystem that dictates how we feel and what we look at. In the digital age, they guide not only our personal habits, but also our political inclinations and engagement, our relationships with each other and our future opportunities. Huxley said that 'only the vigilant can maintain their liberties'. In the era of clickbait and endless cat videos, we need to be more vigilant than ever.

Not all advertising is bad or manipulative. Like political campaigning and propaganda, there is a continuum between marketing and advertising that contributes to a healthy society, and messaging that can ultimately kill millions. And there is no clear divide between commercial and political propaganda. The overlap between the various disciplines of mind control can be seen in some of the key characters who drove the American advertising revolution of the nineteenth and twentieth centuries. Claude C. Hopkins, a former preacher, brought God to the table. And Edward Bernays, the nephew of Sigmund Freud, brought Psyche, the Greek goddess of the soul, with his uncle's insights into human psychology. Their formative years placed them squarely in the traditional spheres of attention capture and control – religion and psychology – laying the path for a new lucrative output for their skills in the advertising industry. These were the new breed of what Tim Wu describes in his book of that name as 'The Attention Merchants'.[28]

Despite its spiritual and political origins, attention capture has never really been a purely ideological endeavour; it has always been intertwined with money. The Catholic Church may have provided a spiritual home for billions through the centuries, but its success has rested equally on its ability to split from the humble roots of early Christianity to accrue vast amounts of wealth and power through the devotion of its adherents. And in democratic societies, political power and financial backing are inextricably connected to the ability to persuade people to vote for you, a trick that is increasingly reliant on the science of marketing rather than the art of political ideology. There is big money in mind control.

Technologists and ethicists have begun to sound alarm bells about the potency of distraction in the digital world. James Williams, the philosopher and former Google strategist, talks about 'freedom and resistance in the attention economy' in his book *Stand Out of Our Light*. And in the Netflix documentary *The Social Dilemma*, Tristan Harris, former Google ethicist and co-founder of the Center for Humane Technology, lays bare the ways that technological design decisions create constant distractions that can be harnessed to twist our minds. On his website, Harris asks, 'How do you ethically steer the thoughts and actions of two billion people's minds every day?'[29] The answer, from the perspective of the absolute right to freedom of thought, is: you don't. Technologists may understand the problems and the reasons why technology has such reach into our inner lives, as they are part of it. But what they fail to see is the ways that human rights and human rights law can provide us with a solid solution.

In the twenty-first century, despite the impending doom of the climate crisis, we are still being sold freedom on roller skates in the plastic wrapping of tampons,[30] or the gas-guzzling promise of an SUV on the open road. Advertising not only manipulates how we think; it changes how we live, and how long we (and our planet) may live for. It uses our desire for freedom to steal that freedom from us, whether the addiction it is peddling is tobacco, online gambling or shopping. Advertising has become the driver of our technological future. We may worry about disinformation and the rise of demagogues who also use the language of freedom to destroy our human rights, but the fuel that drives these phenomena in the modern world is the cold, hard cash of consumer advertising. If we want to take control of building a human future, we need to talk about advertising. It is the thread that runs through all our online interactions. And it is the fuel that drives surveillance capitalism and modern political influence and propaganda. Scratch the surface of any 'big tech' company and you will find an advertising business lurking below. Do we really want publicists like Edward Bernays defining what freedom means for us? As with any threat to our rights and freedoms, we need human rights law and regulation to make sure that the peddlers of persuasion, whether political or commercial, are kept strictly out of our heads.

CHAPTER 5

THE POWER OF HUMAN RIGHTS

... there are no such [human] rights, and belief in
them is one with belief in witches and unicorns.

Alasdair MacIntyre, After Virtue[1]

Some philosophers, like Spinoza, have described freedom of thought as a 'natural right', but for millennia, religion, science, medicine, politics and big business have all played their part in interfering with our right to think for ourselves, individually and collectively. In the previous chapters, we have looked at what it means to live in a world where freedom of thought was under constant threat. But the development of human rights as a legal framework from the seeds of the philosophical and political ideals of liberty and freedom of thought means that human rights law provides us with the practical tools to protect our minds, now and in the future.

Human rights only appear to be real when we recognise them and respect them or when we feel the need to rely on them. The Scottish moral philosopher Alasdair MacIntyre questioned the whole basis of Enlightenment morality in his seminal work *After Virtue*, in which he concluded that belief in human rights was no more justified than belief in unicorns. But the thing about philosophers is that you can generally ignore them with impunity. I never had much time for Nietzsche's maxim that 'sombre clothes and total muteness lead a woman to astuteness'.[2] But the law is different, and ignoring it has consequences. When the law where you live violates your human rights, you need a higher order of law to help you. If I happened to live in a country where women's dress and political participation were restricted by the criminal law, international human rights law would give me the tools to challenge the status quo. Human rights are not just a belief system or a set of philosophical ideas. They are part of a global legal framework designed to let us all be human, regardless of who or where we are, or whether we believe in witches. People who do not believe in human rights have lost their faith because they do not think their own rights are in danger. Their loss of faith is a danger to us all. As Peter Pan famously explained to Wendy, when a baby first laughs, a fairy is born, but there is no longer a fairy born for each child because: 'children know such a lot now. Soon they don't believe in fairies, and every time a child says "I don't believe in fairies" there is a fairy somewhere that falls down dead.' So too with human rights: every time someone is persuaded those human rights do not exist, all our rights are under threat.

While I was celebrating freedom at the Berlin Wall on New Year's Eve 1989, I did not pay much attention to the East German border guards, who had given up on guarding and thrown their winter hats into the party ring. But in the years after the Wall came down, some border guards found themselves facing trial for killing people who had tried to breach the Wall to escape to the West before the party started.[3] They argued that, at the time, East German law and policy allowed (or even required) them to enforce the border by shooting people who tried to escape. But their prosecutions went ahead because, despite the lack of effective human rights protection in East German law, shooting people in the back when they were fleeing oppression was still prohibited under international human rights law. Human rights are real, and even when they are buried very deep underground, they continue to grow. But to really believe in human rights, you need to understand what they mean and how they work in practice. To protect the right to freedom of thought effectively, you don't necessarily need a 'freedom of thought' law, but you do need law. And there are many ways that the law in general and human rights law in particular has been used to give protection to our inner freedom.

Hooded men

Human rights are universal, inalienable and indivisible. The right to freedom of thought is key to protecting our mental integrity and our mental privacy. But cases that deal with protecting our minds from interference do not necessarily explicitly invoke the right to freedom of thought. Other rights, like the right to private life, or the right to be free from inhuman and degrading treatment or torture, may be equally relevant and more familiar to the courts in particular cases. But the human rights protected in law are complementary and interdependent. The right to freedom of thought and the right to freedom of opinion are only now beginning to be invoked by human rights advocates as the language of privacy starts to feel inadequate to deal with the ways that the digital age touches our mental autonomy and our agency. Perhaps because the idea that our inner space could be invaded is so disturbing that we find it hard to accept, or because the idea of freedom of thought can seem nebulous, philosophical and hard to grasp, there have been very few cases that address freedom of thought or freedom of opinion directly. But there are several judgments in international human rights and criminal tribunals as well as cases in domestic courts that reveal how the law can be used to protect the inner sanctum of our minds and guarantee our right to freedom of thought.

Making human rights real for everyone relies on enforcement and the chance for victims to get justice. Ewen Cameron's state-sponsored experiments in the destruction of the soul for the CIA were in clear breach of the Nuremberg Code on medical ethics. And they were without doubt a gross violation of several provisions of the Universal Declaration of Human Rights, including the right to freedom of thought and the absolute prohibition on torture, inhuman and degrading treatment. Cameron destroyed in his victims the reason and consciousness that is the hallmark of humanity. And he put hundreds of people through the slow and excruciating mill of his cruel, inhuman and degrading methods – as much a tool of torture as the medieval iron chair. It does not matter whether the goal was psychiatric breakthrough or protecting national security. These techniques were designed to break and manipulate minds, and there can never be a legal justification for that.

However, for Cameron's victims, who have been trying for more than half a century to get recognition and redress for what happened to them, their rights under international law must feel unreal. Bringing a legal challenge of any kind involves courage, emotional resilience and, in many cases, an awful lot of money. These are things that most vulnerable victims of human rights abuses do not have. More than 50 years after their traumatic experiences, Cameron's victims and their families are still searching for justice. Some have reportedly received settlements tied to non-disclosure agreements.[4] No one says it did not happen, but there is no official recognition of how truly awful it was for these individuals and their families, or of how damaging for the humane fabric of North American society.

For human rights to be effective, they need to be backed up with strong legal mechanisms to make them real, and this is where international tribunals and other mechanisms come in. There are several international and regional courts that rule on human rights law specifically, in Europe, the Americas and Africa. Others deal more broadly with public international law: the International Court of Justice, for example, or, for criminal cases, the International Criminal Court. The case law of these courts and tribunals not only provides access to justice for victims of violations. It also helps to clarify what international human rights law means in practice in the modern day and in particular situations.

One such case, in the European Court of Human Rights, was that of the 'Hooded Men'. In 1971, shocked by reports that the UK government was using the kind of techniques that Cameron had been developing in order to break the minds of terrorist suspects under interrogation in Northern Ireland, the Irish government decided to take the United Kingdom to the European Court using the rarely invoked mechanism of an inter-state complaint. Despite commitments from the UK government that they had stopped the practice by the time the case came to court, the European Court of Human Rights found that the use of coercive interrogation techniques, including hooding, wall standing, sleep deprivation, food deprivation and subjection to white noise (known as 'the five techniques'), amounted to inhuman and degrading treatment in violation of Article 3 of the European Convention on Human Rights.

The recognition in international law that interrogation techniques designed to break minds could be inhuman and degrading treatment is an important principle for the protection of our inner freedom and mental integrity. The five techniques were clearly designed to extract information by coercion, chipping away at the men's mental state in the hope that they would break and reveal what they knew. It was a direct assault on one of the key protections for our inner freedom – the right to keep our thoughts to ourselves. How the courts categorise something is not just academic – it makes a difference to real people on the ground.

In 2014, the Irish government went back to court in an attempt to reopen the judgment. It hoped that, in light of fresh evidence about what the British government knew about the mental suffering the five techniques inflicted on the men, the court would change its assessment of the case to recognise that what the British did was not only inhuman and degrading treatment: it was torture. Torture has a particular place in international human rights law. If a person commits or colludes in it, they are guilty of an international crime. Most governments do not want to be found guilty of human rights violations, just as most people do not want to be convicted of a crime, particularly not a crime that could see them facing prosecution or extradition. The European Court of Human Rights declined to change its judgment, but it did recognise that in the present day it might have made a finding of torture.

Making rights real is as much about access to justice as it is about what the courts say. The Hooded Men had the government of Ireland behind them and a supra-national court system to say that what had happened to them was wrong. Ewen Cameron's victims have not had that chance because the United States and Canada do not subscribe to an international human rights court. Their supreme courts are the ultimate arbiter of what they do in law. And in private cases, non-disclosure agreements can mean that justice may never be seen to be done, the details of what happened and the guilt of those involved locked away tightly behind expensive and impenetrable legal bars. Even in cases where the horrors that victims have endured are well known and publicly documented, you still need an effective legal mechanism to bring the perpetrators to justice. And international courts have ruled not only on the mental cruelty of investigative techniques designed to break down individual minds, but also on the potentially devastating consequences for human rights of propaganda to promote hate.

Radio Machete

When I stepped over the threshold of the 1930 prison in Kigali, Rwanda, in 2007, it was like walking into another dimension. It is an impressive structure – monolithic walls with a crenellated top rising from the red earth that makes fertile east Africa so green. Constructed by Belgian colonialists at a time when Europeans were starting to feel a little less comfortable in their God-given privilege to rule Africa, it was designed to hold the couple of thousand people the Belgians thought might cause them trouble. But the legacy of Belgian colonialism in the form of inter-ethnic conflict meant that by the end of the twentieth century, Rwanda needed to find space for tens of thousands more prisoners.

From the outside, peaceful and serene,[5] it could almost have been a luxury hotel, with a couple of prisoners dressed in soft pink convicts' clothes sweeping the dusty ground. But inside the walls, thousands of men stood tightly packed in quiet groups, makeshift bedchambers racked up against the walls like chicken coops.[6] Walking along the placid spontaneous corridors created by the parting walls of human beings, it seemed incomprehensible that one day just over 10 years earlier, these people could have turned and butchered their friends and neighbours in their hundreds of thousands. They were so compliant in their internal prison organisation that there was no need even for guards. But the deeply scarred dent in the elegant young prison governor's forehead was a constant reminder that humanity can turn with devastating speed and viciousness.

The horror of the Rwandan genocide in 1994 was a stark reminder of the devastating and destructive power of propaganda. More than 800,000 people were murdered over a period of 100 days following a sustained campaign in national newspapers and radio that dehumanised a whole section of the population, the minority Tutsis, and riled the majority Hutus up against them. As the international community finally stirred from its stunned silence, it was not only those who carried out or ordered the violence who found themselves facing trial before the International Criminal Tribunal for Rwanda (ICTR), but it was also those who spread the hatred, poisoning the air waves and print media to turn the beautiful green hills and valleys of the country into a bloodbath. Human rights may be protected not only through holding governments to account with international human rights law, but also through bringing individuals to justice using international criminal law.

In December 2003, the ICTR convicted Ferdinand Nahimana, founder and ideologist of the Radio Télévision Libre des Mille Collines (RTLM); Jean-Bosco Barayagwiza, a high-ranking board member of the Comité d'initiative of the RTLM and founding member of the Coalition for the Defence of the Republic (CDR); and Hassan Ngeze, chief editor of *Kangura* newspaper. Their convictions were for genocide, incitement to genocide, conspiracy, and crimes against humanity – extermination and persecution.[7]

Their convictions were based, in large part, on the way their media activities were designed to affect the minds of their audience.

Of Nahimana, Judge Pillay noted, 'You were fully aware of the power of words, and you used the radio – the medium of communication with the widest public reach – to disseminate hatred and violence ... Without a firearm, machete or any physical weapon, you caused the death of thousands of innocent civilians.'[8] RTLM, otherwise known as 'Radio Machete', was direct in its message to listeners on how to identify Tutsis: 'Look at the person's height and his physical appearance ... Just look at his small nose and then break it.'[9] The station made the call for a 'final war' to 'exterminate all the cockroaches' and gave instructions on where to find terrified Tutsis in hiding. Nahimana was sentenced to life imprisonment for his part in the genocide.

Kangura had run a campaign for years that dehumanised Tutsi people, particularly women. In 1990, it had published an article with the 'Ten Commandments of the Hutu', warning Hutu men that Tutsi women were seductive agents of the enemy, and branding any Hutu man who married a Tutsi woman a traitor. Its front page in 1994 ran with the headline, 'What weapons shall we use to conquer the Inyenzi Tutsi once and for all?'; the answer was provided below with a photograph of a machete, the weapon of choice when the mass murder began. Sentencing Ngeze to life imprisonment, Judge Pillay explained, 'You poisoned the minds of your readers, and by words and deeds caused the death of thousands of innocent civilians.'[10]

But the court, in what was known as the 'media case', was careful 'to distinguish between the discussion of ethnic consciousness and the promotion of ethnic hatred'. An interview Barayagwiza had given on RTLM, which was put forward by the prosecution as part of the case against him, was described in the judgment as 'a moving personal account of his experience of discrimination as a Hutu'.[11] This, the court found, fell squarely under the protection of the right to freedom of expression. But it also recognised that: 'the power of the media to create and destroy fundamental human values comes with great responsibility. Those who control such media are accountable for its consequences.'[12] Speech that destroys the rights of others loses its protection under human rights law.

The men appealed their convictions on numerous grounds, both procedural and factual, some of which were upheld by the appeal court. The appeal court ruling provides some interesting insights into the way hate speech and incitement are considered in international criminal law. It found that direct and public incitement to genocide was a crime that could be established even if genocide itself did not follow from the incitement.[13] And it noted that the cultural context and nuances of the Kinyarwanda language could be taken into account to decide how the words used would be understood by the intended audience, rejecting the argument that only an explicit call for genocide was covered by the statute. The court also looked at persecution as a crime against humanity, and held that hate speech could be considered as serious as other crimes against humanity where it ran alongside a massive campaign of persecution characterised by violence and destruction of property, as it did in Rwanda in 1994.

Nahimana's conviction was affirmed for the crimes of direct and public incitement to commit genocide and persecution as a crime against humanity for RTLM broadcasts made after 6 April 1994,[14] while Ngeze was convicted of having directly and publicly incited the commission of genocide through matters published in *Kangura* in 1994. Some of their convictions were overturned on the facts, though all three were still convicted and sentenced for international crimes. But the message of the media case is clear – if you use your power and your platform to warp the minds and destroy the lives of others, you will be punished, and your right to freedom of expression will not protect you. The next time you hear free speech being touted in modern online culture wars as a justification for spreading hate, ask yourself whether what you are reading, hearing or seeing would really be protected by the right to freedom of expression. Or if, rather, it must be prohibited as propaganda for hatred.

Ensuring freedom of thought and opinion means protecting our minds from manipulation. Human rights law also calls on states to create laws that prohibit propaganda for war and inciting national, racial or religious hatred,[15] providing a double lock to prevent the kind of propaganda campaign designed to manipulate the minds of the masses that was seen in Nazi Germany and in Rwanda. However, organised propaganda to fuel loathing and discrimination most often appears in places where human rights protections have already started to break down. In those cases, international criminal law provides a safety net of accountability. A dictator may think they can get away with a campaign of dehumanisation to provoke violence at home, but would they be prepared to face the consequences of international justice later? International mechanisms, especially the International Criminal Court, have been criticised for their focus on African countries in particular and their inability to hold those from powerful countries to account. If we want to prevent these kinds of atrocities in the future, we need to make sure that the international justice system is strong enough to bring perpetrators to justice no matter where they are or where they are from in the world. Hatred can flare up anywhere, and if uncontained, it can be deadly. International law can be a bulwark against hate as it transcends national borders. But for international law to work, its apparatus needs support – political, financial and practical.

The blood-smeared walls of Ntarama church, where babies' skulls were smashed by paramilitaries, and the shelves full of skulls, bones, bloodied clothes and shoes are a sickening reminder of the 5,000 civilians who were murdered there seeking sanctuary on 15 April 1994.[16] Stepping inside the cool building over 10 years on, the chill went bone deep. It is a visceral horror. My colleague, stumbling out into the sun, was physically sick with the shock of it. This is why it matters that we never, ever stop believing in human rights – because human rights violations are very, very real. Every time somebody says 'I don't believe in human rights', there is a good chance that someone somewhere may fall down dead.

Stained Class

Manipulation of our minds is rarely so direct or so deadly as the messages broadcast by Radio Machete. But human rights are equally important in the private places where everyday human tragedies unfold. Ingrid Bergman's character in the 1944 movie *Gaslight* was unaware that her husband was manipulating her into thinking that she was mad, but the prevalence of this kind of abuse has led to gaslighting becoming a common theme today in public and in private. Recognising the pernicious effect of psychological manipulation in the home, many countries have legislated in recent years to criminalise 'coercive control' as a particular form of domestic abuse.[17] All forms of manipulation play to the subconscious – our hopes, fears, biases and emotional vulnerabilities – but what if it were possible to bypass the conscious mind entirely? What if a message could be delivered directly to the subconscious without us even being aware that we had heard a message at all?

In 1957, marketing man James Vicary announced a new form of advertising that was so painless you wouldn't feel a thing. He claimed to have flashed the slogans 'Drink Coca-Cola' and 'Eat Popcorn' repeatedly during a movie, so quickly that the human eye did not even register it, though the subconscious did, with the effect of massively boosting Coke and popcorn sales. Or so he said. He expected his discovery to be met with delight – no more annoying adverts disturbing your movie experience; now you could be sold things without even noticing it. But the horror of the potential for subliminal messaging to manipulate our minds led to public outrage in the United States and a ban on subliminal advertising in Europe.[18] Several years later, Vicary admitted that his research was sketchy and that he regretted the whole thing.[19] But despite his claims being derided as junk science, the fear and fascination of subliminal messaging continued to concern people for decades.

On 23 December 1985, two young men, Raymond Belknap and James Vance, took a sawn-off shotgun to an empty churchyard in Sparks, Nevada, where they spent the afternoon drinking beer, smoking weed and listening to the music of British heavy metal band Judas Priest before turning the shotgun on themselves. Belknap died immediately, while Vance was seriously injured and died three years later after falling into a sudden and unexplained coma. Their families, devastated by the loss and looking for answers, fell on the suggestion that Judas Priest's 1978 album *Stained Class* contained subliminal backwards messaging[20] promoting suicide, and that this was the reason the men had taken their own lives. The suspicion of subliminal messaging in music had many eighties teenagers desperately listening for spooky backwards messages on cassette tapes and vinyl, but the men's families claimed that far from being an urban myth, Judas Priest's music was infused with subliminal exhortations to 'do it', and they sued the band and the record company for $3.6 million . *Stained Class*, they said, was quite literally a health hazard.

Standing up for human rights is not only the job of international courts in cases of gross human rights violations. Human rights affect all of us; we all have them, and we must also respect the rights of everyone else. Our rights are protected by criminal laws that discourage us from harming others and by civil laws that encourage us to play nicely and treat each other with respect. Human rights, whether implicitly or explicitly, are the daily bread of courts around the world and it is not always easy to spot them. The same can be said for manipulative messages.

Judas Priest, shocked to find themselves at the heart of a multimillion-dollar lawsuit on the other side of the Atlantic involving the death of two fans they had never even met, argued, among other things, that their First Amendment rights to free speech as musicians meant the case should be dismissed. But Washoe District judge Jerry Carr Whitehead was not convinced that the First Amendment would protect subliminal messages at all. Firstly, he found that subliminal messaging does not fulfil any of the functions of free speech – if you are not aware of it, it does nothing for dialogue, exchange of ideas, the pursuit of truth or mental autonomy. Secondly, subliminal messages, because they cannot be avoided, go against the First Amendment right to be free from unwanted speech and are a breach of privacy.[21] The concept of subliminal messaging raises a whole new aspect of the First Amendment – the right not to listen. The US constitution may not explicitly refer to the right to freedom of thought, but the right not to listen or to be free from unwanted speech is an essential part of the right not to have your thoughts, feelings, beliefs or opinions manipulated by others.

The families ultimately failed in their claim against Judas Priest because they could not show that there were intentional subliminal messages on the album, so they could not make a causal link between the music and the men's deaths.[22] But even if they had been able to find the messages in the music, the causal effect of manipulation would be very hard to prove, as critics of Vicary's original experiment have argued for decades. So how can human rights law protect you from manipulation of your thoughts or opinions if you cannot prove it is happening?

Secrets and lies

Your human rights can be violated without you knowing it. And in some cases, the impact of a violation may be difficult to quantify. But human rights must be real and effective; if secrecy was a get-out-of-jail-free card for oppressive governments, our rights would be no good to us at all. And the impact of losing your rights cannot be evidenced or quantified in the same way as the impact of having your purse stolen. So the law has evolved to protect your rights even when it's a secret that they are at risk.

Secret surveillance and interception is, by definition, secret. Unless it is done very badly, with crude clicks on the line or an accidental crossed wire in another language, it would be very hard to prove that you had ever been the subject of surveillance. So, recognising the difficulties in proving incidences of surveillance despite the clear fact that state surveillance does happen, the European Court of Human Rights has established two important principles to address harms that are hard to prove.[23]

Firstly, the principle of lawfulness means that if a state is carrying out activities that interfere with human rights, they must have a clearly codified basis in law. A cloak of secrecy chokes our rights. If a state wants to carry out secret surveillance, it needs to have a law that explains how, why and who it may surveil, and that law must be compliant with human rights standards. Any surveillance interferes with the right to private life. Without law, surveillance will be not just an interference with but a violation of privacy. Law is needed to set out the circumstances where surveillance would be permitted and compliant with the right to private life or other rights. It may seem counter-intuitive as a government to publish all the secret stuff you might do. But if you don't, and you get challenged, your secret stuff will almost certainly be found to be unlawful. This same principle should apply to practices that aim to get inside your head and manipulate you. If the state wants to mess with your head, it needs to explain how and why it will do it in compliance with human rights law. And if companies or individuals want to get inside our heads in a way that would violate our freedom of thought, the state has an obligation to make laws to protect us from that. As digital surveillance techniques, both by the state and by technology companies, are increasingly designed to make inferences about what we are thinking, not just what we are saying, this principle will be increasingly important, not only to protect our privacy, but to protect our right to freedom of thought.

Secondly, a person can make a complaint about the impact of secret state activities on their human rights without having to prove that they have, in fact, been personally and directly targeted. If you can show that you are part of a group of people likely to be affected, that is enough to give you standing as a victim to bring a complaint. In circumstances where huge swathes of the population can be targeted indiscriminately with bulk surveillance powers,[24] almost anyone could, in principle, be affected. The rationale for this approach is not to bring on a wave of complaints (the European Court is already floundering under a huge backlog of cases); it is a reflection of the reality that some human rights violations are hard for individual victims to evidence, and that those very human rights issues can have serious consequences not only for targeted individuals, but for the wider population living in an atmosphere of suspicion and fear. The impact of a breach of human rights may be felt most acutely by an individual victim, but it ripples out through the whole society. When governments, companies or people act in ways that could interfere with our right to freedom of thought, whether that is to find out what we are thinking against our will, to manipulate our opinions or to criminalise them, the whole of society is the victim. The chance of an individual losing their freedom of thought has a chilling effect on all our freedoms.

Witches and unicorns

When we think about protecting the right to freedom of thought, we shouldn't get too hung up on what is real. It doesn't matter whether subliminal advertising actually works. If it is a terrible idea that would destroy human autonomy and freedom of thought, it should be banned anyway. If we wait until our freedom of thought is lost, we will be helpless to get it back. The right to freedom of thought, conscience and belief allows us to keep our inner thoughts private and free from manipulation; and the final plank in the protective fence around our inner lives – the *forum internum* – is that no one should be penalised for their thoughts or beliefs, real or imagined. As the drafters of the right to freedom of thought well understood, people are sometimes persecuted for the beliefs they are perceived to have, regardless of whether they actually have them. And so we come back to witches. There is no point being sniffy about belief in witches while people around the world, including children, are still being persecuted, prosecuted and put to death on suspicion of witchcraft, while others are being killed and dismembered for their supposed innate supernatural properties based on deluded beliefs driven by the desire for power and money.

It does not matter whether supernatural powers are real; as the French noted in the drafting process of the International Covenant on Civil and Political Rights, sometimes people are persecuted based on inferences about their inner thoughts, opinions or beliefs. Belief in and persecution of witchcraft, including legal prosecution, are still common in many countries. The beliefs and the laws go hand in hand. In 2008, the Tanzania Legal and Human Rights Centre concluded that the Witchcraft Act 2002 itself reinforced and legitimised the societal perception that witchcraft is undesirable and those who practise it must be punished.[25] Witch hunts may no longer be as prevalent in Europe as they were in the seventeenth century, but witchcraft is still found in many forms on statute books all over the world. When Romania introduced specific taxation for witches, fortune tellers and astrologers in 2011, the magical community responded by gathering to throw mandrake into the Danube to bring misfortune on the politicians who were looking to cream off 16 per cent of their income.[26] And in 2018, two women in Canada were charged with the criminal offence of 'fraudulently pretending to exercise or to use any kind of witchcraft, sorcery, enchantment or conjuration', the police pressing charges just as the law was slated for repeal as an outdated relic because anything covered by the magical charge would be equally prohibited under the more mundane charge of straightforward fraud.[27]

In 2009, Saudi Arabia established an Anti-Witchcraft Unit to identify the witches in their midst. Perhaps unsurprisingly, most of the hundreds of arrests since then have been of foreign domestic workers, predominantly women from Asia and Africa.[28] Being accused of witchcraft in Saudi Arabia is not a philosophical or fiscal nicety. In 2006, Fawza Falih, a Jordanian woman, was sentenced to death for 'witchcraft, recourse to jinn, and slaughter of animals'. Human Rights Watch wrote to King Abdullah bin Abd al-'Aziz Al Saud, highlighting that 'it is evident that the practice of "witchcraft", if it exists, is by its nature impossible to prove, since it involves the alleged use of supernatural powers'. Like five of the victims of the Zugarramurdi witch hunt four centuries before her, Fawza Falih became ill and died in prison before she could be put to death.

You do not have to believe in witches to believe that Fawza Falih had rights that the Saudi courts trampled over. And you do not have to believe in witchcraft to be persecuted for it. Gary Foxcroft, the director of the Witchcraft and Human Rights Information Network, explains:

> Job losses, illnesses, accidents, relationship breakdowns, and property damage can see a vulnerable person placed at the centre of a witch hunt, but it's estimated that around 70 per cent of witchcraft accusations are triggered by public health problems, like the spread of infectious diseases. People look for someone to blame. It is almost exclusively the most vulnerable members of the community who are accused. Very rarely is it men.[29]

Around the world, children are branded as witches for being subdued or excitable, too clever or not clever enough, and subjected to horrendous abuse because their minds are perceived as different.[30]

It is also true that belief in witchcraft continues to fuel physical attacks, emotional abuse and even murder. In September 2001, the torso of a young boy washed up on the banks of the Thames in London. Police investigating the death found that the boy they named 'Adam' was a six-year-old Nigerian boy who recently arrived in the country after being trafficked from Nigeria via Germany to be killed in what appeared to be a ritual murder. His body had been bled and dismembered, his head was never recovered. Twenty years on, those responsible for his brutal murder have not been identified or brought to justice.[31] Adam's fate made headlines because his body was found in London and the Metropolitan Police continues to look for leads on his case. But his fate is tragically common in many countries in sub-Saharan Africa where the belief that the body parts of sacrificed children can bring wealth, health and political power is growing.[32] In many cases, their disappearance is not even reported, much less investigated or prosecuted. So what does human rights law do to protect innocent victims like Adam from these horrific crimes?

Prosecutions for a belief in witchcraft, whether real or inferred, are a violation of the right to freedom of belief. But prosecutions for the kinds of horrific and brutal crimes carried out in the name of witchcraft are crucial to give justice to the victims and their families and to show that murdering children is not a route to money and power, no matter what you may believe. These hideous practices clearly need to be prevented and prosecuted in law to protect the human rights of victims and their families, including their right to life. But laws prohibiting murder and physical attacks, discrimination or the promotion of violence do not need to be couched in the vague supernatural notion of 'witchcraft'. What children like Adam and their families need are justice systems that make sure people are held accountable for such horrendous crimes, no matter how powerful they may be, and regardless of what they believe. 20 years on, at the time of writing, no one has been charged for Adam's brutal murder.

Human rights law protects our dignity and our humanity from the state, from each other and from the societal oppression that Mill so deplored. In 2021, the UN Human Rights Council passed a resolution on the elimination of harmful practices related to accusations of witchcraft and ritual attacks,[33] calling on states and UN agencies to take action to protect people like Adam and Fawza Falih. If you believe in human rights, you do not need to believe in witches, but you do need to challenge laws and practices that stigmatise and dehumanise people as witches because of inferences about their inner lives. You do not need to penalise belief in witches to design and enforce laws that ban the harvesting of human body parts, child abuse, murder and the persecution of individuals or groups of people for any reason, magical or not. Witchcraft is still an issue that threatens the right to freedom of belief and other human rights around the world, whether you believe in it or not.

And just as our beliefs and cultures change over time, human rights law needs to evolve to meet our modern reality. The right to freedom of thought may have been conceived of long before Mark Zuckerberg was, but if it is to survive in the twenty-first century, it must be able to adapt to address the challenges that companies like Facebook and Cambridge Analytica pose to our freedom to think for ourselves. Luckily, human rights law is designed to do just that.

The living tree

Eleanor Roosevelt famously said:

> Where, after all, do universal human rights begin?
> In small places, close to home – so close and so small
> that they cannot be seen on any maps of the world.
> Yet they are the world of the individual person; the
> neighborhood he lives in; the school or college he
> attends; the factory, farm, or office where he works.
> Such are the places where every man, woman,
> and child seeks equal justice, equal opportunity,
> equal dignity without discrimination. Unless these
> rights have meaning there, they have little meaning
> anywhere. Without concerted citizen action to uphold
> them close to home, we shall look in vain for progress
> in the larger world.

For me, a real understanding of what human rights mean came from very close to home, through a case that has come to define the fault lines of human rights law and policy over the last half-century.

Growing up in the Isle of Man in the 1970s and 80s, we all knew what 'the birch' was – a tool for the police to beat juvenile delinquents. There were two options, a cane for those under 14, or the birch – a handful of sticks bound together – for 14–21-year-olds. As a girl, I didn't need to worry too much; it was only used on boys. Corporal punishment as a criminal sentence had been abolished in England and Wales in 1948 (although it was only in 1999 that it was finally made illegal in all English schools, and even later in Scotland and Northern Ireland). But the Isle of

Man's autonomous status meant it didn't need to follow suit. So in the 1960s, the island amended its laws to allow for more, not less, corporal punishment for young offenders. British newspapers regularly bemoaned the fact that children could no longer be beaten as a punishment for crimes in England, and admired the Manx deterrent. But more than a tool of corporal punishment, the birch at that time was a symbol of the island's unwillingness to be pushed around by outsiders, whether that be British 'yobs' before they moved to the Costas of Spain and the Greek islands, or Europe with its grand ideas about human rights. In the 1970s, though, things started to change.

Three women in the Isle of Man horrified by the practice led a campaign to ban the birch on the island, supported by the British National Council for Civil Liberties. One of them, Angela Kneale, a Belgian woman living on the island, wrote a brave and influential book on the reasons for abolishing the birch that made waves in the civil liberties movement across the water. And then in 1972, they found a case to prove their point. A 15-year-old boy had been caught bringing beer into school with some friends and had been caned by the headmaster. He and his friends then found the boy who had snitched on them and beat him up. The accused boy pleaded guilty to assault occasioning actual bodily harm, and was sentenced and given three strokes of the birch by a policeman. Seeing their chance to challenge what they considered a barbaric practice, the women helped him to bring his case to the European Court of Human Rights.

Corporal punishment had been the norm across Europe when the European Convention on Human Rights was drafted in the 1950s, but by the 1970s, the Isle of Man was an outlier. The Court was asked to decide whether a practice that would have been acceptable to the drafters of the Convention could be considered as inhuman and degrading treatment 20 years on. The boy was not a human rights activist, and over the years it took to get a judgment, he eventually dropped out of the case. But the Court decided to go ahead with the case without him because of the importance of the issue at stake for the value and interpretation of the whole Convention and the wider international human rights project.

The Manx attorney general argued in court that birching was a 'cultural requirement' of the Isle of Man, and produced evidence in the form of a petition signed by a large proportion of the population to show that corporal punishment did not 'outrage public opinion' on the island. But the Court's assessment was damning. It found that the public support for birching could be precisely because of its degrading nature and the assumption that this would make it an effective deterrent, but that, even if it did deter crime, there could never be a justification for violating absolute rights. Degrading punishment would never be allowed.

The Isle of Man lost the argument and the European Court of Human Rights found that it was in violation of the Convention. In a gesture of hurt sovereignty, the island went on to thumb its nose at Strasbourg for the next 15 years, until the law was finally changed. This was the plucky little island standing up for its right to do what it liked to its children. But what I did not understand as a child was that this case, brought from a small place close to home, would have wide repercussions for human rights everywhere.

There are three reasons why the case matters so much for an understanding of human rights, including the rights to freedom of thought and opinion. Firstly, it is a vindication of the rights of the individual person against the tyranny of the masses. Just because the general public think something is a good idea does not make it so. As J. S. Mill so passionately argued, the views of society can be as oppressive to freedom of thought as the law itself. Human rights law is the key to challenging the status quo, no matter how entrenched it is, allowing us to protect the rights of each and every one of us, regardless of how unpopular we may be.

Secondly, if something amounts to a violation of an absolute right, there can never be a justification for doing it. The utilitarian argument that a degrading punishment may act as a deterrent and reduce crime does not matter – it will still be unlawful. Similarly, it does not matter if manipulating someone's inner thoughts might make them a better citizen – if it amounts to an interference with the right to freedom of thought, it will always be unlawful.

And thirdly, times change, and human rights law evolves with the times. Most importantly, the Court stressed that 'the Convention is a living instrument which … must be interpreted in the light of present-day conditions'. The same principle is known in Canadian constitutional law as the 'living tree doctrine':[34] human rights law grows to reflect the changing mores of society; it is not fixed in the monolith of its drafters' context for all eternity. This is what makes human rights law real and relevant over 70 years after the Universal Declaration of Human Rights was agreed.

Even if, as a girl, I was never at risk of birching, I recognise that as a woman I have a lot to thank the living tree of human rights law for: it is the doctrine that allowed women to finally be appointed to the Canadian Senate in 1929. And it is this concept of human rights law as a living tree that allows the right to freedom of thought to evolve to meet the challenges of the digital age.

A twenty-first-century right

We have explored what interferences with the rights to freedom of thought, belief and opinion have looked like in the analogue world through the ages. Punishments for daring to question religious doctrine, cruel interventions to cure wayward thoughts, scientific techniques designed to read and break minds, and psychological strategies to bend the minds of whole populations with deadly consequences. Some of the examples may seem distant and arcane – problems of the past. But many of these threats have been reborn in digital disguises. And they are not someone else's problem. As we will see in the next section, the digital threats to freedom of thought affect us all.

So how should we view the rights to freedom of thought and opinion 'in the light of present-day conditions'? The absolute nature of the rights reflects their fundamental importance. But the absence of jurisprudence and commentary on them makes it harder to pin down their exact scope in a rapidly changing world. Despite the apparent strength of protection contained in the rights, what has not been explored so far is what interference with those absolute rights might look like in the digital age. We don't need new rights to deal with new realities; we just need to understand what the rights we have mean for us today. The right to freedom of thought has been left to languish in the twentieth century, but now it is time for it to step up and show us what it could mean for our future humanity.

If, as individuals and societies, we can start to understand how our freedom is being compromised, we can begin to resist, make choices that minimise the risk and demand better protection. There is an urgent need to consider the ways in which technology can be abused to access and alter our inner thoughts and opinions, and we must take action to stop it. We need to understand the potential risks of technology so that we can make sure that it develops in a way that serves society, not those who seek to control us for their own ends. Once we have lost our ability to think freely and form independent opinions in the privacy of our own minds, we may never get it back. It is in the twenty-first century that the right to freedom of thought must really be allowed to come of age.

Part 2

—

THE DIGITAL

CHAPTER 6

———

FACEBOOK KNOWS
YOU BETTER

A couple of years ago, I met with a politician who commented that human rights had really gone too far, that they no longer reflected what the drafters had in mind in the 1940s and 50s. I replied that if society, and human rights, had not progressed, as a woman I would probably not have been there talking to him, in my job. The conversation moved swiftly on. But I hope it made him think, at least for a minute, even if he may have concluded that it would be no bad thing if I wasn't there after all. The past can give us fresh perspectives on the present and the future. The first part of this book covered where we have come from, the origins of freedom of thought and the ways in which it has been threatened in the past. We may all feel relieved that the dark days of being burned for heresy are largely over – at least in the West – but we cannot afford to be complacent about our rights or our freedom to think for ourselves. Threats to human rights are nothing new, and many of us are in a much better place, enjoying vastly greater rights and freedoms than our ancestors or even our parents. But the world has been transformed in my lifetime by the ubiquity of digital technology.

And in September 2021, the UN High Commissioner for Human Rights, Michelle Bachelet, described the way that data is collected, used and shared against the background of rapid growth in AI as 'one of the most urgent human rights questions we face'.[1]

We are moving very fast into a new digital age where we need to decide what human rights mean to us and to the future of humanity. The complexity of the big data economy and the algorithms that dictate our modern lives, as well as the veil of secrecy drawn over the inner workings of the digital world by big tech companies and governments, makes it hard to understand exactly what the threats are to our human rights. But in the modern world, you don't need to be a philosopher, a wise woman or a social misfit to have negative inferences drawn about your mind that could dictate your future life chances. Big tech is reading us all everywhere, all the time. And the potential to scale up attacks on our freedom of thought is almost limitless. Once we lose our freedom of thought, we lose what it means to be human.

We are at a crucial juncture. In 2010, Facebook founder Mark Zuckerberg claimed that privacy was no longer 'a social norm'.[2] Six years later, the General Data Protection Regulation made it clear that, in Europe at least, we are not so ready to give up on human rights in our daily lives. The incursions of technology into our freedom to think for ourselves, in private and without judgement or penalty are very real. We cannot allow freedom of thought to become an anachronism, a Luddite concept not suited for the modern age. Without freedom of thought we may find ourselves in a world where the violations of human rights discussed in Part 1 will seem petty compared with the scale of human rights abuse that may be perpetrated at the click of a mouse or the tweak of an algorithm. If we want to understand how to protect our freedom of thought for the future, we need to know where the current threats are, and in the digital age, they are everywhere.

Today, the internet makes it harder to escape your past, as British 'canoe man' John Darwin discovered when he faked his death for an insurance claim.[3] His fraud was revealed by a stunningly misguided decision to appear smiling in online photos in Panama years later. But social media does give us unprecedented opportunities to create new, ideal versions of ourselves online while comparing ourselves with the picture-perfect existences of friends and family, whose lives and lips appear flawless through the filters of Instagram. Our social media lives may feel comfortably cut off from the grimy and messy realities of our daily lives. But while we post unreal filtered pictures of ourselves online, social media runs on the crude oil of our thoughts and feelings and the trails of them we leave in our greasy data footprints.

I have a brown leather suitcase I inherited from my grandfather that contains my memories from before Facebook. Full of letters, journals and photos that document my social interactions over three decades, it has been carried with me through several countries and what now feel like several different lives. It lives at the back of the cupboard and is rarely opened. But when I did open it recently, looking for a lost part of my life, I was moved by the memories of people I have never quite forgotten and the moments we lived together. An envelope stuffed full of love letters reminded me acutely of who I was when I was 20, and glamorous photographs at 30 showed a completely different image from the one in the accompanying journal entries filled with self-doubt. A snapshot from a diary entry at 18 revealed how far I have come since then and how little I have really changed. The memories in my suitcase are indelible. I can touch them, and the various flavours of handwriting scurrying across reams of paper trigger flashbacks of the people who wrote them. But they are not for sharing. The letters were addressed to me; they are deeply personal and they are about the connection I had with the writer. My journals were never designed to be read by anyone else; they were only ever a means of understanding my own thoughts, not a way of presenting myself to the outside world. Not everything we record needs to be shared.

When Winston Smith, Orwell's hero in *Nineteen Eighty-Four*, buys a pen and a notebook and starts a diary, he finds himself writing over and over again: 'DOWN WITH BIG BROTHER'. But it doesn't matter what he writes, or even whether he writes. The mere fact of buying the pen and the notebook, of setting pen to paper away from the omnipresent eyes of Big Brother, away from the telescreens and the speakwrite machines that record every thought and emotion, means he has already committed 'the essential crime that contained all others in itself. Thoughtcrime …'

The arrival of the reality show *Big Brother* on our TV screens at the turn of the century gave us all a delightful frisson, with the awful idea of constant surveillance and public sharing of individual lives that Orwell had described in his novel now made flesh in a fun and palatable format for mass media – or as Orwell called it in newspeak, 'prolefeed'. At the time, the participants seemed like strange beasts. How could they cope with that degree of exposure? Why would they do it? There was an irrepressible horror at the idea – cameras and microphones in the bedrooms and bathrooms, constant judgement from the outside world. Yet somehow, since then, we have all allowed our lives to become microcosms of the Big Brother house without even realising it.

Whether you engage on social media or not, the minutiae of your life as it is lived online, and in the real world in the company of your ever-present smartphone, are monitored and recorded and parsed for signs of who you are, how you might behave and how you could be manipulated.

Nothing to hide, nothing to fear

So why are people so free with their private lives? Is it the initial rapture at connecting with strangers and friends across the ether? Or the opportunity to curate a perfect image of ourselves for public consumption? The cult of fame has gradually become mainstream – if we are prepared to open up and bare our souls, we can be famous for Andy Warhol's notorious 15 minutes. All it takes is a few moments of brutally honest exposure, or a carefully timed casual quip on Twitter, and the riches of global adulation can be yours. But this exposure not only has an impact on our privacy, it reveals and affects how we and others think in ways we may not even realise.

Sharing has become the norm without us noticing. And sharing somehow feels private when it is done in the night from our beds, on a device that is practically a part of us. Research done about people holding their phones in public, even when not using them,[4] points to only one thing we prefer to phone holding – hand holding with a significant other (if they are physically there). Our phone use has become a surrogate for intimacy. It is the way we get close to people, and we can only get close if we open up and share. But how many of us would speak openly on a phone call if we really believed someone else was listening in and interpreting the subtext in our private conversations? Would we feel comfortable with the idea that someone else was taking notes as we whispered sweet nothings down the line, analysing our tone, comparing it with another call we made the year before, triangulating our emotions and desires, recording it for posterity?

If we thought about it, we probably would not. Our communications would be adapted; heightened or dumbed down. We would not be authentic, if we chose to talk at all. Yet what is happening with our interface with technology is much more intrusive than that. It is not the content we post or even the personal information we provide that matters. Every piece of information about every action we take, or hesitate to take, every thought we explore online, every place we visit, the speed we move at, every word we utter near a voice-activated device can be brought together and analysed in an effort to give a clear picture of our thoughts and desires, our levers and buttons. It is the metadata that bares our souls.

In 2015, the news was peppered with stories claiming that Facebook knows you better than your friends and family.[5] Researchers at Cambridge University (including Michal Kosinski, whose controversial research on politics and sexual orientation feature in later chapters) had discovered that analysis of the things you've 'liked' on Facebook was a pretty good predictor of your personality and other personal attributes based on the 'Big Five' personality traits of openness, conscientiousness, extroversion, agreeableness and neuroticism. The results of the study show just how hard it would be to cover our online personality tracks as we click and scroll. We are not consciously telling Facebook our innermost thoughts; rather these are being extracted through an algorithmic analysis of our online activity and turned to profit, though not for us. While you might expect that liking a Facebook page for a campaign supporting gay rights could in some way be a predictor of sexual orientation, how would you know that liking curly fries would be a predictor of high intelligence, while liking Harley Davidson or 'I Love Being a Mom' would allow someone to assume you were not so bright?[6] Although perhaps the fact that liking 'Being Confused After Waking Up From Naps' is a strong predictor of male heterosexuality is less surprising than many men might like to think.

More seriously, the researchers' conclusions highlight both the positive and the negative potential of AI inferences being drawn from online behaviour. They claim that a wide variety of personal attributes ranging from intelligence to sexual orientation can be automatically (and they say accurately) inferred based on the digital traces we leave, including Facebook likes, browsing histories, search queries or purchase histories. But their description of the uses these inferences could be put to is particularly revealing. On the positive side, they suggest that 'online insurance advertisements might emphasize security when facing emotionally unstable (neurotic) users but stress potential threats when dealing with emotionally stable ones'. While this may be useful for insurance companies trying to sell their services, it is not necessarily good for the consumer being lulled into a false sense of security by adverts playing on their psychological quirks for money.

On the negative side, the researchers noted the risks associated with automated profiling of personal attributes, particularly when this 'can easily be applied to large numbers of people without obtaining their individual consent and without them noticing. Commercial companies, governmental institutions, or even one's Facebook friends could use software to infer attributes such as intelligence, sexual orientation, or political views that an individual may not have intended to share.' Consent is crucial in drawing the legal line around our inner lives. We cannot give consent to something we do not notice and are not aware of. That is why legislators in Europe were so disturbed by the idea of subliminal advertising being used to bypass our critical faculties regardless of what it might have been trying to sell us. Freedom of thought and opinion gives us the right to decide which parts of ourselves we want to reveal about our inner worlds, and to whom. It lets us choose when it is safe to share what is going on inside our minds. Making these inferences on an industrial scale without consent is, effectively, a massive violation of the rights to freedom of thought and opinion. And it's a violation that most of us are subjected to each time we interact with technology.

Perhaps one of the most revealing conclusions from the study is the fact that these predictions can be dangerous, regardless of whether they are rubbish or not. As the researchers admit:

> One can imagine situations in which such predictions, even if incorrect, could pose a threat to an individual's well-being, freedom, or even life. Importantly, given the ever-increasing amount of digital traces people leave behind, it becomes difficult for individuals to control which of their attributes are being revealed. For example, merely avoiding explicitly homosexual content may be insufficient to prevent others from discovering one's sexual orientation.[7]

In the modern world, it is practically impossible to avoid leaving traces of yourself that may be used to profile and even punish you. Privacy settings will not help. The way these inferences are made and used is beyond our personal control. It needs serious laws and effective regulation to draw the lines around what is acceptable from a human rights perspective for us as individuals and for our societies. This research lights up the bottom line for social media companies – the business model is not about supporting community and connection; it is about understanding and exploiting how the user thinks and feels. How we think and how we can be made to think and behave is what is commercially valuable. Because if you can understand and control how we think and feel, you can control what we buy, what we do and how we vote.

Cyberball

The 'likes' are not only about what we like. They have a dual purpose. The things we like tell Facebook who we are and what we think, while the likes we receive give us social validation along with a dopamine hit and leave us craving more, effectively locked into the platform. And that craving is very real and acutely felt. In the past twenty years, psychologists have started to recognise that the pain of feeling left out socially can have the same impact as actual physical pain.[8] In one experiment, volunteers were given an fMRI scan while playing an online game called Cyberball. This involved a three-way virtual game of catch, with two players gradually starting to pass the ball just between themselves, excluding the third. The researchers found that the brains of those who had been excluded showed an increase in activity in the dorsal anterior cingulate and the anterior insula – a brain response commonly associated with physical pain.

Further research has shown that we feel social pain, albeit fleetingly, in our daily interactions when a stranger passes us without eye contact, or perhaps when the person we are with picks up their phone. It doesn't even matter whether the perceived slight comes from someone we really, really don't like. The connection between social and physical pain is apparently so intimate that actually taking painkilling medication has been found to reduce the social pain just as it does physical pain.[9] But reaching for the Tylenol is not the natural response to social slights; a more likely reaction is to chase the buzz of validation, and in the world of social media, this means the ultimate tonic of the drip-feed of constant 'likes' or the steady build-up of an army of followers. FOMO (fear of missing out) craves 'likes' and 'follows' and drives more and more social media time chasing them, which feeds deeper and deeper algorithmic insights about our thoughts and feelings that social media giants can harvest as hard cash.

It is not just Facebook likes that reveal our inner selves. Research published in 2020[10] confirmed earlier studies that show similar personality predictions can be gleaned passively just from the way we use our phones. By taking data from mobile phones, including communication and social engagement, music consumption, app usage, mobility, overall phone activity and the times of the day and night when you use your phone, the researchers showed that they could predict the personality of a user with a fairly high level of accuracy. It is not what you say, it is what you do or don't do, along with when, how and how often you do it. Our phones offer a window into what and how we think and how we can be manipulated. And we religiously carry them in our pockets to help them do it better.

In 2012, Harvard law professor Eben Moglen said at the re:publica conference, an international festival of internet and digital society: 'They own the search box and we put our dreams in it. And they eat them, and they tell us who we are right back.'[11] In 2020, it is not the search box, it is the shiny screen glued to our hands that extracts our dreams like a Vulcan mind meld. We may think we are carefully tailoring a public image, but it is no longer a question of who we think we are, but who they think we are and who they will turn us into.

This algorithmic assessment of who we are and what we are thinking or feeling poses a serious threat to our right to freedom of thought. In our normal social interactions, we may be constantly interpreting the people we speak to and engage with, trying to understand what they think and feel so that we can respond appropriately. But social media does something different. It is an industrial-scale attempt to get inside our minds for purely exploitative reasons. There is nothing social about Facebook's drive to understand us; it is purely commercial.

The information that we do not choose to share is taken anyway. Our social pain is profitable too. Lack of engagement, our moments of private loneliness, can be as revealing as the over-sharing. And this hoovering up of our likes, our data and metadata, our searches, our idle notes, our daydreams, our downtime is an interference with our absolute rights to freedom of thought and opinion. The former UN Special Rapporteur on freedom of opinion and expression, David Kaye, noted that in the digital world, our exploration of ideas and information, while falling short of expression, belongs to that inner realm where we need the freedom to develop and hold our opinions freely and in private.[12] But it is our inner world that is the basis of what the economist Shoshana Zuboff calls 'surveillance capitalism'.[13] Extracting our thoughts without our informed consent is absolutely a violation of our right to freedom of thought. You may have consented to the terms and conditions of Facebook, YouTube, Google or any other platform you use in your daily life, but even if you took the 76 working days per year required to actually read the terms and conditions and privacy policies,[14] you likely did not really understand the potential consequences. There was no informed consent. Signing away control over your mind in return for cat videos or the pain of virtual social isolation is no more a legitimate legal contract than signing your soul over to the devil. The reason the right to freedom of thought entails the right to keep your thoughts private is because it is through knowing or inferring the contents of someone's mind, their personality, opinions and feelings, that they can be manipulated, controlled and punished.

Emotional contagion

The problem is not only what social media companies infer about us; it is also the way they use that information to influence us and how they can make us feel. Facebook feeds me a stream of heart-warming stories about regional farm animals – a rabbit in Wales who hangs out with sheep, a Shetland pony in Scotland who takes people with mobility issues to the beach – and it is certainly more uplifting than the news about Afghanistan in my newsfeed. On Twitter, I am fed stories about older women dating younger men – perhaps inspired by the divorce certificate I received by email. We are becoming more and more acclimatised to the strange choices and personalised content that we find directed at us through social media. Personalisation is often billed as a way of 'improving user experience', but we need to think carefully not only about what our social media use says about how we think and feel, but also about how it could be used to make us think, feel and ultimately behave differently.

Millions of us now find ourselves 'just checking' our phones in the spare moments in our days when we used to stare idly out of a window watching a robin or sit quietly studying the person across from us on the train. We no longer have spare moments because social media fills them for us with the illusion of connection to our friends and family or the sense that we have our fingers firmly on the minute-by-minute pulse of the news cycle. Those spare moments might have given us a little space to reflect and let our thoughts lead us down the yellow brick road of creative optimism, or perhaps narrower, darker alleyways of despondency. Instead, our idle moments are no longer really ours at all; they are carefully (or even casually) curated and managed by algorithms that have other ideas about what we should be thinking or feeling. The feelings of dejection we might experience may not only be down to the niggling thought that we are wasting our time; they could also be due to the way our social media feeds are designed and delivered to us. As technologist turned philosopher James Williams puts it: 'The effect of the global attention economy – i.e., of our digital technologies doing precisely what they are designed to do – is to frustrate and even erode the human will at individual and collective levels, undermining the very assumptions of democracy. These are the distractions of a system that is not on our side.'[15]

The idea that our emotions may be manipulated or that our autonomy could be compromised is something that makes us all uncomfortable, but however much we may mock the sometimes absurd personalisation results and bemoan our reliance on our phones, the wholesale manipulation of emotions in the distraction economy is more or less the mainstay of social media, and it is not even hidden. The combination of design decisions that make social media 'sticky' to keep us online when we don't really want to be and the ability to tweak our emotions and opinions is what makes the current model so dangerous.

In 2014, Facebook published the results of a study entitled 'Experimental evidence of massive-scale emotional contagion through social networks'.[16] The study showed that Facebook could alter the emotional state of users by manipulating their newsfeeds. Just under 700,000 users were targeted in a two-week experiment that monitored how those users felt according to how their newsfeed was arranged. Researchers manipulated the feeds of this random sample and found that those shown more negative posts posted more negative comments, and vice versa. When the research was reported, there was a backlash from Facebook users unhappy with this evidence of control and manipulation of their emotional states. Facebook apologised and said the experiment should have been 'done differently'.[17] But it did not distance itself from the conclusions of the study and its capacity to socially engineer emotions en masse. Arguably, an experiment that sought to manipulate users' inner space without their knowledge should not have been carried out at all. There is no real way it could have been done differently in compliance with the right to freedom of thought. But while the Irish Data Protection Commission and the UK's Information Commissioner's Office (ICO) reportedly opened investigations into the legality of the experiment, they ultimately went nowhere. For Facebook, after a small blip of negative press and regulatory interest, it was business as usual.[18]

We are all fodder for social media data-guzzling, and whether we use the platforms as a matter of course or not, Facebook and Google will know who we are through our friends and through other aspects of our behaviour that their monopolistic control of the online space gives them access to. But some groups of people are more acutely vulnerable than others to the lure of the 'like' and the pain of exclusion, and their online activity is likely to be the most lucrative of all.

Teenagers and young adults are particularly susceptible to the hurt of social exclusion. The desperate search for meaning and validation is an imperative in an exciting and emotionally fraught world that seems eternally new. As a teenager growing up on a farm in a remote rural community with no computers, I only had to suffer social exclusion on the school bus, or when I inadvertently walked past the bus shelter in the village at the wrong time of day. For the most part, home was a haven where I didn't need to know what anyone who mattered really thought of me. And as a teenager, what my family thought of me was obviously completely irrelevant. Of course, I didn't see it as a haven at the time; it felt more like being stranded on Alcatraz, and the desire to get out and engage with the world, for crumbs of attention from pointless boys who didn't know I existed, drove me into a variety of dangerous teenage exploits involving Pernod and motorbikes that now make my maternal blood run cold. Teenagers need the world urgently, and there is a fair chance that it is going to hurt them along the way. But now that the social opportunities and dangers have moved online, what does that mean for the turbulent teenage inner world?

Despite our fears about the dangers our children face online and the spectre of online grooming leading to offline harm, in some ways the shift of social life to social media platforms has reduced the real-world risks of the need for social validation. In my teens, my mother used to drop me off in town every week for my Saturday-night pub crawl, not because she was particularly encouraging me to drink, but because she felt it was less likely to result in stomach-pumping or pregnancy if I was in a pub in town with a licence to protect and security on the door rather than in the village bus shelter. Statistically, where I grew up, these were fairly high risks for a teenage girl, and perhaps thanks to my mother's pragmatic approach, I managed to avoid them both. The idea of teenagers conducting their social intercourse somewhere monitored and regulated is something most parents would welcome.

In the 2020s, however, those particular teenage risks have dropped significantly, at least in Europe and North America.[19] Getting pregnant or making yourself sick with litres of Diamond White are very unlikely to happen when your social life is conducted almost exclusively via a screen from a bedroom in your parents' house. But is social media the twenty-first-century equivalent of the village bus shelter in terms of the emotional exploitation of our youth?

In 2017, *The Australian* newspaper broke a disturbing story,[20] based on leaked Facebook documents, that appeared to show Facebook offering real-time insights into teenagers' emotional states for sale for targeted advertising. Understanding when a teenager might be at their lowest ebb could be gold dust for selling them products and services that might make them think they'll feel better. The document claimed that Facebook's algorithms could identify 'moments when young people need a confidence boost' and share this with advertisers. The list of teenage emotional states that the documents indicated Facebook could deduce from use of its platform will be horrifyingly familiar to anyone who either remembers their own teenage years or currently has a teenager in their life: 'worthless', 'insecure', 'defeated', 'anxious', 'silly', 'useless', 'stupid', 'overwhelmed', 'stressed' and feeling 'a failure'. We may all suffer from these feelings at different times in our lives for greater or lesser periods, but there are few times when they are so frequent and intense as adolescence.

Mark Zuckerberg famously created another platform around the same time as Facebook, with some people maintaining it was an early incarnation of its more famous big brother. 'Facemash' was a platform for Zuckerberg and his fellow Harvard students to rate girls according to their appearance in their annual college photos – an online 'hot or not' game that he later described as 'a prank'. While writing the software for Facemash, Zuckerberg reportedly blogged, 'I almost want to put some of these faces next to pictures of some farm animals and have people vote on which is more attractive.'[21] I wasn't at Harvard in 2003, or indeed ever, but I did experience my own Facemash live when, arriving at my first dinner in a boys' boarding school that took girls in sixth form, we were forced to run the gauntlet of score cards held up to grade the new girls. There are few things as a teenager more likely to make you feel like you need a confidence boost than having your attractiveness publicly rated. I have little doubt that that experience pushed me straight to the tuck shop to binge on Boost bars for the next two years. Using technology to exploit young people's emotional states is in Facebook's DNA, and so perhaps *The Australian*'s article should come as no surprise.

The company's response to the story was to deflect. In a public statement, it said that the article was misleading because 'Facebook does not offer tools to target people based on their emotional state'.[22] Although the documents were apparently drafted by Facebook Australia executives for engagement with advertisers, Facebook claimed that the researcher had not followed its internal research protocols, and promised to address this oversight. But whatever the public statement said, the published research shows that Facebook not only knows when we are at our lowest ebb, but it also has the power to manipulate our moods and put us there.

Surveillance advertising

Advertising is the bottom line of social media and the online environment. Big tech companies like Facebook and Google are, ultimately, advertising companies. And if you have ever been online, you will recognise that feeling that advertisers seem to read your mind. If the adverts you see appear to reflect your thoughts and preoccupations, that is no accident. The way online advertising works is based on the information advertisers have about you from all your other technological interactions. What is known as real-time bidding (RTB) is the mainstay of ad tech (advertising technology), and RTB allows advertisers to target you based on inferences about how you're feeling and what you are interested in at any given time. This is the way most websites sell advertising space to grab our attention. Digital advertising exchanges generate detailed online information about you, such as what you're reading, watching or listening to, your unique pseudonymous ID, your profile's ID from the ad buyer's system, which can include details of the kind of person you are, what you are interested in, your location, device type, operating system, browser, IP address, and so on. As the organisation European Digital Rights (EDRi) explains:

> Every time you visit a website that uses RTB, your personal data is publicly broadcasted to possibly thousands of companies ready to target their ads. Whenever this happens, you have no control over who has access to your personal data. Whenever this happens, you have no way of objecting to being traded. Whenever this happens, you cannot oppose to being targeted as Jew hater, incest or abuse victim, impotent, or right-wing extremist. Whenever this happens, you have no idea whether you are being discriminated.[23]

And it's easy to buy this kind of information. In 2021, Reset Australia, the Australian arm of a global initiative combating digital threats to democracy, released a report[24] showing how it was able to purchase advertising slots on Facebook to target teenagers between 13 and 17 with adverts based on their identified vulnerability to extreme weight loss, gambling, and online dating with wealthy older men. While Reset Australia never ran the adverts, their research showed how easy it was to target vulnerable young people with advertising for dubious and even dangerous activities for less than the cost of a tank of petrol. If you could combine the definition of interests and vulnerabilities with a real-time assessment of how susceptible someone might be at any given moment and top that off with the ability to tweak their moods to suit the market, just imagine how effectively you could sell your services.

The scale of the problem is utterly unimaginable. The digital rights activist Duncan McCann has been reporting on it for the New Economics Foundation for years. In 2018, he reported that an average of 164 RTB auctions happen to each person in the UK per day.[25]

Surveillance advertising is not only affecting us as individuals through targeting us based on our weaknesses; it is also undermining our societies by funding disinformation around the world. Jake Dubbins, co-chair of the Conscious Advertising Network, noted that 'advertisers have helped fund the misinformation that stoked fires in the US Capitol', while NewsGuard found that over 4,000 brands – including in some cases major pharmaceutical companies – 'bought ads on misinformation websites publishing COVID-19 myths'.[26] Disinformation spreads like wildfire when the right targets are identified and targeted through their profiles. The Global Disinformation Index has estimated that '$76 million in ad revenues flow each year to disinformation sites in Europe'.[27] And this is made possible by a business model that runs on the fuel of personalised surveillance advertising – you can target those most vulnerable because you have already gathered the information on them for lucrative advertising. And the more popular your website is, the more money you will make. Outlandish claims make money.

Digital soma

The use of data and metadata to read and predict our personalities, thoughts and changing moods, without us knowing and consenting to it, is an interference with our right to freedom of thought. While we may be happy to let people know that we liked a post about Salvador Dalí and another about kittens, we may not be so comfortable with the fact that this information will be analysed to reveal psychological traits or fleeting states of mind that will, in turn, be used to manipulate our behaviour or to tell others how they should treat us. And the interpretation of our online activity is not restricted to conscious and public expressions we make online. It is not only what we say we like through hitting the 'like' button that is recorded, but also what we look at but don't choose to like, how long we linger over particular content and the conversations we have around our mobile devices.[28]

All this information is being extracted and analysed as part of our daily interactions with technology. And as we will see in this section, technology touches every sphere of our lives. Every time we interact, we teach the machine to interpret our thoughts more completely than we understand them ourselves. And it is not only our own actions and inactions, but those of everyone we connect with online, the people who frequent the same shops as us, or live in our streets, or share our DNA that feed into this rich picture. With social media, you don't need a torturer's chair or a lie detector; we are all informing on each other and incriminating ourselves all the time.[29] If social networks are to be used in a way that allows users to protect their right to freedom of thought as well as their privacy, we need to ask exactly how far algorithms that monitor, interpret and mould our activity can go. We need to understand the present and possible future capabilities for extracting information from the data we hand over. Only then can we ascertain what is and is not permissible from the perspective of freedom of thought.

In Aldous Huxley's *Brave New World*, 'hypnopaedic conditioning' ensured that people were content and compliant consumers. Regular conditioning, obligatory promiscuity and top-up doses of 'soma' ensured that society worked like clockwork – everyone knew their place and enjoyed the thoughts and ideas that were fitting to their station in life. It is a vision that resonates in the way our digital world is developing. Mindless messages are tailored to distract us, confirm our biases, inspire our consumer needs and control our emotional reactions by either reassuring us that everything will be OK or riling us up to hate the other. They are teaching children that their bodies are not perfect and that sex is meaningless, through endless access to porn and reality TV. We are constantly fed the next great thing we need to buy, believe or vote for through tailored advertising that targets our individual subconscious. Meanwhile, there are more and more stories of tech billionaires limiting their families' access to their own technology[30] and buying up huge tracts of land in remote locations so that they can retreat to a tech-free island when society implodes.[31] As Huxley's vision of the future appears to take shape, mediated through our screens, are we heading towards a world where only the super-rich have the right to think for themselves?

CHAPTER 7

THE MINISTRY OF TRUTH

It's 16 June 2016, and I'm starting to feel uneasy. I am in Paris, at a seminar discussing human rights and the fight against terrorism. Outside, the city is on high alert, heavily armed police patrolling streets lined with Parisian café society. But I am in a closed room with no windows and no Wi-Fi. Inside the room we are all on the same page. We are worried about the way the world is going, with increased surveillance, anti-migrant rhetoric, the steady erosion of human rights and the rule of law. We have all been talking and writing about it for decades. But it is starting to feel more real.

Brexit hovers in the air and there are jokes about who will have to marry whom and who will have to emigrate if it really happens. There's an undercurrent of excitement about the referendum, because nobody really believes that the British public could actually vote 'leave'. Surely it's a bit of whipped-up political hysteria that will calm down when the nation of shopkeepers goes to the polls.

For months I have been talking about it with European colleagues. Joking with arched eyebrows about what could happen 'post-Brexit', rolling my eyes at Nigel Farage on the radio yet again, laughing at Boris on a zip wire flying the flag. But none of us seriously considers that it could happen. Ten years earlier, Britain was cage-rattling in Brussels about the 'power grab' that was the proposed 'European constitution', but then it was rebranded as the Lisbon Treaty and it all went quiet. Surely this time common sense and British pragmatism will prevail again. And anyway, everyone we know on Twitter and Facebook agrees with us. So it will all be just fine.

But when I return to my hotel and connect to the Wi-Fi, the news starts to pour into my devices. The MP Jo Cox is dead – shot dead in the street. My heart stops. This doesn't happen in Britain. But it does now.

Back home a week later, I find myself delivering leaflets on the morning of the referendum, unnerved by the fact that despite something so momentous as the murder of a British politician, apparently for her support for tolerance and unity, the train of debate about Brexit has carried on unquestioningly. I have never delivered leaflets before and my stand is a small one, too little, too late, spreading the word for openness in a leafy suburb of London that was always going to vote overwhelmingly to remain. But I feel afraid. For the first time in my life, I feel as though I have no idea what is going on.

That night, I check my Facebook account and go to bed early, sure that in the end, the country will vote to remain in the European Union. Facebook tells me what I want to hear, and I sleep soundly. But in the morning, it is clear that the country does not agree with me or my Facebook feed.

Brain signatures

While I had been living safely in the social media bubble of my 'remainer' and European friends, just down the road in real life, researchers from Kingston and Essex universities had been looking not at what people said they thought about Brexit, but at what their brain activity said about their voting intentions. In the five weeks before the referendum, they had brought in 62 volunteers aged between 18 and 55. Using a cap with electrodes to measure brain activity through the scalp, the researchers recorded the volunteers' brain responses to 112 short pro- and anti-EU statements. They wanted to find out whether a brain signature that flagged up disagreement with a person's social values, known as N400, would be an accurate predictor of voting behaviour. Predicting which way someone would vote, they hoped, would be shown by how much they disagreed with the messaging from the other side.

At the start of the experiment, 18 of the volunteers expressed an intention to vote remain, 18 to vote leave and 26 declared themselves undecided. But the results indicated something revealing and disturbing about the way the brain makes our minds up without us necessarily even knowing it, or at least admitting to it. The study explained for the first time that brain activity in response to politically charged statements could predict voting behaviour not only in participants who said they were already sure, but, crucially, in those who said they had still not made up their minds. It found that tracking brain activity was a better predictor of voting behaviour than asking people how they planned to vote.[1]

If I wanted to know how people in my neighbourhood would vote, it seemed that rather than knocking on their doors and asking them, all I needed was an electrode cap and a set of questions, some of which they would be sure to disagree with. It was a small study and the participants consented to their participation voluntarily in exchange for a modest fee of £25, understanding that the researchers were looking for a biological window into their minds for the short period they were wearing the cap with electrodes. They arguably gave the researchers access to their thoughts willingly, in the same way they might in agreeing to answer a question, albeit with a higher risk of a Freudian slip or a gambler's tell to cast doubt on the truth of their answers.

This study is not the only one to set off alarm bells about the potential for brain scans to be used as a source of information on a person's political leanings. In a 2012 study entitled 'Red Brain, Blue Brain: Evaluative Processes Differ in Democrats and Republicans', led by Dr Darren Schreiber of the University of Exeter, researchers looked at the predictive power of both the structure and activity of the brain to identify the political ideology of 82 participants from the United States. These participants, unlike the volunteers in the study on Brexit, had not agreed to have their brains read for traces of their political leanings, and were not presented with political questions as part of the study. They had originally consented to fMRI scans to explore the way different brains respond to risk-taking. But the researchers were curious to find out whether the results of the scans on risky behaviour could also shed light on the volunteers' political views. So, taking the scans from the original experiment, they checked their results against publicly available voter registration and electoral turnout records. Their findings were astonishing.

One of the most established methods for predicting political partisanship is through the political ideology of a person's parents, which results in around 69.5 per cent successful predictions of self-reported choices between the Democratic and Republican parties. Similar levels of accuracy emerge from research comparing the brain structure of politically liberal and conservative people, with a 71.6 per cent predictive success rate.[2] That research showed that liberals have a more developed left posterior insula, the part of the brain typically associated with perceptions of internal physiological states, while conservatives have a more developed amygdala, connected to fear conditioning. But the researchers who looked at the brain scans in the risky behaviour study observed that by adding in brain activity to the analysis of brain structure, they correctly predicted 82.9 per cent of the observed choices of party.[3]

It seems the way conservative and liberal brains are wired to respond to risk is fundamentally different. This doesn't mean they will make different choices about risk – so you cannot tell whether they are conservative or liberal purely by the choices they make in a risk-taking environment. But their brain responds differently to the activity, so you can tell whether they are conservative or liberal by watching the way their brain lights up when they are asked to take risks. In this case, you do not need to fit the cap with electrodes and ask politically charged questions; you just need to have access to brain scans acquired for a completely different purpose.

That experiment was carried out on a relatively small sample of people, and brain scans are still difficult to acquire at the scale needed to swing an election. But in 2021, a study by the Stanford researcher Michal Kosinski claimed to show that it could predict political orientation based simply on a photo of your face. Kosinski used a facial recognition algorithm to predict the politics of over a million individuals based on their photos scraped off Facebook and dating websites from the US, Canada and the UK. The study indicated that 'political orientation was correctly classified in 72% of liberal–conservative face pairs, remarkably better than chance (50%), human accuracy (55%), or one afforded by a 100-item personality questionnaire (66%) … Accuracy remained high (69%) even when controlling for age, gender, and ethnicity.' As Kosinski noted, 'Given the widespread use of facial recognition, our findings have critical implications for the protection of privacy and civil liberties.'[4] That is somewhat of an understatement. Whether accurate or not, in the wrong hands, inferences about political opinions drawn from photos of our faces, whether online, through surveillance cameras or on our ID cards, could be dangerous for us as individuals and devastating for our democracies.

The results of these studies are both fascinating and terrifying. The development of techniques that can extract voting intention or political ideology from our brain or even our face without us deliberately sharing and before we have even consciously decided how to vote poses very serious risks both to an individual's right to freedom of thought and freedom of political opinion and also to our democratic rights and democracy itself. If you can tell how someone will vote by studying a photo of their face, you can decide, on an individual basis, who you might want to turn up on polling day, or even who you would prefer to eliminate altogether. Reading political opinions from a photo of your face is a clear breach of the right to keep your opinions to yourself, and a disturbing new take on the age-old pseudo-science of physiognomy.

Neuropolitics

In the twenty-first century, political campaigning entered a whole new era. Focus groups and pollsters had been big business for decades, fine-tuning electoral campaigns to the vagaries of public opinion. But as a series of wildly inaccurate predictions in the US and the UK in 2016 sounded the death knell for political polling, it was time for the behavioural and neuroscientists to step out of the political shadows.

'Neuropolitics' is a relatively new field, but it is one that feeds into the urgent desire for political power. Over the first two decades of the twenty-first century, the academic studies showing that voting intentions and political affiliations can be predicted based on physical responses in the brain or other parts of the body, even before people know it themselves, have fed into a nascent neuropolitical consulting industry. The neuroscience studies of the past decades on conservative and liberal brains show that reading a person's brain scans by looking at both the structure and the activity in response to certain stimuli can give you a pretty good idea of an individual's political leanings. But what is not clear is how much these different structural and activity markers come from nature and how much from nurture. Are we born liberal or conservative? Or are we made that way?

As the 'Red Brain, Blue Brain' study noted, 'acting as a partisan in a partisan environment may alter the brain, above and beyond the effect of the heredity'.[5] This raises fundamental questions about the way our brains reflect our politics, but also to what extent our brains may be influenced by the political ideology around us on both a structural and activity level. The political messages we receive may well leave an imprint on our brains, literally changing their shape. It is unlikely that targeted messaging would switch us directly from being liberal to being conservative or vice versa. However, certain prompts do seem to nudge us in one direction or another – for example, fear has a tendency to provoke more conservative responses, even in people with a liberal ideology. But what is more likely is that our environment could build on our natural tendencies and prejudices to make them ever stronger. As the political environment is increasingly partisan and delivered to us online with the use of artificial intelligence designed to understand and influence our emotional reaction and to favour extreme responses, could the physical differences in liberal and conservative brains become even more marked? If so, this has implications for us as individuals, but is also a significant threat to the ability of any well-meaning politicians (or others) to bring divided societies together. And it opens up new avenues for tyrants to drive us apart or persuade us to turn on each other at the flick of a politically charged psychological switch.

In 2015, journalist Kevin Randall published an article in *The New York Times* titled 'Neuropolitics, where campaigns try to read your mind',[6] explaining how a Spanish company, Emotion Research Lab, provided insights to political campaigns in Mexico by installing cameras in an electronic billboard that allowed the company to read the emotional responses of passers-by who looked at it. The idea was that while you were reading the message on the billboard, the billboard was reading you. Less than two weeks after Randall's article was published describing this 'neuromarketing' campaign in Mexico, in a follow-up article he reported that the party that had been using the technique had dropped it.[7] Politicians may want to employ these methods to understand the electorate, but they know there is something uniquely disturbing about them, something that we, the voters, will not like, so they are extremely reluctant to admit publicly that they are using them. They may believe these campaign tactics are strictly legal, but they also understand that they are fundamentally immoral.

Regardless of the morality, the people working in neuropolitical consultancy, and their clients, are operating in unknown territory as far as the law is concerned. In an interview for an article in *The New Yorker* in early 2020, Spencer Gerrol, the CEO of SPARK Neuro, a start-up neuromarketing consultancy that launched in 2017, talked about the dystopian risks of working for political parties and candidates: 'It's a slippery slope. When have we gone too far?

... Each leader of any given company doing work like this needs to figure out where to draw the line for themselves ... It's contingent on us to try to make that line as hard as we can and not cross it.'[8] Leaving these decisions to be made by the leaders of companies who stand to make fortunes out of subverting democracy would be a serious dereliction of the duty that states have to protect our rights. It is not up to captains of industry to decide on the moral limitations of their activities; it is for the lawmakers. And ultimately, it is for the public to push the lawmakers to build the kind of society we want to live in and put limitations on the political practices that threaten our rights and our democracies.

Orwell's Winston Smith in *Nineteen Eighty-Four* observed that in the world of Big Brother, 'Nothing was your own except the few cubic centimetres inside your skull.' In the 75 years since Winston Smith was born in George Orwell's free-thinking mind, even those few cubic centimetres have become prime real estate available for sale to the highest bidder for both commercial and political ends. The development of research and the sale of services that promise access to the inner workings of the minds of the electorate is a serious threat to our individual rights to freedom of thought and opinion and to our democratic societies.

Behavioural microtargeting

By the night of the 2016 American elections, I no longer believed my Facebook feed, and I suspected what was coming. We have all now heard how Cambridge Analytica's famous 'secret sauce' brought together the research on altering emotional states through Facebook[9] with research on psychological profiling and Facebook likes[10] in a technique called 'behavioural microtargeting'.[11] This technique is based on the premise that by harvesting information on Facebook users and their friends, you can build detailed pictures of millions of members of the voting public and use that information to influence their voting behaviour through personalised targeted advertising. The effectiveness of the technique has been questioned.[12] But providing a service designed to access our thoughts on an individual level without our knowledge and use that information to manipulate our thoughts, emotional states, opinions and therefore our voting behaviour without us realising it undoubtedly amounts to interference with our right to freedom of thought on a grand scale.

Guardian journalist Carole Cadwalladr broke the inside story in 2018, winning the Orwell Prize for Journalism for her tenacious reporting.[13] Since then, our newsfeeds have been filled with parliamentary inquiries around the world, glossy documentaries like *The Great Hack* and crime-drama-style photos of ICO officers raiding Cambridge Analytica's offices in bomber jackets. Finally, in 2019, Cambridge Analytica closed under the pressure and the newsfeeds moved on. But the fundamental problems that the saga revealed about the way technology can be used to play with our minds and swing our elections did not.

Behavioural microtargeting did not start or end with Cambridge Analytica. Many liberals all over the world were delighted when Obama became president in 2008, but his presidential campaign was the first to use microtargeting techniques on a grand scale.[14] If you feel uneasy about political behavioural microtargeting when it delivers Trump, you need to question the ethics of using this technique at all, regardless of the politics of the candidate involved. This kind of technique, using social media as a means of knowing and influencing people individually on a grand scale, particularly when it is used in political campaigns, is not just an issue of data or finances. It is an attempt to interfere with the rights to freedom of thought and opinion of individual voters, scaled up to hack the political opinions of whole swathes of society to swing elections.

What Cambridge Analytica was selling to its clients was the promise of a bloodless coup through a mass violation of our rights to freedom of thought and opinion. And Cambridge Analytica was just one of many companies offering their services to try and hack our minds. Violations of electoral spending codes and data protection regulations are just symptoms of the problem; they do not go to the heart of it. We need to shore up our democracies with adequate legislation to protect freedom of thought in the electoral process, and that means limiting the way big data can be used to access our minds. But can we trust our politicians to do that?

Law and politics

Human rights law puts a positive obligation on states to take action to protect the rights of people under the state's control. This means not only refraining from doing bad things, but also taking action to prevent bad things by bringing in laws, changing existing laws and building effective enforcement frameworks to address the gaps in the system. Countless reports from regulators, parliamentary inquiries and civil society organisations have highlighted political behavioural microtargeting as an area that needs urgent regulation. In the UK, even the advertising industry body, the IPA, called for a moratorium on political behavioural microtargeting adverts.[15] But this practice is like a great white shark that has somehow bypassed the protective nets of democracy entirely. We all know it is there, but we are still swimming in the shark-infested sea. At least for now, it remains a tempting and lawful tool for political parties in many countries, including the UK, the Netherlands, the US and others. And far from banning the practice, some countries are taking steps to embed it even more strongly into the legislation that governs their political life.

At the height of the media furore about Cambridge Analytica, the UK's Data Protection Act 2018 passed through the UK Parliament with barely a whisper. But tucked away in an unassuming little section, there was a get-out-of-jail-free card for political parties – the 'political parties exemption clause'. What this clause means in practice is that British political parties have the right to harvest massive amounts of data about us as individuals that reveal our political opinions, and to use that information for their political campaigns. While the ICO's 2018 report, *Democracy Disrupted?*,[16] laid out in disturbing detail the minutiae of data on your life that the main political parties could access and use to profile and target you for political purposes, the new law, rather than dealing with the disruptive impact of this data grab, effectively rubber-stamped it. While British politicians were prepared to talk the talk in front of the cameras, they were certainly not ready to walk the walk in the voting chamber.

The exemption for political parties in the Data Protection Act was explained as a means to help politicians to engage with the electorate and a hangover from analogue political campaigning. It was sold as a method for promoting rather than subverting democracy – allowing political parties to understand what will get us engaged with the political process. But there are other ways of addressing voter turnout than microtargeting. In some countries, like Australia, voting is compulsory. This means that even if individual voters may not be particularly engaged in the political process, and may even decide to spoil their ballot, they are obliged to put their minds to the question of who they want to vote for, at least for the moments before they drop their voting slip in the ballot box. Behavioural microtargeting is not a straightforward tool to promote public engagement in politics. It can be used as effectively for voter suppression as it can for getting the vote out. It is very much the dark underbelly of political campaigning. But it is very appealing to those who see pound signs and political power in big data and those who already have the spending power to leverage it.

The model set by British politicians, with its promise of digital influence campaigns without the limitations of tedious data protection and privacy laws, resonated with politicians in other countries too. Within the year, Spain and Romania had adopted similar laws. But in Spain, at least, constitutional protections offered a chance to curb the political hunger for information on the electorate. In March 2019, the Spanish Defensor del Pueblo, the ombudsman tasked with protecting the rights guaranteed in the Spanish constitution, swung into action with a challenge to the new laws. He argued that, far from being a tool for democracy, the broad powers given to political parties to access and use citizens' data without the usual limitations of data protection law amounted to a breach of several rights protected under the constitution, including the right to protection of personal data, the right to private life, the right to 'ideological freedom' and the right to political participation. Explaining his reasons for bringing the case, he commented:

> [T]he possibility, or even the certainty, as shown
> by the recent case of Cambridge Analytica, that big
> data techniques can be used to modulate, or even
> manipulate, political opinions demonstrates the need

for normative guarantees and legal restraints to be
appropriate, precise and effective in relation to the
collection and processing of personal data related to
political opinions by political parties in the context of
their electoral activities.[17]

The constitutional court, recognising the importance of the case for Spanish democracy, agreed with him and reached a unanimous decision.[18] In a record two months, the new provisions were declared unconstitutional, putting an end to the free-for-all on political data in Spanish electoral campaigns. While the court recognised that personal data on political opinions may be collected and processed in the context of electoral activities according to EU law, it stressed that this was only permissible where it was in the public interest and the law provided sufficient safeguards. A general exemption for political parties to data protection regulations could not fulfil those requirements. In its judgment, it stressed that the right to protection of personal data was important both as a stand-alone right and as a right that guaranteed the effective enjoyment of other constitutional rights such as the right to 'ideological freedom' (the Spanish constitutional equivalent of the right to freedom of thought or opinion in international law). This judicial recognition of the interplay between data protection and the right to freedom of thought and opinion was a turning point for our absolute right to keep what goes on inside our heads private and free from manipulation. It is not the connection with our private lives that makes data so valuable for political campaigns; it is its role as the key to our minds.

Law provides the guardrails around the kind of societies we want to live in. But the law has so far been slow to respond to the existential threats posed to our democratic systems by the rise of neuropolitics, behavioural psychographics and microtargeting in political campaigning. That needs to change.

Disinformation and hate

Politics does not live only in the ballot box. It is when political opinions are manifested in real life that they are at their most potent. And that potency can be harnessed for good and for evil. In Orwell's *Nineteen Eighty-Four*, people were obliged to join in the Two Minutes Hate every week. It was a moment where workers stopped what they were doing and focused on a message of vitriol. As the protagonist Winston Smith noted, 'The horrible thing about the Two Minutes Hate was not that one was obliged to act a part, but that it was impossible to avoid joining in.' This is the power of propaganda and brainwashing: their ability to sweep the individual up in the collective tide of hatred. The pinnacle of propaganda in *Nineteen Eighty-Four* is Hate Week, where months of preparation go into winding the crowds up into a frenzy of loathing for the caricature enemy of Eurasia. At the peak of a mass rally, the memo comes in that Oceania is now at war with Eastasia, not Eurasia. But the speaker doesn't miss a beat in the shift of hate from one focus to another. It doesn't matter who you hate; it is the feeling of hatred that matters. Once people are wound up into this enmity, it can be turned on anyone.

Online disinformation in the twenty-first century makes the power of Orwellian Hate Week available to pretty much anyone, at a price. Populations can be whipped up and turned on the tweak of an algorithm. The level of heat in online debate can be diverted to new and senseless targets in the blink of an eye, whether through deliberate coordinated campaigns or through the accident of an algorithm designed to sell more adverts. The rise of the Yellow Vests in France brought central Paris to a standstill for month after month in 2018 after a change in Facebook's algorithm shifted to favour local messaging that literally set France alight.[19]

In 2020, at the start of the coronavirus lockdown in the UK, a conspiracy theory infected the socially distanced social media sphere with the idea that the virus was not a natural phenomenon emanating from a wet market in Wuhan, China, and spread by person-to-person contact. Rather, it was a Chinese conspiracy disseminating the deadly virus through the 5G towers that were popping up across the country. Who knows where exactly the online conspiracy virus began, but the scale of its reach was driven by the power of a few gullible social media influencers[20] and the endless wisdom of the algorithms that amplify extreme and sensationalist content to drive user engagement for powerful platforms. As with the most effective manipulation techniques, this particular disinformation story preyed on existing prejudice and anxiety, bringing together underlying fear of the Chinese state and anxieties about the power of technology. Together, these fears ignited hatred in the hearts of socially isolated individuals, who burned down 5G masts and attacked telecoms engineers in the real world.[21] Disinformation thrives where fear and hate are already present – in India, rather than burning down 5G masts, the disinformation networks linked the coronavirus with Muslims, giving a terrified population a new reason to hate and attack their Muslim neighbours.

Stoking hate is not new, but the signs and appalling consequences of its pervasiveness online have been increasingly apparent across the world in recent years. In Myanmar, a country of 35 million people, Facebook boasts 20 million users. As a UN fact-finding mission put it, for most people there, 'Facebook is the internet',[22] their source of social contact, news and information. So when, on 25 August 2017, a militant group of Rohingya Muslims launched coordinated deadly attacks on security outposts across the northern Rakhine State,[23] the 'immediate, brutal and grossly disproportionate' response of the Myanmar security forces played out both in the real world and online through Facebook feeds, with devastating effect.

Hatred and prejudice against the Rohingya in Myanmar was nothing new. But the scale of what happened in 2017 was astounding. By mid-August 2018, nearly 725,000 Rohingya had fled to Bangladesh, while the death toll in Myanmar was in the tens of thousands. The description of the violence in a UN report makes horrifying reading:

> People were killed or injured by gunshot, targeted or indiscriminate, often while fleeing. Villagers were killed by soldiers, and sometimes by Rakhine men, using large-bladed weapons. Others were killed in arson attacks, burned to death in their own houses, in particular the elderly, persons with disabilities and young children, unable to escape. In some cases, people were forced into burning houses, or locked in buildings set on fire …
>
> Rape and other forms of sexual violence were perpetrated on a massive scale … Sometimes up to 40 women and girls were raped or gang-raped together. One survivor stated, 'I was lucky, I was only raped by three men.' Rapes were often in public spaces and in front of families and the community, maximizing humiliation and trauma. Mothers were gang-raped in front of young children, who were severely injured and

in some instances killed. Women and girls 13 to 25
years of age were targeted, including pregnant women
… Victims were severely injured before and during
rape, often marked by deep bites. They suffered serious
injuries to reproductive organs, including from rape
with knives and sticks. Many victims were killed or died
from injuries. Survivors displayed signs of deep trauma
and face immense stigma in their community. There are
credible reports of men and boys also being subjected to
rape, genital mutilation and sexualized torture.[24]

The scale of the real-world violence and hatred in Myanmar was
something that for most of us is simply an unimaginable horror.
Sadly, in the human history of mass atrocities and human rights
abuses, it is not unique. We have seen how radio fanned the flames
of hatred in Rwanda and in Nazi Germany. And what really stands
out in the UN assessment of this 'human rights catastrophe' is that:
'the role of social media is significant. Facebook has been a useful
instrument for those seeking to spread hate, in a context where, for
most users, Facebook is the Internet.'[25] Where a population's access
to information is channelled through only one source, the potential
for that source to be hijacked and polluted is enormous. Those
stoking hate in the country understood this very well. Albert Speer's
warning about the potential of technology as a tool to manipulate
minds rings very true in Myanmar. In an interview about their
investigation, one of the UN team said that Facebook had 'turned
into a beast' in the country.[26]

Facebook has accepted that it did not deal quickly enough with
the misuse of its platform to spread hate and incite violence in
Myanmar, and it has promised to try to do more to take down

inappropriate content and stop what it calls 'coordinated inauthentic behaviour' on the platform. The term seems hopelessly inadequate for the kind of consequences that online disinformation can have anywhere in the world. And lest you think this is a phenomenon of the developing world, the evidence suggests otherwise.

On 6 January 2021, the real-life impact of political disinformation played out across our screens from the US Capitol as American democracy was stormed by an angry mob, resulting in five deaths. The Capitol riots may have caught the eye of global media, but they were really the tip of the iceberg in terms of the real-world impacts of disinformation networks in the United States. The campaign group Avaaz teamed up with Guns Down America in 2021 to document the experiences of nine survivors of what it calls 'tech harms' in the United States.[27] Carmen Palmer and her family went to protest peacefully as part of the Black Lives Matter movement in Kenosha, Wisconsin. Before they could join, they were met with armed militias who had organized on Facebook. Hannah Gittings lost her partner at the same Kenosha shootings and is now suing Facebook to enforce their policies and remove hate groups and violent content. What happens online to our minds cannot be separated from what may happen offline. Twisting minds is a very dangerous business wherever it happens.

Good citizens

Democracy may not have done much for Socrates' freedom of opinion, but throughout the twentieth century, more and more countries adopted democracy and respect for human rights as the basis for their political and governance structures. To support these shifts, electoral laws developed to protect the democratic ideal of free and fair elections. Limitations on the levels or sources of funding for political campaigns in many countries reflect fears that either oligarchic elites or foreign powers could exert undue influence on the opinions of the electorate. In liberal democracies, there are commonly laws that prevent campaign tactics that might either entice voters to turn out or discourage others from going to vote. These safeguards are crucial to prevent corruption in the election process through votes being either bought or suppressed. The secrecy of the ballot is absolutely fundamental in a functioning democracy to ensure that no one can be punished for the way they did or did not vote. For politicians in countries where a bag of rice might be enough to buy you favour, if the ballot is truly secret it can be very difficult to know whether your investment has paid dividends – you may buy vouchers for votes, but you can't guarantee that they will be cashed in as promised. The details around guaranteeing a free and fair vote in democracies around the world may vary, but what never changes is the principle that a democratic election relies on the freedom of thought and opinion of each individual voter. Without freedom of political opinion, there is no democracy.

While election observers have been tutting over the more blatant ways that some less democratic countries seek to influence the electorate with intimidation, bribes or straightforward ballot stuffing, they have failed to pay sufficient attention to the hijacking of the democratic processes in countries once famed for their democratic credentials. In 2021, we saw how online disinformation stoked political extremism with the storming of the US Capitol by self-styled 'patriots' who refused to believe that Donald Trump had really lost the election. And neuropolitics and behavioural psychography have become bywords in lawful political campaigns in the United States, though they may undermine the freedom of thought and of opinion of the electorate just as surely as a stuffed ballot – but without such an obvious trace.

In most cases, the danger is subtle. It is not the threat of technology turning us all from liberals to conservatives or vice versa. In a democracy, small shifts in voter turnout in a handful of areas can be enough to swing an election. Neuroscience is promising ever more insightful evidence of where a person stands on the political spectrum or how they feel about a particular candidate or message. Behavioural microtargeting claims to be able to shift behaviour of voters on a granular level, changing or reinforcing the thoughts and behaviour that really matter to a campaign. But where it is particularly useful is in tweaking the way people feel about voting, not for voter engagement, but for voter suppression. If you can remind the anxious people you don't want in the polling station that voting is stressful, there's a fair chance they may just stay at home.

In Orwell's Oceania, one doctrine – Ingsoc, or English socialism – has taken over the political space entirely. But its domination is only possible thanks to its complete control of the personal and emotional space of the population. Orwell's vision of that control of the hearts and minds of the people is the ultimate portrait of a world without the right to freedom of thought. That control both starts and ends with our ability to reach out, connect and love each other. And in the digital age, technology may hold the key to your heart too.

CHAPTER 8

CONSENTING ADULTS

I remember watching the film adaptation of Orwell's *Nineteen Eighty-Four* on a date in the back row of a small cinema in the Isle of Man in 1984, with teenage insouciance and a mild sense of relief that Orwell's vision, like so many predictions of the end of the world over the years, had simply not come to pass. But that was an age when most of us had not even dreamed of the internet, let alone had access to it.

Dating was a very different and more direct experience in the 1980s. With no dating apps, mobile phones or social media, I spent my evenings blocking up the family landline as I chatted for hours with the boyfriend who took me to the cinema. I still remember his three-figure phone number that I would dial religiously every day. We used to meet up the hill on a deserted country lane between our homes. With no contactless bank cards, CCTV or GPS mapping my movements, the only risk of monitoring was a passing farmer sharing information about my whereabouts if they happened to come across my parents in the village shop. Growing up on a small island, it felt as though everyone knew your business and there was nowhere to hide. But at the time, I had no idea that this sensation would become the norm for everyone, everywhere.

As we discovered during the pandemic, technology can make

distances disappear. It opens new opportunities for connecting and new chances to hide. My great-grandfather managed to get around a bit at the turn of the last century, between failed enterprises in North America, unexplained trips to Africa and his ultimate banishment from the north of England to the Isle of Man. The only traces left of what he was up to are a handwritten diary of a boat trip that ended mysteriously with the boat weighing anchor off Conakry on the west African coast, and a photo of a child taken in Canada with the inscription 'To Daddy' on the back (which is not a photo of any known relative). People lie, cheat and manipulate in their personal relationships, perhaps more than in any other sphere of their lives. While online dating sites are full of married people posing as singles, these days, once you have a name, you don't need to be a private detective to find out quite a lot about someone through their online footprint. The online dating world may feel anonymous, but it is not.

I have never been a fan of weddings, but they are a place where many people, beyond the bride and groom, find their future partners. One friend made an extra-special effort when I flew in for her wedding, sitting me next to the only remaining eligible bachelor at the party. He started out fairly civil, asking me what I did, but when I told him I worked on human rights and counter-terrorism for an international organisation, he said, 'I bet you read *The Guardian*, don't you ...' before turning away and ignoring me for the rest of the evening, clearly unimpressed with what he had inferred about my thoughts and opinions. I didn't mind. This real-life swipe-left meant I avoided a long and tedious conversation and was free to spend the night dancing to Abba with people with whom I was more politically and spiritually aligned, regardless of their relationship status, gender or sexual orientation.

In the twenty-first century, online dating has surpassed meeting through friends and family as the most popular way to meet a partner in the United States,[1] and its popularity is catching up elsewhere around the world.[2] It's the best place to present an ideal version of an attractive, carefree you: the photo with your cousin's dog that makes you look affectionate; the holiday shot that makes you look adventurous, with the all-inclusive resort walls just out of shot; or the perfect pout with the wrinkles filtered out. In a world where people rarely look up from the screen stuck to their palm, the most efficient way to attract the attention of a potential love match is through their screen. And in lockdowns around the world, where it was not only unlikely but practically illegal to bump into a stranger in real life, it became the only way to connect.

There is little more intimate going on inside our minds than the search for love and acceptance. The yearning for someone to touch your skin; the fear of what they might find, or how you might feel, if they do. The ineffable quality of another person's features that makes their lips appealing as a ripe cherry to one person and as repulsive as snogging a snake to another. It is both complex and utterly basic.

Sigmund Freud put sex at the heart of understanding human psychology, and the mid-twentieth-century dystopian authors understood that sex is a tool for social control. Sex is not only personal; it is political, and it sells. In *Nineteen Eighty-Four*, 'desire was thoughtcrime', sex and love were discouraged among party members with strict controls on what was acceptable, and the Anti-Sex League was there to police anyone who might feel romantically inclined. In Huxley's vision of a *Brave New World*, social control was orchestrated by more sex, not less, but it was sex devoid of love or real desire. The fortnightly 'Solidarity Service' at the 'Fordson Community Singery' is essentially an obligatory drug-fuelled orgy that leaves the hero, Bernard, 'much more alone, more hopelessly

175

himself than he had ever been in his life before'.[3] Our twenty-first-century reality is, perhaps, a combination of the two. Online pornography floods the psyche with meaningless sex, while teenage pregnancies plummet. Sexting will not get you pregnant, though it may well ruin your life when it comes back to haunt you. In the online dating world, the shift to superficiality is made flesh. But while swiping may seem like harmless browsing, the potential for social control through online dating apps is no less real.

The virtual gaydar

As we increasingly love, connect and express ourselves digitally, inferences are being made on a constant basis about our inner lives. And the potential consequences of those inferences being shared in a world where people are still attacked, imprisoned or sentenced to death for who and how they love should never be underestimated. The right to freedom of thought includes the right not to be punished for our thoughts and feelings. We may be punished for what we do, but not for who we are on the inside. But once inferences are made about our inner lives, it is extremely hard to know what will be done with them.

The research published by Michal Kosinski in 2021[4] analysing political opinions from photos of individual faces was based on training algorithms to judge people from photos scraped off dating sites in the UK, Canada and the US. If you've ever posted a photo of your face online looking for love, there's a fair chance your photo was used to train a machine to identify people's political opinions without their knowledge. This is the kind of technique that could be used for voter suppression or even genocide, allowing authoritarian regimes to identify political opponents and eliminate them before they do or say anything to challenge the regime. It is not very romantic. That cute selfie on your dating profile is your biometric data, and it can and will be exploited.

Aside from academic researchers like Kosinski, there are large companies making serious money from massive databases of online photos. In 2021, four Canadian privacy commissioners issued a report[5] finding that one such company, Clearview AI, had breached privacy laws by collecting photographs of Canadians without their knowledge or consent. But despite their findings that Clearview's collection of biometric data was a violation of human rights on a massive scale, the commissioners noted that Canadian law did not provide them with adequate enforcement powers. They could not even use financial sanctions to force Clearview to comply with their recommendations to delete all photos and cease to operate. What Clearview was doing was wrong, but there was very little the commissioners could do to stop it.

The Clearview case in Canada should be a wake-up call. We cannot protect our own rights when we engage online; we need governments to make laws that will protect our rights online as they do offline. And the ways your dating profile photo can be used go way beyond privacy. Your data can be analysed to make intrusive inferences about your inner life, and it can be used to train algorithms to discriminate and destroy the human rights of others on an industrial scale all around the world.

And it is not just about your politics. In 2017, Kosinski and Yilun Wang, a fellow researcher from Stanford, published a study that claimed AI could predict sexual orientation,[6] with 81 per cent accuracy in men and 71 per cent accuracy in women, based only on a single photo of your face.[7] The researchers trained AI on a dataset of photographs, again scraped from online dating sites, as well as a set of photographs from their mypersonality.org site, which had collected psychological questionnaires and Facebook profiles from hundreds of thousands of volunteers. They were then able to check the AI's assessment of sexual orientation against the dating profiles to see whether the individuals were looking for same-sex or opposite-sex partners. The technology, dubbed the 'virtual gaydar', is part of a wave of research around facial recognition technology that claims to be able, essentially, to read our minds and personalities through our faces. It is the modern-day revival of the widely discredited practice of physiognomy.

A researcher in South Africa sought to replicate the virtual gaydar experiment in 2019, but his study cast doubt on the Stanford results, indicating that it was possible there were other factors in the photos used as the dataset that might give clues on sexual orientation, apart from facial characteristics. In justifying his experiment, he said:

> From an ethical point of view I take the same standpoint as he [Kosinski] does, I believe that societies should be engaging in a debate about how powerful these new technologies are and how easily they can be abused.
>
> The first step for that kind of debate is to demonstrate that these tools really do create new capabilities. Ideally we would also want to understand exactly how they work but it will still take some time to shed more light on that.[8]

The issue with the virtual gaydar is not whether it works; it is whether such activities should ever be allowed. The potential for regimes to co-opt these ideas with murderous consequences does not depend on the accuracy of the results – try arguing from a prison cell in an authoritarian state with homophobic tendencies that the computer misread your face. The precautionary principle[9] makes it clear that experiments that could lead to significant societal harms or human rights abuses should not be carried out. Training technology to infer things about our inner lives opens Pandora's box. The answer is not to prise the box open with a wrench to see how dangerous the contents might be. Rather, we need to set legal limits on the avenues of technological discovery and development to ensure that technology cannot be used to breach our absolute right to freedom of thought.

Kosinski and Wang recognised the difficult history of science that tried to infer personal traits from faces and argued that their experiment was designed to reveal just how dangerous developments in facial recognition AI could be. They say they wanted a debate on the capabilities of AI. But there are very serious ethical problems with pursuing research that purports to be able to get inside our minds to see who, or what, we might like. From a human rights perspective, there is no need for a debate – AI that infers sexual orientation from faces is an interference with the absolute right to inner freedom and mental privacy, undermines human dignity and opens up the potential for wholesale discrimination or even genocide. Academic freedom is an important principle and is itself key to promoting freedom of thought, even when the ideas being pursued may be offensive to some. But academic freedom does not give academics carte blanche to pursue avenues of research that will destroy the rights and lives of people directly impacted by their research. The risks are not just a by-product of otherwise benign uses. In this case, it is hard to imagine a good use case for discerning sexual orientation based on a photo. Using images that have been posted on a dating website for this kind of experiment, without permission, also raises serious questions about consent. Would you want your photo to be used to train AI to destroy other people's human rights? Is that what you thought you signed up for?

Sexual orientation is not only a deeply personal issue; it is also an acutely political one. For many people around the world, keeping their sexual orientation private could be a matter of life or death. I remember very clearly the news in 1992 that the Isle of Man had legalised homosexuality; too late for one of my teenage friends, who had decided to leave the island so they could live as themselves. And I recall the palpable fear on the Pride march in Warsaw in 2006, walking in solidarity with friends and colleagues between the solid black police cordons keeping back hostile crowds. Working on human rights in Uganda, every season brought a new threat to the dignity and safety of the LGBTQ+ community as the government tried to bring in legislation that would allow the death penalty for the offence of 'aggravated homosexuality'. The Human Dignity Trust was founded to challenge the continued existence of laws criminalising consensual sexual activity between adults in 73 countries around the world, of which 12 have the potential to impose the death penalty.[10] But the risk is not only about criminalisation; stigma and discrimination can also be deadly.

In 2020, a new outbreak of coronavirus in South Korea, initially connected to LGBTQ+ clubs, sparked a homophobic backlash facilitated by the wealth of data provided through contact tracing apps to identify people who had tested positive for the virus.[11] The consequences of having a positive coronavirus test meant potentially being identified as gay or lesbian, losing your job and being attacked. In those circumstances, would you want to go to get tested? And how would you feel about AI that claims to be able to out you just by scanning your face?

Even in places where attitudes are relatively tolerant of people's sexual orientation, things can change quickly. While the Berlin of the early twentieth century was one of the most liberal cities in Europe, boasting many gay and lesbian bars and organisations, by the 1930s, everything had changed. In Nazi Germany, an estimated 50,000 gay men were rounded up under new criminal laws and imprisoned in terrible conditions, while 10,000–15,000 were sent to concentration camps, where many were castrated, subjected to medical experiments and ultimately died.[12]

And the idea that homosexuality can or should somehow be 'cured' has tragically not yet been consigned to history. In May 2020, Germany brought in legislation criminalising the practice of 'gay conversion therapy' on under-18s.[13] The kind of practices banned under this law include hypnosis, electric shocks and even 'corrective rape' to try to change a person's sexual orientation or gender identity. A German human rights organisation, the Magnus Hirschfeld Foundation, estimated that around 1,000 people were subjected to this type of treatment each year in Germany alone, many of them young, vulnerable people who were coerced into it by others. The German law has been criticised for not going far enough, with some arguing that the age limit is too low. But incredibly, for such an inhuman practice, designed to coerce and manipulate a person's inner life through brutal force, in many countries there is still no such legislation.

Creating AI that says it can tell if someone is gay based on their photo not only risks criminalising them, putting them at risk of death and discrimination, but it also opens up the prospect for others to decide what is best for them and to try to reach inside them to 'fix' who they are. This is a very real risk, and it shows us why we need laws not only to prevent coercive practices like conversion therapy but also against the use of AI to make inferences about our sexual desires at all. Our sexual orientation and gender identity live firmly in the inner realm, and it is up to each individual how much and with whom they want to share that.

Norway v. Grindr

To connect with others, we do need to be able to open up and share, but we also need to be able to choose when, how much and with whom we share our thoughts, feelings and desires. We may be consenting adults, but do we have any idea exactly what we are consenting to when we sign up for online dating? Using a dating app leaves a pungent trail of our emotional lives to be tracked in real time across the online wilderness. Two days after I finally gave in and downloaded a dating app, the Norwegian Consumer Council confirmed my worst fears in a disturbing report[14] detailing the extent of information shared about users by major dating apps for targeted advertising, among other things.[15] As well as the obvious question of who or what you are looking for, in some cases apps ask for sensitive information like political views, religion and health questions like HIV or COVID vaccination status. This is the information that makes dating profiles and their photos so useful for researchers like Kosinski, and what makes them so dangerous. Users clearly choose to reveal this information to the service, but can they be said to have really consented to the way it is stored, analysed and used in the wider ad tech and big data ecosystems?

The broader sharing of what you say on your profile about you and your inclinations raises serious privacy concerns, but the way this information is potentially mingled with all the other data and metadata available about you in real time is what takes the intrusion beyond the external private sphere to the heart of your inner world of thoughts and feelings. As the Norwegian Consumer Council report highlighted, the data being shared by dating apps like Grindr and others included things like 24/7 GPS tracking, which tells third parties where you are and potentially who you are with, and a list of all the other apps you have on your phone, allowing triangulation of data and giving a pretty good insight into what your interests are, declared or otherwise. When I installed the dating app on my iPhone, the automatic setting was for the phone to learn from my app use. Learning from the way you use an app can help to understand what you, and people like you, are thinking and feeling about themselves, the world around them and the profiles they are looking at and talking to at any given time. Swipes can be as lucrative as likes. What does an intensive burst of night swipes at 3 a.m. at home in my bed say about my emotional state? This activity, when combined with information about my shopping habits, social media activity and geolocation data gives a rich picture of who I am, how I think and what I may be feeling minute by minute. I unclicked the 'learn from your use of this app' toggle, but I didn't feel reassured.

But at least in Norway, things are starting to change. The Norwegian Consumer Council's report led to an investigation into Grindr's data-sharing activities by the Norwegian Data Protection Authority. This resulted in a fine of £8.6 billion, or 10 per cent of the company's global turnover, being served on Grindr for breach of Norway's data protection laws.[16] The Norwegian Data Protection Authority was not convinced that the scale of the data sharing was lawful. And it did not buy Grindr's argument that the sensitive data shared would not reveal sexual orientation because, despite being a gay dating app, not everyone on the platform was necessarily gay. Article 19, an international NGO campaigning for freedom of opinion and expression, has reported on the serious threats lesbian, gay and bisexual people using apps like Grindr face in the Middle East and North Africa.[17] As the drafters of international human rights law recognised, incorrect inferences about your thoughts and opinions can be as dangerous as accurate insights in the wrong hands. Such a large fine is a serious signal that the standard business model of many apps, in particular dating apps, is not something we need to just accept. Law and regulation can help to reshape an industry promoting new developments and fresh innovation in directions that will help us find love without having to sell our data souls in the process.

Monstermatch

The online dating business model thrives on continued use, not on successful relationships. Dating apps are only lucrative when they are being used. If you find true love and ride off into the sunset, the app company will have lost its tether on your heart and your value will be limited. Dating apps mine our minds and they also influence the way we behave, both in terms of how long we give them our attention, and the direction in which our desires are guided. Online dating can not only read us; it can also profoundly affect the way we think and feel and the choices we make about who we might like. The dopamine hit of a match drives compulsive swiping. But hours of wasted time laced with feelings of rejection and the sense that people are disposable is a pretty toxic combination in the dark days of winter. Finding love has always been fraught with rejection and the fear of it. The timeless imagery of Cupid's arrow piercing an unsuspecting breast, or the painful bleeding of a broken heart, reflect how acutely we feel the pain of love and rejection. We hurt each other every day, whether we mean to or not. But in the real world, our hopes and actions are calibrated around the context and the cues we receive from the person in front of us. In the online space, we run blindfolded into a brick wall.

What is really problematic in the online dating space is not the actual rejections by real-life potential matches but the algorithmic decisions that can leave people feeling rejected and excluded simply because their profile has been downgraded by the system. It is not only our peers in the online dating pool who are judging our photos or our wit or desperation levels. The algorithms are equally important to our chances of romantic success, if not more so. And the algorithmic judgement is trained on the biases of people we don't even know and may not like very much.

In the MonsterMatch game created by technologist Ben Berman for Mozilla in 2019, the problem of 'collaborative filtering' in online dating is laid bare. Collaborative filtering uses majority opinion to dictate what you will like and predict who you might be interested in. The game uses werewolves, zombies and vampires looking for love to demonstrate the way real-life dating apps work. For example, if a werewolf swipes 'yes' on a zombie then 'no' on a vampire, from now on, when a new user swipes 'yes' on the zombie, the algorithm will assume they also dislike the vampire, and so the new user never sees the vampire profile.[18] What is more, far from presenting us with a neutral bias-free experience of dating, the way in which algorithms decide who we can match with and who we won't even see reflects the biases already inherent in our societies. A study by OkCupid in 2014[19] confirmed that biases in dating selection hugely disadvantage Black women and Black and Asian men, with real-world biases being amplified in the online dating world. The pain of racism in the real world is then reinforced by the passive-aggressive choices of the technology imposing the biases of the majority on us all. Our options and opportunities for love are being effectively curated by the prejudices and tastes of the people who have gone before us. It is not personalisation; in fact it is biased generalisation. And these are the algorithms that will help to decide the future of our relationships and ultimately of our societies.

Online dating affects not only how we view relationships and potential partners; it also affects how we feel about ourselves. Tinder, for example, faced years of controversy over its mysterious 'ELO', or desirability, score. This is the score an algorithm gives you to decide whether you even get to the next stage of human judgement. In 2019, Tinder announced that it had changed its controversial ELO score so that it now used a new 'match score', which would decide which profiles you saw and who saw you based on your activity and preferences, with no reference to your ethnicity or earning power.[20] But while this solution might go some way to addressing the discriminatory aspects of the algorithm, it does nothing to address the psychological impact of curated rejection on the site. The new score prioritises heavy users of the app – in order to improve your chances of being chosen by someone you like, you now have to commit more time to suffering the pain of repeated rejection. More time and activity on the app equals more real-time personal data and more potential for targeted advertising revenue for the platform. It may no longer matter whether you're 'black, white, magenta or blue'[21] on Tinder, but in online dating, it seems the house always wins.

The way this kind of system works means that people suffering the very real pain of rejection in online dating may in fact be experiencing not the natural knocks of human interaction but an artificial system of exclusion. When you think of this regular pain of rejection in terms equivalent to physical pain, it is unbelievable that this model of online dating is allowed, and used by millions of people worldwide. Sean Rad, Tinder's founder, reportedly claimed, 'The beauty of Tinder, after all, is that rejection has been removed entirely from the process, since you have no idea who dismissed your profile.'[22] But, as research on the Cyberball experiment shows,[23] digital experiences like algorithmic rejection may be felt as keenly as real-world rejection, even though unlike most of our experiences in the real world, it is coordinated and designed that way. If you can imagine the experience of rejection or exclusion on a dating app as an electric shock, it is easy to understand the kind of long-term damage this can cause to mental health.

Jonathan Badeen, Tinder's senior vice president of product, reportedly recognised the very real influence of the platform's algorithmic choices: 'It's scary to know how much it'll affect people … I try to ignore some of it, or I'll go insane. We're getting to the point where we have a social responsibility to the world because we have this power to influence it.'[24]

When that power is used to manipulate the ways that we think and feel, to alter our societies, we cannot afford to leave it in the hands of a few private companies. We need guardrails to dictate the way relationship broking will evolve, with serious consequences for companies that step over the lines. Law and regulation need to make it clear that freedom cannot be sold. The freedom to form and hold opinions about our bodies and each other without manipulation must be protected absolutely. As in the political sphere, messing with people's minds around sex and relationships can have very serious real-world consequences for them and for their societies.

And it is not only dating apps that affect the way we view each other and think about sex.

Rough sex

When British backpacker Grace Millane went on a Tinder date in New Zealand the night before her 22nd birthday, she texted a friend at home to say 'I click with him so well. I'll let you know what happens tomorrow.' Tragically, Grace didn't make it to tomorrow. She was murdered by strangulation by the man she had met online, who was posing as an oil executive. He claimed it was an accident, rough sex gone wrong. But the court heard how, in the hours after her death, he had taken intimate photos of her dead body and watched pornography while she lay dead in his room. And he managed to fit in another Tinder date before burying Grace in a suitcase in a shallow grave out of town. The jury didn't buy his defence and he was convicted of murder.[25] But it's not the fact that she met the man on Tinder that was the real threat for Grace; the nature of her murder was symptomatic of a broader shift in attitudes to sex and women driven by another online phenomenon – porn.

The rise in the use of the defence of 'rough sex' for killing women, particularly by strangulation, is documented on the campaigning website We Can't Consent To This.[26] And Grace Millane is not the only woman killed on a first date arranged online. In the UK in the past decade, there has been a 90 per cent increase in killings of women involving 'sex games gone wrong' defences.[27] The feminist thinker and CEO of Culture Reframed, Gail Dines, puts the normalisation of strangulation during sex down to two avenues – for men, violent pornography; and for women, magazines telling them that's what men want.[28] Erika Lust, one of an extremely small number of female porn directors, explained in an interview with *The Guardian*, 'Face slapping, choking, gagging and spitting has become the alpha and omega of any porn scene and not within a BDSM context. These are presented as standard ways to have sex when, in fact, they are niches.'[29]

For many people today, their first exposure to sex is through hardcore porn when they look for answers online in the absence of adequate sex education. As Lust points out, this teaches our kids that 'men should be rough and demanding and that degradation is standard'.[30] It is perhaps no wonder that a European Parliament report on gender equality in 2013 proposed that pornography should be banned to eliminate gender stereotypes in the EU's 27 member states.[31] Although that proposal was ultimately rejected, we do need to think carefully about the impact of pornography on our minds, behaviour and ultimately our societies.

The internet has provoked new debates around finding the balance between the threat of hate speech and the risks of censorship because of its power to twist minds, not through its content, but in the way it delivers messages and the scale of its impact. Free speech allows for a range of views to be aired, but there are limits: in particular, international human rights law obliges states to prohibit hate speech. The European Parliament's 2013 report reflected wider debates about whether violent pornography should be considered as hate speech because of the way it affects attitudes to women, sometimes with fatal consequences. This is a conversation we cannot afford to have silenced.[32]

It is perhaps obvious that attitudes and behaviours around sex might be moulded by the constant stream of pornography and sex for sale online, whether you are seeking it out or not. But whether online pornography, particularly violent pornography, has an impact on the way our brains work is a hotly contested issue. Studies have shown differences in brain structure in regular consumers of porn, but they have not been able to say definitively whether the differences were caused by pornography or were a pre-existing condition that made porn more rewarding.[33] And the direct connection between the ubiquity and often violent nature of online porn and the increase in 'rape culture' of the kind highlighted by #MeToo and Everyone's Invited is not proven. However, researchers from the Max Planck Institute for Human Development in Berlin found that the results of a range of studies taken together 'support the assumption pornography has an impact on the behaviour and social cognition of its consumers. Therefore, we assume that pornography consumption, even on a non-addicted level, may have an impact on brain structure and function.' Something so ubiquitous, with such potentially profound impacts on individuals and societies more broadly, would seem an obvious area for law and regulation, just as we regulate drugs and gambling. Regulating and legislating around pornography is not the same as regulating sex or artistic expression; it is about supervising big business distributing a product that has worrying impacts on our societies.

Online pornography acts like a lightning rod for the battle for our souls between free-speech libertarians and those who feel governments need to take control of the online space to guarantee our safety. But perhaps in the future we will view the defenders of online pornography in the same light as those women who marched down Madison Avenue with their Lucky Strike 'torches of freedom' a century before. For now, though, there remains a strong protective ring around online porn.

When the Icelandic interior minister Ögmundur Jónasson announced that Iceland was planning to ban online pornography in

2013, there was uproar. An open letter was sent to Jónasson signed by over 40 human rights lawyers from around the world criticising the proposal as censorship, saying that the methods that would be used were technically identical to those used by totalitarian regimes like Iran, China and North Korea. The signatories pointed out:

> On the Internet, censorship has taken a new guise. It doesn't merely prevent publication, but also restricts people's access to the information they seek. Rather than silencing a voice, the result is depriving the population of material they can see and read. This is censorship, as it skews the way people see the world … The right to see the world as it is, is critical to the very tenets and functions of a democracy and must be protected at all costs.[34]

But the argument that we have the right to see the world as it is applies equally to the positive obligation to protect our rights to freedom of thought and opinion from online manipulation through the tsunami of online depictions of violence against women. We cannot afford to view the challenge of limiting the distribution of certain types of content on the internet to a binary question where all or nothing must be allowed. International human rights law does allow for limitations on freedom of expression and the freedom to seek, receive and impart information, where restrictions are needed to protect the rights of others and for the protection of public health or morals.[35] But the right to hold opinions without interference is absolute. The problem with some kinds of content on the internet, in particular pornography, is that it is extremely difficult to avoid on an individual level. Dealing with spam mail, aggressive pop-ups and malware requires a degree of technical know-how that many people do not have. And deciding on the way we want our society to grow and flourish is a part of the democratic process in a liberal democracy. We do not all have to make the same choices, and 'the world as it is' can look very different depending on your perspective.

Iceland is a liberal democracy and a strongly feminist society. The ways in which countries draw the lines around the limits of freedom of expression, in particular to protect the rights of others, vary widely around the world. In Iceland, the printing and distribution of pornography has been illegal since 1869, with the law updated twice over the past 150 years to prohibit pornographic performances and child sexual abuse images. The Icelandic Supreme Court defined pornography under the law in 1990 as 'aggressive representation of sex to make money, without love, tenderness or responsibility'. This was in contrast to erotica, or the 'sexual art of literary or artistic expression of love'.[36] It is not that Icelanders don't like sex; they just don't see the value in violent pornography, and they see the risks it poses for their society. Their approach to lawmaking is backed by a strong democratic process. Banning online pornography would be a logical way to update their existing law and reflect their cultural approach to the issue.

If the people of Iceland don't want their screens bombarded with violent pornography, should that not be their choice? The pervasiveness and intrusiveness of pornography in the online environment makes it particularly toxic. The purveyors of online porn don't wait for you to seek it out; they use any means possible, like malware, spam and pop-ups, to get it in front of your eyes. The right to freedom of opinion relies on our ability to access information to help us form our own opinions. But it also requires the possibility to choose the material we want floating around our minds – the ability to exclude images that we don't want to see and may not be able to unsee.

As the American legal scholar Patrick M. Garry has explored in his book *Rediscovering a Lost Freedom*, the American courts have laid the foundations for recognising that, in the home, our right to censor should outweigh anyone else's right to shout through our windows. The US Supreme Court has found that, despite 'the value of exposing citizens to novel views, home is one place where a man ought to be able to shut himself up in his own ideas if he desires'.[37] And in a case involving an ordinance that prohibited the use of sound trucks in a neighbourhood even if they were delivering highly protected political speech, the court upheld the regulation because the 'unwilling listener is practically helpless to escape this interference with his privacy by loud speakers except through the protection of the municipality'.[38] It didn't matter that many people wanted to receive the information; it was enough that some found it objectionable and there was no other way for them to avoid it. Cumulative influence and the sheer scale and ubiquity of information delivered has a very different impact on our freedom to form and hold opinions or beliefs than merely the content of a particular message.

The European Court of Human Rights has found in the context of religious speech that a line, albeit a difficult one, has to be drawn between preaching and brainwashing.[39] Returning to pornography, the issue here is not about the content per se, but about the manipulative effect of delivery methods and the realistic prospect of keeping your home and your mind free from it if that is what you want. At the moment, that is a practical impossibility. When I complained to the police, Apple and my internet provider in 2020 about malware that spammed a device

193

in my home with pornographic websites, despite heavy parental controls and even when it wasn't in use, I could hear the shrug down the phone line. I was told that it sounded like I was doing all I could. And the horrific experience of Zoom-bombing with child abuse images on a conference organised by .ORG, a digital rights organisation, confirmed that even a few seconds of exposure to particularly disturbing material has a lasting and deeply upsetting impact on the viewer. If we cannot realistically eliminate intrusion from pornography, violent pornography or even illegal images of child abuse into our homes as individuals, we do need the state to look at ways to legislate and regulate businesses profiting from the multibillion-dollar porn industry to help us do that.

In Iceland, the international clamour to protect free speech won the day and the proposals were ultimately dropped. But the polemic around online pornography and the concerns about its impact on individuals and whole societies has not gone away. As we become increasingly aware of the ways that the design and delivery of information online, including pornography, can affect our minds, we need to have a serious debate about how we can control that, whether as individuals or societies. To protect our freedom of thought and opinion, we must be able to choose what we don't want to see or hear as much as what we do want. The right to see the world as it is must include the right not to see idealised bodies and violent portrayals of sex, and not to have the people we interact with indoctrinated by those images either. Amia Srinivasan, professor of social and political theory at Oxford University, has written about the challenges of the 'porn wars' in her illuminating essay 'Talking to My Students About Porn'.[40] She notes that a key issue is not just the nature of the sex portrayed in online porn, but the medium itself, pointing out that while filmed sex appears to open up a world of sexual possibility, instead, by exposure to sex on screen, 'the sexual imagination is transformed into a mimesis-machine, incapable of generating its own novelty'. Srinivasan acknowledges that there are no easy solutions, either in law or in education, to open up the possibility for sex to be 'more joyful, more equal, freer'. But she also recognises that, 'rather than more speech or more images, it is their onslaught that would have to be arrested'. Looking at online pornography from the perspective of inner freedom, the right to cultivate your own sexual imagination rather than the right of others to impose their fantasies on you, could open up new possibilities for future generations. It is a difficult debate, but if we believe in the universality and indivisibility of all human rights, it is a debate we must allow to happen in a way that can explore the intricacies and find different solutions in different places for different people. That is how the world, and sex, really is.

Connections

Sex and relationships are messy, and they can be exploitative and transactional in real life too. But they are also the core of what it is to be human. The choices we make about our sexuality and our emotional life are deeply personal. Loving other people is where our inner worlds collide and where we experience *ren*, the Confucian idea of treating others with humaneness that Chang sought to embody in the Universal Declaration of Human Rights. The digital world does offer us new opportunities to connect and can open our minds to new people. Despite the discriminatory algorithms, there is some research indicating that online dating may be driving a surge in new connections outside people's social and ethnic groups, with jumps in the rate of interracial marriage in the United States (banned in some states until 1967) coinciding very clearly with leaps forward in online dating.[41] If we want to protect our right to freedom of thought and that quality of humaneness in our sexual and emotional relationships online and off, we don't need to get rid of online dating and we don't need to ban sexual or erotic images online. But we do need to think very carefully about how we want them to affect our societies and our human rights, and we do need to regulate the industries that monetise them to make sure that human connection can continue to flourish to the benefit of us all. And that applies not only to the romantic sphere, but to all the ways that new technologies affect our lives and our communities.

CHAPTER 9

SOCIAL CREDIT

When I returned to the UK after several years living and working in Uganda, I filled out an online form for a new bank account, looking forward to all the perks of British banking and a decent interest rate on the salary from my new job. But when I hit enter, the computer hesitated for a few moments, and then it said no. I called the number and spoke to a friendly woman who was sure there would be no problem if she inputted the data manually – after all, the salary was coming from the Financial Ombudsman Service, the UK body charged with ensuring that banks treat their customers fairly and reasonably. How could there possibly be a problem? But there was a problem. The computer did not care who I was or what I did. When it crunched my data, it was concerned about where I'd been and what that might say about my trustworthiness. So it spat my application straight back out.

If you've ever found yourself faced with a 'computer says no' experience, you'll know how frustrating it is. But it is not only frustrating. It can make you feel uneasy, ashamed, left wondering if you have done something wrong. There was no chance of redemption for me that day. The security and financial checks I'd gone through to be appointed as an ombudsman counted for nothing with the algorithm. And it didn't matter that in Uganda, I had been working on combating corruption as a diplomat for the European Union. The computer had decided that people arriving from Uganda were inherently suspicious, and there was no way round it.

It wasn't the first time it had happened to me. In my twenties, I had struggled to open an account in the UK because, as a barrister, I was self-employed and didn't have a salary slip. Much of my life had been lived in the Isle of Man, abroad or in shared accommodation, so I didn't have a solid UK paper trail. I had opened accounts in France, Spain and Belgium, where I had ID cards to prove my existence. But in the UK, it was always a problem. British banks disapproved of my nomadic existence, my Manx origins and my aversion to salaried employment. So when I started out as an ombudsman, for the first few months my salary was paid into the only British account I had, an account with the Isle of Man Bank that I'd opened for my first ever job, in Woolworths at the age of 15. I lived in fear of the inferences that could be made about having my salary paid into an offshore bank account, until finally I found a UK bank that would have me.

Apart from the shame and frustration of rejection, my experience did not adversely affect my life. But as an ombudsman, I saw how devastating it could be for others when the computer says no. These decisions can affect whether you have a home, how you can feed your family and how the world sees you, or how you see yourself. They can start to take your life out of control. In the cases I dealt with, the bank could sometimes point to their reasons – connections with Iran, asylum-seeker status, being married to a foreigner – so that they could be considered, found wanting and corrected. But there were other cases where they could not explain. The algorithm said no, and if the algorithm said no, there must be a reason, just one too complex for mere humans to understand. Automation bias, that tendency to believe the computer's analysis over the proof before our own eyes, is a recognised problem.[1] But at least in the UK there is the potential for accountability. If the decision cannot be explained, it is unlikely to be found to be fair and reasonable by an ombudsman, and the algorithm will just have to think again. But when the computer says no in somewhere like China, it really means no.

Re-education

In 2014, the Chinese State Council revealed plans to establish what has been called the 'social credit system' – national scores of trustworthiness for each individual, based on a complex set of data extracted from a wide range of sources including information about wider family and social connections as well as your own behaviour. The Chinese government claimed the score would 'allow the trustworthy to roam everywhere under heaven while making it hard for the discredited to take a single step'. This national score would dictate your access to services, jobs and opportunities and would give priority to those people who most chimed with the official Chinese social system. In 2019, *The Guardian* newspaper reported that, by the end of 2018, people had been barred from buying flight tickets 17.5 million times for social offences, while social credit offence blacklists had resulted in 5.5 million people being prevented from buying train tickets.[2] US Vice President Mike Pence lashed out at what he called China's 'Orwellian system premised on controlling virtually every facet of human life'.

China has developed and deployed technology in a way that does not include even a thin veneer of consumer choice or social freedom. The scale of surveillance that the predominantly Muslim Uighur population in the province of Xinjiang is subjected to provides a very dark window onto the potential for a human future controlled by technology. In 2019, Human Rights Watch reported on the IJOP app that Chinese officials use to fulfil three broad functions: collecting personal information, reporting on activities or circumstances deemed suspicious, and prompting investigations of people the system flags as problematic.[3] It is a security system, but it feeds off information gathered outside the security sphere. In 2021, online investigative news organisation The Intercept[4] reported on the type of information collected, purportedly to identify extremism, but more often used to flag religious activity or signs of political dissent. This included biometric and health data, financial data, banking records and communications records, as well as details of hardware. And in Xinjiang, it is not only what you yourself might be thinking that matters; the surveillance maps your connections to check what they might be thinking too, and what that could say about you. The line between social and economic activity and security is almost entirely erased. The granular surveillance is used to identify those who may be thinking in ways the state disapproves of so that they can be interned in 'political re-education camps'. There is no conceivable way that a political re-education camp is going to be compliant with the right to freedom of thought.

Outside of the broader human rights problems related to technology in China, it is not entirely clear how far China's programme to develop its planned national social credit system has actually gone, or what it consists of in practice.[5] Companies like Sesame Credit have experimented with credit reporting systems, including data such as purchasing history and social media activity. They operate as loyalty programmes offering perks to individuals they deem worthy of trust. But this kind of credit scoring is not unique to China; credit reference agencies and data brokers around the world are increasingly drawing on massive troves of our data and metadata to decide what we are like and what we deserve. The human rights abuses happening in China are horrific, but we need to look very carefully at the way algorithmic decision-making in both the private and the public sector is developing social credit systems in our own back yards. It is not only in China that your social credit score could affect your travel plans if the algorithm doesn't like you, or your friends and family.

Air miles

We all need a holiday sometimes, but that idyllic cottage you had your eye on may only be yours for the weekend if Airbnb deems you trustworthy. Airbnb owns the patent of an algorithm known as a 'trait analyser', which scrapes the internet and any available databases for information about you that can be filtered through its system for signs of untrustworthy characteristics such as 'neuroticism', 'narcissism' or 'Machiavellianism'. If you're a porn star looking for a relaxing break, Airbnb may decide you are just not the kind of person who deserves one.[6] Of course, if you are a holiday let landlord, like British actor Miriam Margolyes,[7] trying to avoid your property being used as a drug-smuggling hub, the commitment to spotting suspicious behaviour before it happens may seem reassuring. But this is what social credit looks like in action. And when you are denied that spa break because an algorithm doesn't like the look of your kid's Instagram feed, the process may not seem quite so reasonable.

Being deprived of an Airbnb break may not seem too dramatic, but our governments also make judgements about our trustworthiness for travel, whether with algorithms or with analogue human surveillance techniques. Borders are at the front line of technology that seeks to understand who we are and whether or not we are welcome.

Travel blacklists and no-fly lists are not new – they have been a thing in Europe and many other countries since the 2001 terrorist attacks on the United States. The sharing of passenger name records (PNR) across the Atlantic has been one of the fault lines between European data protection law and global security.[8] While politicians in Europe were keen to share our data with North America in the interests of security, the Court of Justice of the European Union agreed with campaigners that to do so would be a breach of human rights as protected under EU law.[9] In 2020, the UK government was forced to ditch an algorithm used to filter visa applications when it was legally challenged about the system that automated years of prejudice and preconceptions about people from particular countries.[10] If you were from a country where people had been refused visas in the past, you were highly likely to have your visa refused regardless of the merits of your individual application – you would be deemed too risky.

Your social network, on- or offline, can have devastating consequences when you cross borders. Maher Arar, a Canadian–Syrian dual-nationality engineer, had no idea why he was held up transferring flights at New York's JFK airport in September 2002 on his way home to Montreal. It would be over a year before he would finally make it back to his family in Canada. He was detained by American security services and flown around the world to be tortured and interrogated in dark sites in Jordan and Syria, one of the only victims of the US global rendition programme to have been picked up on American soil. Why was he singled out? The Canadian authorities had tipped off their American counterparts that the person Arar had listed as a guarantor on his tenancy agreement was someone they were investigating for links with terrorism. For Maher Arar, it was not what he knew, or what he'd done; it was who he supposedly knew that threw him into a cycle of mental and physical torture that he imagined would never end.[11] In 2006, the Canadian Commission of Inquiry found that Maher Arar had no links to terrorism or extremism, and in 2007, the Canadian government issued a formal apology for their part in his horrific ordeal, along with $10.5 million compensation plus costs.

Arar's case is a chilling lesson in the brutal consequences of inferences drawn about your thoughts and opinions as a result of bad data about you and anyone you've ever known. This is how severe the idea of 'social credit' could be in practice. And his experience was the consequence of human error in a time of analogue data-processing. The chances of such an error happening to you expand exponentially when the pool of data and connections for such inferences to be drawn from becomes limitless, and the ability to automate the process means profiling millions of people. This is the reality of the technological panopticon that China's Uighurs live under, but Arar's case shows that it is not only in China where such systems can lead to gross human rights abuses.

Since 2017, US border guards don't even need to rely on intelligence from their neighbours – they can know everything they need to know through the increasingly common practice of a 'digital strip search' of your devices.[12] Accessing social media, phones, tablets and laptops is an increasingly common phenomenon at borders, and it allows officials to decide whether or not you, or your friends and relations, have the kind of opinions they want in their country. The next step on from parsing devices for clues of malicious intent is to digitally strip our face, posture, voice or gait for clues as to what we are thinking. The nascent field of emotional analysis through artificial intelligence seeks to understand what we are thinking and feeling by analysing data such as photographs and video footage. The European Union funded research on the potential use of video technology as a lie detector, using emotion analysis in border controls to decide who should be allowed into the European Union through the iBorderCtrl programme.[13] Public money funded this controversial research, despite the fact that, if proven to be effective, it would completely undermine the basic principles of the Union supposedly founded on human rights. Technology that purports to read your mind so as to take decisions that will affect your life is never going to be human rights compliant, whichever country it is designed or deployed in.

When life gives you lemons ...

It is not only border control officials who are interested in how honest or how risky you are. Right across our lives, in financial services, employment, social support and any other sphere where our trustworthiness might matter, AI is increasingly being used to decide what kind of people we are and what we are thinking. In 2021, American digital insurance start-up Lemonade drew harsh criticism[14] when it bragged about its digital claims technology, tweeting that it could gather 1,600 data points on individuals through them answering 13 questions by video as part of the claims process. They maintained that 'Our AI carefully analyzes these videos for signs of fraud. It can pick up non-verbal cues that traditional insurers can't, since they don't use a digital claims process.' The tweet was deleted, and Lemonade backtracked on its claims in response to the Twitter backlash from the tech ethics community. Interestingly, when Lemonade went public in 2020, it did so as a public benefit corporation – a company that could turn a profit for the public good. It would take the lemons of big data to disrupt the insurance industry for the good of all. But how exactly Lemonade does use the data it collects from and about its customers remains opaque. Let's hope that its Twitter disaster goes beyond a lesson in how to manage social media. To be truly disruptive for the public good in the insurance industry, we need start-ups that step away from what is essentially personality profiling, whether it's based on biometric emotional analysis or on profiling through big data. So far, we are a long way away from that.

What you put into your supermarket trolley says more about you than you may think. Have you ever stood in the checkout queue and idly compared your shopping basket with the person ahead of you? Perhaps it made you feel smug at the complex array of herbs and fresh food that you were taking home to recreate the latest Ottolenghi inspiration while listening to Vivaldi's *Four Seasons*. Or maybe you felt slightly diminished by your multibuy of Doritos and margarita mix compared with their healthy choices. In the era of online shopping, loyalty cards and data aggregation, it is not only you who is being judgemental, weighing up your diet choices to compare them with the yoga teacher two doors down. Loyalty schemes can seem great, but as we rush out to rack up points on our cards for the next shiny free opportunity, do we ever stop to think that there really is no such thing as a free lunch, even from your favourite supermarket? What you buy is a reflection of who you are. It gives a window onto your inner life, your mood, your sense of responsibility, your reliability. In sum, it says a lot about how risky you are as a person. The mathematician Hannah Fry, in her book

Hello World: How to Be Human in the Age of the Machine, explains how what you buy can be used as an indicator of your inherent reliability, with fresh fennel topping the chart. If fresh fennel in your shopping cart is the best indicator of reliability,[15] what did those Doritos say about you? And our choices change over time and don't necessarily conform to stereotype. As a fancy-free student, I had an awful lot of time for an occasional delicate orange and fennel salad, though I may not have been entirely reliable, and the regular haggis suppers from the chippy did not appear on my supermarket loyalty card. Now, with a focus on food that can be produced quickly with a high likelihood that everyone in the house will eat it, there are more baked beans (sugar free, of course) than there used to be on my shopping list, and barely a whiff of fresh fennel.

Big data offers the promise of a certain future, a world without risk, and delivering on that promise touches on all three aspects of the right to freedom of thought – it makes inferences about your inner life that can manipulate the way you see yourself and the world and that may be used to penalise you for who you are or who the algorithm deems you to be.

The analysis of millions of data points on an individual builds a picture of how risky it is to make inferences about their inner lives. If you have ever taken out a car insurance policy, you will know that everything you fill out on your application will be weighed against the rest of the world to put a price on whether you are a risk worth taking. If, like me, your work could put you into any one of several categories on the professional drop-down menu, you will be aware that whether you describe yourself as a barrister, an arbitrator or an author may have a significant impact on how risky the company thinks you are on the road based on its previous experience of your colleagues. That in turn will dictate the cost of your premium. Some categories of differentiation are unlawful in some jurisdictions. You can no longer offer pink-themed discounts on car insurance for careful lady drivers in the European Union since the European Court of Justice ruled sex-based distinctions amounted to sex discrimination.[16] This ruling was billed by the British media as a blow to women's rights to lower premiums, but interestingly the insurance industry never considered lowering everyone's premiums to avoid discrimination, and anyway, there are plenty of data points that act as proxies for gender that can still be fed into the risk algorithm without crossing the legal line. Do you buy tampons? Buy pink razors? Is your name Sarah? If you answer yes to all three, there's a fair chance you might be a woman.

Although discrimination is against the law, the mysteries of the algorithm can often mask it. The range of data points available to insurers through data enrichment companies makes the number of variables attached to each individual consumer almost impossible to unpick. But, as the *Sun* newspaper revealed in an investigation in 2018, the cost of insuring a car in the UK if your name is Mohammed is vastly higher than if your name is John. Comparing around 60 quotes for car insurance in different names, the newspaper revealed that the additional cost of driving while Muslim in Britain is up to £919, with Admiral the worst example.[17] It seems that faith in the afterlife has ceased to be a sign of trustworthiness since the days of J. S. Mill.[18] Insurance companies know they are not allowed to discriminate against drivers based on faith, race or ethnicity. But the business of risk assessment based on big data, emotion recognition or other technological techniques designed to get under our skin to know if we are a risk worth taking is perilously close to penalising people based on inferences about their inner lives.

In late 2016, British car insurer Admiral announced the launch of a new product called 'firstcarquote', targeting young drivers who might find it hard to get affordable car insurance. A shiny new Facebook app offered the promise of reduced premiums for new drivers in exchange for access to their social media activity. But the information the app would assess would not include photos of the driver knocking back a tequila shot while waving around their parents' car keys, or pictures indicating a marked interest in Formula 1 racing. What Admiral was looking for was a much more subtle and granular indication of the kind of person they would be insuring. It was reported[19] that the company would identify certain personality traits by assessing posts and likes for particular tells. Short sentences, lists and precision when arranging to meet friends would suggest someone was conscientious, so less risky. Exclamation marks and a lot of categorical statements using 'always' and 'never' could indicate overconfidence, which might translate into higher insurance premiums. Although Admiral claimed the app would only lead to reductions, not increases in premiums, Facebook decided that it breached its privacy guidelines and Admiral ultimately pulled the product hours before the launch.[20] But whether or not the information is gleaned through a Facebook account, financial services companies still have access to a massive trove of information on you, and what that data says about you and your inner life may well shape your future.

Oracle

The scale of 'digital exhaust'[21] we leave about ourselves is beyond any real comprehension. It includes the things we don't know we give away and even some things we may not know about ourselves. And at the heart of global big data is the data broking industry. While you may have been worrying about whether to delete your Facebook account, have you ever questioned what Oracle might have on you? Is the modern-day corporation as insightful and prophetic about our individual and collective futures as the oracles of ancient Greece it is named after? Could data broking be the modern equivalent of communing with the gods?

In the financial sector, many of us have learned to rely on companies like Experian, Oracle and others to persuade banks that we are deserving of their credit. As Privacy International has highlighted in its campaign work on what it calls the 'hidden data ecosystem',[22] these companies work in the background, away from the limelight of social media. Nevertheless, they hold the key to our secret identities and their activities threaten both human dignity and autonomy. The mass of data they have on us is far beyond our credit records. Oracle, the American computer software company, claims to sell data on more than 300 million people globally, with 30,000 data points on each individual, covering over 80 per cent of the US population.[23] And the kind of information they have can be disturbingly intimate. When Belgian privacy campaigner Paul-Olivier Dehaye requested his personal information from advertising technology company Amobee, he found a prediction that, on a particular date, he was likely to be more susceptible to advertising for drinks. On further investigation, it appeared this information came from data from IBM's Weather Company predicting how weather conditions in his location might affect him that day so that he could be targeted for drinks sales.[24] Did you know that the weather app on your phone could be selling information on where you are and just how much you might need the toilet? In 2020, the Weather Company settled a privacy lawsuit filed by the Los Angeles city attorney's office that claimed the company 'deceptively' gathered personal and geolocation data through its app which, at the time, had 45 million active users.[25]

Data brokers often use the argument that the data they deal in is 'anonymised', but whether or not this is true, the data that is being collected and attributed to us by unique identifier numbers can still be used against us. You don't need to know someone's name to violate their rights. The scale of surveillance is so all-encompassing and the desire to judge and rank us so powerful that it is virtually impossible to avoid. As anyone who has tried to get credit for the first time will know, staying out of the system won't help you – without the data to judge you by, you are deemed to be deeply suspicious. If you never buy your groceries with a bank card or online and you have no loyalty cards, that in itself says something about your personality when it comes to Judgement Day. And the tracking and data gathering is not only online. Increasingly, it is in the streets and in our shops, a constant assessment of our worth, our mood and our risk in real time.

In the 2002 adaptation of Philip K. Dick's *Minority Report*, Tom Cruise walks through a shopping mall as he tries to escape his destiny, but he cannot escape the all-seeing surveillance advertising and personally tailored adverts flashing up all around him, calling his name to lure him in to buy something he doesn't want and doesn't need. In 2022, this is no longer science fiction. The cameras in today's malls can be trained to pick up your anticipation as they scan your face for emotion to understand what they may be able to sell you, and how much you may be able or willing to pay. But if the credit algorithms have decided that you are not worthy and your card is declined, the shop's camera running your image through its AI may see the kind of despair that can lead to shoplifting, so the security guard might check your bag just in case.

This scenario may seem far-fetched, but companies like Emotion Research Lab[26] in Spain already sell services that claim to read emotions in real time to improve customer experience or maximise sales, while others, like Vaak, a Japanese start-up, say they can predict shoplifting before it happens by identifying suspicious body language through surveillance cameras.[27] The line between shopper and suspect is a fine one, and it is not only the police who are interested in detecting crime. In the digital age, security is not solely in the hands of the state. Our shopping experience is increasingly about 'optimisation', but it is the access to our minds that is being optimised, to promote sales and prevent business losses, rather than our personal experience.

Banks decide whether to give us credit, how much and at what price, based on a risk assessment of our individual circumstances combined with their institutional risk appetite. If you have a secure job and a history of paying off loans reliably, you are likely to have access to more and cheaper credit than someone whose fortunes, and credit repayments, fluctuate according to their latest flutter on the horses. It is reasonable for businesses to judge our creditworthiness based on our financial circumstances and our financial history. But is it fair to judge us on all our data – whether individual data points like a taste for fresh fennel, or machine learning that draws together everything we have ever thought or done alongside everyone we have ever met to assess whether we are a risky person on aggregate? Faith in the algorithm, like faith in God, cannot be easily unpicked. If it is impossible to explain what it is about a person's circumstances that led to a decision about their credit, it is unlikely to be 'fair and reasonable'.[28] Without clear, identifiable reasons, a risk assessment becomes just a prejudiced judgement on someone's inherent riskiness.

Digital welfare dystopia

It is not only businesses whose decisions on our trustworthiness can affect our financial futures. In the twentieth century, many countries adopted the idea that we should all contribute through our taxes to supporting not the ruling elite, but the most vulnerable in our societies. Social welfare schemes of various types developed around the globe. But as the AI revolution has swept the world, inevitably governments have shifted to automate the process, with potentially devastating results. As the UN Special Rapporteur on extreme poverty, Philip Alston, put it, we are at risk of 'stumbling, zombie-like into a digital welfare dystopia'.[29] When you need welfare support, if the computer says no, it may leave you unable to afford basic, life-sustaining provisions.

Social welfare is expensive and welfare fraud is a pernicious problem that governments all over the world struggle with. The US state of Michigan thought it had the answer when in 2013 it installed an automated fraud detection system for $47 million, which made around 48,000 accusations of fraud against those claiming unemployment benefit – a five-fold increase on the previous system. Those accusations resulted in action to claw back the money, in some cases over $150,000 worth of repayments straight from wages, bank accounts and tax refunds, without any human checks. Imagine the devastation of waking up one day to find you owed the state tens of thousands of dollars because you had tried to claim benefits. The fallout on those affected was dire – divorce, eviction, homelessness, bankruptcy and even suicide. But a later state review of the system found that 93 per cent of the fraud determinations were wrong. People's lives were destroyed because the data suggested they were dodgy and nobody thought to check why.[30]

In the Netherlands, the government introduced an automated system known as the System Risk Indication (SyRI for short) to identify people most likely to commit benefit fraud based on the full range of data points available to the state. But when the system was challenged by a group of non-governmental organisations (NGOs),[31] the district court of The Hague ruled that the legislation that governed SyRI violated the higher law of international human rights.[32] The inability of people to know whether or not they had been profiled or identified as risky along with the absolute lack of transparency about the algorithm and data used meant that the legislation was unlawful in breach of the right to private life. The court was not convinced that the Dutch government had shown that the measures were justified, necessary in a democratic society or proportionate to the aim of combating benefit fraud. This case was argued primarily on the basis of the right to private life, a limited right, so there was a balancing act to be done between the need for public order and the rights of the individuals. But when the algorithmic black box approach was weighed up, it was found to be wanting. The right to a personal identity and the right to personal development are elements of the right to private life, but where they refer to things that go on inside our heads, our thoughts, personality and inclinations, they may equally be considered as aspects of the rights to freedom of thought or opinion in the inner realm.

Often a particular set of facts may raise issues under several different rights. In the SyRI case, having found a violation based on the right to privacy, the court did not go on to consider the other arguments put forward about discrimination and fair trial because it didn't need to. But if an automated welfare system was found to be an interference with the absolute protection of the *forum internum*, there would be no need for a balancing exercise – it would always be unlawful. Privacy arguments are more familiar to courts for now, but as the discussions develop to consider other rights, including absolute rights like freedom of thought, society will have a new and powerful weapon with which to fight back against abuses by big tech. And what is sometimes referred to as 'mental privacy' can equally be considered as the right to keep our thoughts, opinions and inner lives to ourselves. Poverty law professor Michele Gilman has documented the ways in which 'data-centric technologies add scope, scale, and speed to negative inferences about poor people'.[33] She observed that 'when people experiencing poverty are targeted for predatory products based on their digital footprints – or conversely excluded from mainstream opportunities such as housing and jobs – they lose the freedom to make sound decisions that best serve their families and their economic stability'. This is why the right to freedom of thought could be a useful addition to the legal arsenal for challenging the harms of automated decision-making on low-income communities in fields as diverse as consumer law, family law, immigration surveillance and education, in the United States and beyond.

Algorithmic risk assessments are not only potentially discriminatory, they have far-reaching implications for our inner freedom. The further they are removed from objective risk factors that can be explained and identified, the closer they come to nebulous inferences about our inner states. Those inferences about the inner realm are used as the basis for decisions on our future life chances and opportunities. And we may be penalised not only for how risky the algorithm deems us to be, but also how clever.

F**k the algorithm

When I moved from my local comprehensive in the Isle of Man to a private boarding school in England, I remember the pause on the other end of the line when the private school called to ask for my O level results. 'Can you repeat that?' I was never quite sure if the problem was my Manx accent or the fact that girls from schools like mine were not supposed to get grades like that. I recognise that I am privileged in that this kind of thing rarely happens to me; for others it is a gruelling daily reality. Bias and inequality are deep-rooted societal problems, but when they are branded as artificial intelligence, they take on a whole new dimension.

Algorithms that settle our life chances based on inferences about 'people like us' murder ambition, innovation and social mobility. In 2020, high school students across the world were prevented from sitting their final exams because of the COVID-19 pandemic. In England, the government's answer to the problem was to gather assessments of what teachers expected their individual students to achieve and then run those through an algorithm that rounded them up or down according to the historical scores of a particular school or region. As a result, 40 per cent of students found their dreams shattered as their qualifications were downgraded by the regulator's algorithm.

In 2020, it seemed, you would not be graded on your previous personal achievements or your potential; you would be taught to know your station as you were classed with your peers. If you were a pretty average student at the elite school Eton, the algorithm would grade you in light of the privilege around you that had produced so many prime ministers over the years. If you were a brilliant student from a deprived area where no one had ever gone to a top university, you would be downgraded based on the assumption that people like you are intellectually useless. One quarter of students from state schools were downgraded, but only 1 in 10 from private schools, with some private school students seeing their grades inflated by the algorithm thanks to the success of their predecessors. This was the British class system translated into code.[34]

But the students were not having it. Masked up against COVID-19 (and coincidentally against London's ubiquitous facial recognition cameras), they took to the streets chanting 'Fuck the algorithm', while legal teams with the organisations Foxglove and the Good Law Project sent letters setting out the legal reasons why the algorithmic injustice would not pass. After a week of official obfuscation, the government U-turned. Students would be graded as individuals based on teacher assessments, however flawed those may be. This was perhaps the first time in Britain that so many people had woken up to the way algorithmic inferences about our mental potential can affect us all. This was a human rights fight the whole country got behind, and won.

But the kind of assumptions made by the exam-grading algorithm have not gone away; they are just deployed in more subtle ways that are harder to identify. For example, the problem with targeted advertising is not only about the people who are targeted, but also about the people who are excluded from ever knowing that opportunities exist. If you never see that great job advertised, you are not going to apply, and you will never get it. If you never knew about the option of student finance, you may never imagine yourself as an MBA graduate.

Gravitas

In 2018, the American Civil Liberties Union (ACLU) sued Facebook for allowing targeted advertising for jobs to be shown only to men, in violation of the US Civil Rights Act.[35] Bobbi Spees, one of the women bringing the charges, said she realised that she was not seeing employment openings on Facebook when she compared notes with her husband, who was also job-searching online.[36] Without her husband, she might never have known. Lawyers from the ACLU and the Communications Workers Union were able to collect many examples in order to bring the complaint by checking the information Facebook provides when you ask 'Why am I seeing this ad?' where it specified that the adverts targeted men in a certain age range and geographical area. However, in general, we have no idea of the adverts and opportunities that we don't see – personalised ads are the great 'unknown unknown'. Targeted advertising for exclusion makes sure that people stay in their own lane because they never get to see an alternative route.

In early 2019, Facebook agreed a $5 million settlement on five discrimination lawsuits.[37] But by August the same year, a new suit was launched claiming that the problem persisted and seeking compensation for individual Facebook users as a discrimination class action.[38] Facebook is getting used to responding to bad press and lawsuits. Where possible, it apologises, tweaks the algorithm and moves on with business as usual. But this does nothing to address the underlying problem of the wider threat of social engineering posed by granular online profiling and targeting and the embedding of bias in algorithmic decision-making. You can remove direct targeting on the basis of sex or race, but what about other data that act as a proxy? This is not the same as traditional advertising that might choose a publication or a geographical area with a particular demographic; it is about targeting and controlling information and opportunities on an individual basis. You might usually search for job adverts in your local paper, but there's nothing preventing you from checking the adverts in the *Financial Times*. With targeted advertising, you have no way of knowing or accessing the adverts for which you have not been deemed worthy. An interest in Sephora cosmetics (one of the factors in Michal Kosinski's research on Facebook likes) might indicate that you're likely to be a woman. And pick a brand designed for darker skin and you are probably a woman of colour. Choosing a halal menu on a flight may give an indication of your religion or ethnicity. Even if you step away from direct discrimination, the inferences made about our inner lives based on the mass of data available on us still have the potential to condemn us and limit our life choices. Following a football team may be a sign that you're more likely to be a man, but targeting based on interests alone is harder to identify as discrimination.

Just because you can't explain the discrimination does not mean it is not there or that it is not affecting the way you think. And the discrimination does not only come from the ways you see yourself; it's also about the ways the world is guided to see you. As Dr Safiya Umoja Noble has documented in her book *Algorithms of Oppression: How Search Engines Reinforce Racism*,[39] the way that people search for information about the world through major search engines like Google can reinforce biased world views. When Noble searched for 'black girls' on Google in 2011, the first result was 'hotblackpussy.com'. A year later, she found the algorithm had been changed.[40] Noble's work explains how algorithms not only affect the way women, and in particular women of colour, see themselves; they also shape the way others see and treat us all as individuals. Propaganda and disinformation operate by hijacking information flows to manipulate minds. In the twenty-first century, where Google is the portal for so much of our information, what Google thinks about someone has great power to manipulate the way we all think about them.

When I got through to the final round of interviews for a senior public appointment a few years ago, I was thrilled to have got that far. But when the feedback came through from the interview panel, I felt very differently. They told me they thought I was wonderful but that they had ultimately decided to go with a candidate they felt had a bit more 'gravitas'. I didn't need to wait for the public announcement to know they had appointed a man. In 2013, when Janet Yellen, an extremely well-qualified female candidate, was passed over to head the US Federal Reserve, the reason given for choosing a man instead was again 'gravitas'.[41] Meeting a friend for lunch the day after the decision, he clarified for me why the experience had left me so uncharacteristically upset: 'It's what direct discrimination feels like, Susie.'

Many large international companies are switching to automated recruitment processes based on emotional and psychological analysis of candidates provided by companies like HireVue to try to tackle human bias.[42] The assumption is that people are prejudiced, but surely a machine must be neutral. But as recruitment becomes increasingly automated, the risks of bias are rising, not dropping, as artificial intelligence learns about our discriminatory attitudes and amplifies them. You're not going to be seen as having gravitas if the first thing Google gives up about people like you is porn. While many companies attempt to neutralise the inherent human bias in recruitment by removing details like name or place of education that could be loaded with connotations and value judgements, the rush to use machines to correct our human failings simply exacerbates the problem. It is laudable that organisations should try to address the issue. But the way automated selection works, including so-called emotional analysis, just consolidates the problem.

For the public appointment I had applied for, there has never been an appointee who was not a white man of a certain age. So any machine learning trained on prior appointments to identify good candidates based on qualities like 'gravitas' will know exactly who is 'perfect' for the job. If gravitas looks like a white male in his fifties, nothing else will fit the bill. Amazon famously had to ditch its own executive recruitment AI when it found that it did not recognise women as executive material, penalising résumés that included the term 'women's' so that people whose listed interests included things like 'women's chess club' or who went to all-female colleges were automatically downgraded by the algorithm.[43] If we don't fit the learned template, the automatic inference about our potential and our inner state is that we are just not quite right.

Companies like HireVue sell technology that is designed to read people's faces, voices and demeanour in video interviews, using emotion recognition technology and AI to predict which of them will have the right characteristics to be a good hire. They sell their systems as a direct portal into the human mind without the clutter of our inherent bias. But what they offer entrenches exclusion and is built on claims about the science that experts say are both overblown and dangerous.[44] Researchers in the field of affective AI like Meredith Whittaker, the director of the AI Now Institute, are raising their voices in concern, 'calling out the unregulated, unvalidated, scientifically unfounded deployment of commercial affect recognition technologies. Commercialization is hurting people right now, potentially, because it's making claims that are determining people's access to resources.' Emotional analysis is hard enough to do with your own family, but if you've ever crossed a national border, you will be well aware that facial expressions, eye contact, smiling, shrugging, voice tone and inflection, as well as choice of language – all data points that HireVue's technology takes into account – mean very different things in different cultures or for different groups of people. In many societies direct eye contact is perceived as rude, so algorithms trained to judge a lack of eye contact as shifty are automatically going to rule those people out as untrustworthy. If you are a woman, I'll bet you've been told to smile by a stranger at least once in your life, and maybe you've learned to do it automatically to avoid criticism. But smiling does not really give you gravitas and the AI knows that. The biases we live with as human beings are not cured by AI; they are excused and industrialised by it.

There is already legislation in some places preventing the use of polygraph testing in most recruitment processes, and HireVue's technology is essentially a new and flashier version of the Marstons' polygraph, designed to get under a candidate's skin to understand how their mind works.[45] However, the fundamental question is not whether HireVue's technology can really understand you on a deeper level; it is whether it should be allowed to try to read your mind at all. In *Nineteen Eighty-Four*, Winston Smith learned to 'set his features to the expression of quiet optimism'[46] that it was advisable to wear in the presence of the ubiquitous telescreen. And in 2021, it was reported that the tech company Canon had installed 'smile recognition' technology in its Chinese offices so that only smiling workers could enter or book meeting rooms, thus guaranteeing that everyone would be, or appear to be, happy at work all the time.[47] Emotion analysis will not eliminate risk and improve our lives; it will just reward insincerity and conformity and drive our humanity and our diversity underground.

Shoshana Zuboff tells us that surveillance capitalism is all about 'human futures' – predicting them and making them happen, whether actively or passively. If the algorithm infers that you are a loser, it will help to make sure that is what you become. Freedom of thought is the freedom to be, or, even more importantly, as Charles Malik put it, the freedom to become. As the British drafters of human rights treaties noted, freedom of opinion can be interfered with by managing information flows. This affects not only your opinions about the world around you, but also your opinion of yourself, your self-worth, your potential and your future. It is not only affecting you, it is changing the ways everyone around you sees their world and the way they look at you. And when the world starts to look at you with suspicion, it could be your liberty that is on the line.

CHAPTER 10

PRE-CRIME AND PUNISHMENT

My first crown court trial as a junior barrister was never meant to be a trial at all. I had been sent to court to request an adjournment, as the colleague who was instructed for the defence had been rushed into hospital that morning. But prosecution counsel, smelling my inexperience and reading the terror in my eyes, decided it would be an easier job to get the trial done there and then and successfully persuaded the judge to refuse the adjournment, giving me just an hour to prepare for a three-day trial. Criminal culpability, in most cases, relies on proving a state of mind. For guilt to be proven for most offences, you need to show both that the accused did the act they are accused of and that they did it with a guilty mind. A judge or a jury in court weighs up the evidence to decide whether both the physical and mental aspects of a crime are proven beyond reasonable doubt. The whole UK criminal justice system is built around ideas of criminal responsibility, the weighing up of evidence and, in an adversarial system, persuasion.

My client was accused of receiving stolen property. He had been found in possession of a shiny, nearly new stolen BMW that he had thoughtfully acquired for his doting and heavily pregnant wife. He had the car, and it was clear it was stolen. All the prosecution had to prove beyond reasonable doubt was that he had knowledge or belief that the goods were stolen and that he had acted dishonestly. Over three days the prosecution built a picture of circumstantial evidence that would indicate his likely knowledge that the car was stolen – how much he had paid for it, whether or not his fingerprints were found near the vehicle identification number, and where he'd got it from. The fact that he had a list of previous convictions as long as your arm or that the police had happened across the car when searching his house (successfully) for cannabis plants were all facts kept from the jury; knowing he had committed other crimes would be likely to taint their view of his mindset, prejudicing them against him while not really providing proof that he knew, or ought to have known, that the car was stolen.

Once all the evidence had been presented, whether thanks to my persuasive advocacy skills or my client and his wife being charming enough when they gave their evidence, the jury did at least debate for a couple of hours before finally convicting him. As his list of previous convictions and the pending drugs charge were read out by the judge considering whether or not to give him bail pending sentencing, a ripple went through the jury, some faces settling into expressions of comfortable vindication while others looked at me with an air of betrayal as if they felt they had very nearly been duped.

Mind-reading

Human assessments of honesty are notoriously inaccurate.[1] But would it have helped if the court had been presented with evidence from the defendant's brain that showed he knew the car was stolen? Or that there was something about the shape of his brain that indicated criminal propensity, or showed that he just couldn't help himself? And if this kind of proof had been presented, how would it have affected the way the jury weighed up all the other evidence? Would this be enough to remove reasonable doubt? And what would that mean for justice? Neuroscience has developed at an exponential rate in recent decades, particularly in the field of crime and security, with some researchers making proud claims that their technology can cut through the chatter of human language and prevarication to directly reveal the secrets of the brain. Attempts to access the criminal mind have taken many forms over the centuries, as we saw with the history of physiognomy and lie detectors. But the most modern and cutting-edge techniques are based on leaps forward in brain scanning technology, particularly the use of fMRI to show in unprecedented detail how and what the brain is doing. So is the use of brain scanning, polygraphs or other forms of lie detection in the criminal justice system something we should embrace, with its potential to bypass human obfuscation and deliver justice? Should we deny the innocent the chance to exonerate themselves by revealing the truth as an irrefutable, abstract, brightly coloured image of their brain? In the twenty-first century, these questions have become increasingly urgent.

In 2008, Aditi Sharma, a young Indian woman, made criminal justice history. Her story, a dramatic love triangle, was the stuff of movies. The judge at her trial in Mumbai explained how the MBA student, engaged to be married to Udit, had fallen in love and eloped with another student, Pravin. When six months later her ex-fiancé was found dead, Aditi and Pravin were accused of his murder. It was alleged that she had lured him to a McDonald's at a shopping mall to give him a food offering known as a 'Prasad' laced with arsenic, an accusation that she strenuously denied. The tale of the alleged crime had everything you might want in a cinematic murder mystery, but it was not the crime itself that made global headlines; it was the evidence used in the trial.

With primarily circumstantial evidence and the fairly thin motive that Aditi had previously been in love with the victim but had left him, the police needed to find something more solid to base their case on. So both Aditi and Pravin were subjected to psychological tests to try to ascertain whether their stories were true. The polygraph test involved sensors being attached to their bodies recording a baseline and the changes in response to a series of 'yes' or 'no' questions. Their physiological responses were supposed to reveal whether their answers were true. Pravin's results were inconclusive, but the analyst decided that Aditi's responses indicated deception.

So, based on the results of the polygraph test, she was given an additional new type of test, known as the brain electrical oscillation signature test, or BEOS, developed by an Indian neuroscientist building on methods developed earlier by American scholars.[2] Sensors are attached to the subject's head through a cloth cap, placed to detect the electrical activation in various parts of the brain in response to a set of questions. The test is supposed to be able to distinguish between two different aspects of memory. Conceptual memory is related to semantic processing, involving the recollection of words and language. This type of memory would indicate a recognition of information received through the media or people talking about an event. Experiential knowledge, by contrast, reflects participation in an activity or event. The designers of the BEOS system claim it can distinguish between the brain's responses to conceptual memory and experiential knowledge. So the test is designed to tell whether a person's brain remembers being involved in a crime, or if their knowledge of it is passive, based on information they have received from other sources.

Alone in a room with her head wired up to 32 sensors, her eyes closed, Aditi was instructed to remain silent and let her brain speak for her as statements about the alleged crime were read out. As the luminous patterns of her brain waves rushed across the screen, she no doubt hoped that they could wash away any doubts of her innocence. Instead, they condemned her. The processing of her brain's responses to the prompts was fully automated, and according to the expert testimony, they showed that she remembered what was being described. The judge explained that the findings of the BEOS showed that Aditi had experiential knowledge of the affair and Udit's unhappiness about it. She was also found to have experiential knowledge of planning, preparing and carrying out the murder as well as of the emotional experience of being relieved and scared about giving Udit the 'Prasad'.[3]

The judge, sentencing her to life in prison, found that 'the psychological evaluation tests of Aditi thus clearly prove her involvement in Udit's murder as indicated by deceptive responses on the relevant questions in polygraph test and by the presence of experiential knowledge on the target probes in BEOS in terms of having a plan to murder him, collecting "Prasad" and arsenic, meeting Udit and giving him the Prasad'. She became the first person ever to be convicted primarily on evidence of her mental culpability extracted straight from her brain. But just a year later, she was released on bail pending appeal based on the unreliability of some of the evidence against her. It turned out that the 'Prasad' tested for arsenic was not the same as that which she had allegedly given the doctor on the night Udit fell sick.[4] Later that year, two other people were convicted of Udit's murder using the same evidential technique with brain scans. Aditi Sharma's conviction was ultimately quashed.

The reliability of both polygraph and BEOS testing is hotly contested. Sharma's experience highlights the concerns that have been reflected in jurisprudence around the world about scientific evidence that claims to reveal deliberate deception or criminal knowledge. Much of the discussion in court and in academia around scientific evidence that claims to reveal the workings of the human mind has focused on whether it can actually deliver on its promise. In their book *Brainwashed: The Seductive Appeal of Mindless Neuroscience*,[5] the psychiatrist Sally Satel and psychologist Scott Lilienfeld briefly mention concerns about mental privacy or mental integrity in their analysis of these techniques. They conclude that the current flawed state of neuroscience is not a threat to our inner freedom because it cannot, in fact, read our minds. But that conclusion is based on a misunderstanding of how rights and freedoms work in law and practice. The results of a lie detector test may be unreliable rubbish, but for the person subjected to the test, the stress and uncertainty and the risk of being condemned for a read-out of their brain activity are very real. Regardless of reliability, there is a fundamental question as to whether these techniques could ever be compatible with human rights, including the absolute right not to reveal one's thoughts.

In a seminal judgment in 2010,[6] the Indian Supreme Court set out the legal arguments that had been developed in courts in North America, the UK and India as it decided a set of appeals relating to the administration of scientific techniques, namely narcoanalysis, polygraph examination and the brain electrical activation profile (BEAP) test for the purpose of 'improving investigation efforts' in criminal cases. The Supreme Court justices grappled with questions relating to 'mental privacy', human dignity, personal liberty, the prohibition on self-incrimination, the right to be presumed innocent until proven guilty and the potential of such techniques to undermine the fact-finding role of a judge in a fair trial. Explaining their reasoning for ruling that the use of these techniques was not compatible with Indian law, the justices said, 'We must recognise the importance of personal autonomy in aspects such as the choice between remaining silent and speaking', and concluded that there should be no legal scope to forcibly interfere with someone's mental processes to force them to make a statement, especially where they might be penalised for doing so.[7]

In the United States, the right against self-incrimination is protected by the Fifth Amendment, and the US Supreme Court came to similar conclusions in a judgment delivered by Justice William J. Brennan Jr, who said, 'To compel a person to submit to testing in which an effort will be made to determine his guilt or innocence on the basis of physiological responses, whether willed or not, is to evoke the spirit and history of the Fifth Amendment.'[8]

Much of the case law around the admissibility of this kind of test in the United States has come from the defence wanting to use such evidence as proof of an innocent mind and claiming that the refusal to admit it violates an accused person's Sixth Amendment right to present a defence (a right reflected in international human rights law within the right to a fair trial). The US Supreme Court, however, found that the rule against such evidence served legitimate interests in the criminal trial process, including 'ensuring that only reliable evidence is introduced at trial, preserving the jury's role in determining credibility, and avoiding litigation that is collateral to the primary purpose of the trial'. Deciding on the credibility of witnesses and the mental state of a defendant are fundamental parts of the criminal justice system, but these decisions must be made by the jury in the United States and by the trial judge in systems like the

Indian system. Using technology to try to see inside people's minds to convict them of crimes instead of relying on a human assessment of the evidence is a very clear leap into the absolutely protected realm of our inner world. It replaces the human assessment of credibility with an automatic read-out. The evidence is not informing the tribunal's assessment; it is effectively substituting its own.

Both the US and Indian courts agree that this kind of technique should not be compelled, but the question of what amounts to compulsion remains open. The Indian Supreme Court recognised that, even if these read-outs were accurate, accepting them in court might lead investigators to be tempted into using shortcuts. Those in themselves could be violations of other rights, such as the prohibition on torture, inhuman and degrading treatment, and the court pointed out that the right against self-incrimination or the right to remain silent is a vital safeguard against torture and other 'third degree methods' to extract information.[9]

While the court recognised the need to exclude compelled testimony of this kind to avoid the risks of coercive behaviour by investigators, it left open the possibility of using the results of this type of test in criminal trials where they were done voluntarily. In Aditi Sharma's case, she agreed voluntarily to undergo the psychological tests, but did she really have any choice? If the results of the tests are allowed in a trial, a refusal to undergo the tests may in itself be used as evidence to infer a guilty mind. And the Indian Supreme Court also left open the possibility for lie detectors or other neuroscientific techniques to be used in situations where they were not relied on to achieve a criminal conviction. These procedures are not restricted to the criminal justice system in a couple of jurisdictions; they are currently in use and in development in many contexts and countries around the world.

In the United States, polygraphs are used to screen employees for government jobs requiring a high level of security clearance.[10] In the UK, they are used on sex offenders convicted of serious offences,[11] and it is planned to use them on convicted terrorists[12] to gauge compliance with conditions of release or to understand if a convict is trying to trick their parole officer. And in India, these techniques have been used in divorce proceedings to prove a state of mind.[13] These examples highlight a problem that is much more fundamental than the reliability of evidence used to convict someone. The issue goes beyond the right against self-incrimination. There is something uniquely invasive about what is, essentially, mind-reading. It undermines both mental integrity and human dignity in ways we may understand more fully if we step away from the criminal justice context and imagine what it might feel like for us.

In 2019, a participant on the UK daytime TV programme *The Jeremy Kyle Show* killed himself after failing a polygraph test he had hoped would prove his faithfulness to his estranged partner. The episode was not aired, and the show was pulled amid criticisms about the ethics of this kind of reality TV. But the tragic outcome shows how deeply distressing it can be to fail this kind of test, no matter the circumstances. This was an example of a voluntary test, but the impact of failing it was profound, not only because it could have destroyed any possibility of reconciliation with his former partner, but also because it put a question mark over his personal integrity and destroyed his dignity. Who would voluntarily put themselves forward for a lie detector test if they weren't sure they would pass it? Catching someone out in a lie based on evidence is one thing – the possibility of that is the basis for human interactions and trust in criminal justice, business, education and love. We know that people lie all the time (some much more than others, according to researchers)[14] and we need to be able to spot and infer deception in others to manage and mitigate that in our lives. But using a technique designed to extract the lie directly from the mind is something very different. The judge in the Aditi Sharma case described the BEOS technique as 'non-invasive'. But in a moral sense, the BEOS is just as invasive of the mind as cutting the head open would be invasive of the brain. Refusing to take the test is an indication of guilt; taking the test is a coin flip on condemnation. There is no escape.

It is notable that, in the UK, police departments have claimed that even the threat of using a polygraph has led to an increase in reporting of breaches of parole conditions among sex offenders.[15] While the police put this forward as a justification for using such techniques, it also shows the coercive effect of the threat of a polygraph. Policing is about protecting the public from crime, and that is a part of the government's positive obligation to protect all our rights. But the way in which that duty is delivered must in itself be compliant with human rights.

Since the signing of the Universal Declaration of Human Rights, huge leaps have been made in building an international framework to ensure effective protection for other absolute rights. The United Nations Convention against Torture describes in great detail the steps that states must take to make the prohibition on torture, cruel, inhuman and degrading treatment or punishment a reality in practice, not just in theory. One key to this framework is the inability to use evidence extracted through torture or ill-treatment. I remember the shock expressed by one prosecutor on an international training course on human rights and counter-terrorism when I explained how human rights law prevents the use of torture evidence in court. 'But how can you get anyone to confess if you can't beat them?' he asked, quite dismayed.

If you cannot use evidence obtained using coercive techniques to convict someone, the motive for using these methods drops away in many cases. And the answer to the prosecutor's conundrum is to develop more effective legitimate investigation techniques so that you can prove guilt in a fair trial. Conviction of innocent people based on false confessions extracted through torture or indications of guilt taken straight from their brains through hi-tech sensors do not make the world a safer place for anyone. Just as we cannot tolerate the use of torture in our criminal justice system, we should not tolerate investigative techniques that breach the right to freedom of thought. The debate on 'mind-reading' techniques in the criminal justice system and beyond needs to move on from the technical questions around reliability to address the more fundamental questions of the general legal and ethical validity of these procedures to decide whether they can ever be acceptable.

Facecrime

In the criminal justice sphere, it is not only your brain waves that might give you away. If your face doesn't fit, it could land you in big trouble. Facial recognition technology has become ubiquitous in many parts of our lives, from using our face to open our laptop or pass through a border, to policing and security through fixed cameras and mobile facial recognition devices. Privacy and human rights campaigners have been raising the alarm about the risks of such widespread surveillance to democratic societies for years. They have highlighted the chilling effect on the right to protest as police record gatherings and check faces against vast databases. And researchers like Dr Joy Buolamwini, founder of the Algorithmic Justice League, and Timnit Gebru, an AI ethicist, have laid bare the technical failings and bias in facial recognition, which is practically incapable of recognising Black women's faces as women, or even as faces at all – an issue that Buolamwini describes as 'the coded gaze'.[16]

The use of facial recognition technology as a way of identifying a face in a crowd is deeply concerning and raises a myriad of human rights and other legal questions. But facial recognition technology is not only about identification and physical surveillance; it is also about mental surveillance. In Europe, the Reclaim Your Face[17] movement is campaigning to ban biometric mass surveillance within the European Union as an urgent measure to protect human dignity and human rights. We saw how facial recognition technology can pose problems for rights and freedoms in the world of work and commerce, but it is in the security and criminal justice sphere that the implications of this technology are most dangerous. The consequences for anyone being assessed as criminal on the basis of their face – arrest, imprisonment, the death penalty – are just unthinkable. But for now, at least, the industry continues to develop tools to read us. For example, one Israeli company claims: 'Faception offers a breakthrough computer-vision and machine learning technology that goes beyond biometrics. Our solution analyzes a person's facial image and automatically reveals his personality, enabling security companies/agencies to more efficiently detect, focus and apprehend potential terrorists or criminals before they have the opportunity to do harm.'[18]

It may seem trite to describe this technology as Orwellian, but it is certainly something that Orwell's Winston Smith would have recognised. In *Nineteen Eighty-Four*, he observed, 'It was terribly dangerous to let your thoughts wander when you were in a public place or within range of a telescreen. The smallest thing could give you away. A nervous tic, an unconscious look of anxiety, a habit of muttering to yourself – anything that carried with it the suggestion of abnormality, of having something to hide.' It was known as 'facecrime'. This is something that the Uighurs, subjected to China's biometric panopticon, are already terrifyingly familiar with, and it may soon be a threat to all of us.

In 2020, the pushback against the use of facial recognition more broadly came to a head as the protests following the murder of George Floyd in the United States spread across the world. Global companies like IBM, Microsoft and Amazon all announced an end to providing facial recognition technology to the police amid concerns about privacy, discrimination and racial bias. In the UK, the NGO Liberty successfully supported Ed Bridges in taking South Wales police to court over its pilot of facial recognition to compare faces in crowds against a 'watch list'. Mr Bridges' face had been scanned while he was Christmas shopping and while attending a peaceful anti-arms protest, though police accepted he was not a person of interest.[19] And in June 2020, research at Harrisburg University in the United States on the use of AI to predict criminality through facial recognition provoked the Coalition for Critical Technology to write a letter signed by over 1,700 academics criticising the research on both scientific and ethical grounds, resulting in the paper being rejected for publication by the academic publisher Springer.[20] The Coalition for Critical Technology has called on all publishers to refrain from publishing similar studies based on spurious science with potentially huge human rights implications.

But despite the pushback, this type of technology is still being developed and trialled across the world in a variety of settings, including situations where security measures are taken outside the strict confines of the criminal justice system. You may think this is not your problem, but the chances of you being subjected to this kind of technology as you go about your daily business are increasing as biometric surveillance technology spreads around the world. What if the AI perceives you as angry or shifty? Will you be arrested at the entrance to the polling station to prevent trouble? What if it gets you wrong?

There is growing research to show that AI makes a racially biased assessment of a person's emotional state based on photographs. This bias is not limited to problems identifying Black faces; the automated attempts to understand Black faces are even more sinister. In a recent paper,[21] researchers showed that AI was typically much more likely to infer 'anger' or 'contempt' from photographs of Black male basketball players than it was for white male basketball players when adjusted to reflect similar facial expressions. Even if their smiles were just as wide as those of their white counterparts, Black men's expressions were categorised as threatening no matter what. The reasons behind this were unclear, but what is clear is that the machine has learned how to denigrate and misinterpret the emotions and intentions of Black people as effectively as any racist cop. And the technology does it with a thin veneer of scientific credibility in exactly the same way that the physiognomists of the nineteenth and twentieth centuries dressed up their deadly prejudice.

The potential for discrimination in these systems is obvious, but arguments about addressing bias in the system miss the more profound problem with inferring criminality based on what someone looks like as opposed to what they do. Facial recognition technology employing emotional analysis or personality analysis undermines human dignity. The attempt to get behind the face we show to the world to criminalise and stigmatise some aspect of our inner lives is a clear step into the absolutely protected realm of freedom of thought. What is needed to address the problem is not better data to feed the machine learning beast; once again, we need clear red lines around the purposes for which AI can never be used. One such purpose is emotional analysis in the criminal justice system.

PreCrime

In Philip K. Dick's sci-fi novella *The Minority Report*, Police Chief John Anderton of the newly minted 'PreCrime Division' tries desperately to escape from a future in which he will commit murder. In Dick's world, a group of three 'Precogs' are capable of seeing into the future and predicting crimes before they happen. They are kept in a temple, from which footage of their visions is fed out to the PreCrime Division so that police officers can take action to prevent the predestined murders from happening. The use of this system wipes out murder from the streets, but its success and continuation depends on public belief in its infallibility. If the Precogs could be wrong, the whole system fails. Sometimes the Precogs disagree with each other, but to protect the integrity of the system, in these cases the 'Minority Report', or dissenting voice, is suppressed and erased from the record. To admit fallibility would be to lose the superhuman power to override justice.

We could not countenance people being locked up on a human hunch that they might be about to murder someone, but if algorithms flagged it up as a high possibility, we would be stupid not to, wouldn't we? While we may not have access to Precogs, the tools are being developed right now to establish our own versions of the PreCrime Division. 'Pre-crime' in the twenty-first century comes in two main forms. In its analogue manifestation, modern pre-crime shifts the law from criminalising behaviour to sanctioning ideas that may or may not lead to criminal behaviour in the future. This can be seen in many laws around the world relating to extremism suspected of being the first step on the path to terrorism. And in the digital sphere, predictive policing, or the use of algorithmic risk assessments in the criminal justice system, purports to give police and security agencies the infallible prescience of the Precogs, using data to identify circumstances or individuals likely to pose a risk of criminal activity. Both are a threat to our rights to freedom of thought, conscience, belief or opinion and both have a disproportionate impact on particular people or groups in our society.

The field of criminal justice has perhaps the most dramatic impact on individual rights of any of the areas covered in this book, but it is also the easiest thing for most people to ignore. If you think, or feel, that you are not the kind of person who would land up before a judge on criminal charges, you may not care too much about the rights of someone who does. But perhaps a more accurate analysis is that you are not the kind of person who is suspected of criminality; in other words, the police are not going to infer a criminal mind from the way you look, where you live or who you know. You are beyond suspicion. In a country like the United States, where police carry guns and the death penalty is still in force, the perception of innate criminality is literally a matter of life and death. And if you are perceived as the 'wrong' kind of person, there is little you can do to avoid it. In one particularly horrific example, Rayshard Brooks, murdered by police in Atlanta in June 2020 in his car, was actually asleep when he was approached by the police officers who went on to kill him. But still he was perceived as a criminal threat.[22]

Bias in policing is not new, but in criminal justice systems around the world, the slide into 'pre-crime' and predictive policing that uses data and artificial intelligence to identify risk as the basis for arrest and prosecution is gathering momentum, propelled by technologists' claims that they can see inside our souls to understand who will commit crimes before they even happen. And the result is not less bias, but automated bias served cold at scale.

In Los Angeles, a community activist group, Stop LAPD Spying Coalition, is making strides to challenge the tidal wave of surveillance in policing and the inevitable discriminatory impact it has on the ground. The police in LA have been using two different types of predictive policing. The first, known as Operation Laser, was person-based predictive policing where individuals were subjected to a risk assessment based on past interactions with the police and criminal justice system to decide whether or not they should be targeted as at high risk of recidivism. These risk assessments led to 'chronic offenders' being included on lists kept in patrol vehicles, and an array of intrusive surveillance techniques like CCTV, IMSI-catchers that intercept mobile phone traffic and track mobile location data and other measures being deployed so that individuals could be targeted and stopped on the street.

The second type, known as PredPol, was location-based, identifying hotspots for intensive policing. If you lived in an area designated a problem area, you were likely to be stopped and frisked, and each time this happened, your risk assessment score rose. Minority groups living in deprived areas were stuck in a vicious cycle where every interaction with the police set off the next. The Stop LAPD Spying Coalition won a lawsuit against the police, who had refused to share the details of their predictive policing records. What they found when the details were finally revealed was a list of 679 individuals, 90–95 per cent of them young Black or brown people.

In an interview with *MIT Technology Review* in June 2020,[23] the founder of the Coalition, Hamid Khan, explained how surveillance and information gathering are used as tools of social control over minority and marginalised groups in society. Describing the organisation's aims, he said: 'one of our last guiding values is that our fight is rooted in human rights. We are fiercely an abolitionist group, so our goal is to dismantle the system. We don't engage in reformist work. We also consider any policy development around transparency, accountability, and oversight a template for mission creep. Any time surveillance gets legitimized, then it is open to be expanded over time.'[24] In a testament to the power of their abolitionist work, Operation Laser was dismantled in April 2019, and the end of PredPol in LA was announced in April 2020.

The approach taken by the Stop LAPD Spying Coalition is an important one. They want predictive policing to stop because it is inherently wrong. And there are other signs of progress. In June 2020, Santa Cruz became the first US city to bring in a ban on predictive policing and facial recognition technology, and others are following suit. But for every step forward, another threat looms. Predictive policing continues to grow in many other US states and countries around the world. And similar techniques are used to decide sentences, parole and prison conditions for millions of people in the criminal justice system based on automated risk assessments drawn from an unfathomable mass of data to grade their mindsets.[25] The key difference between the rise of surveillance in the West and the horrific, all-encompassing surveillance state in Xinjiang province in China is that, in the West, we can still use the law and activism to challenge it.

For many, pre-crime has been a de facto reality for years, with racial profiling and other forms of systemic discrimination rife in our criminal justice systems. The 2017 Lammy Review[26] of racism in the British criminal justice system was a depressing confirmation that, if anything, things have become worse since my time as a criminal barrister in the late 1990s, when the Stephen Lawrence inquiry report[27] was published, highlighting the very serious problem of systemic racism in British criminal justice. Even then, without the help of algorithms, I saw pre-crime effectively in action in our courts. It is clear, if you spend any time at all in the criminal justice system, that there is an assumption that for some parts of society, it is a question of when, not if, you will commit an offence. In one British city, Bristol, Black people were eight times as likely to have been fined for breaching the coronavirus lockdown regulations than white people.[28]

The numbers of people fined, arrested, stopped and searched are the basis for the data that drives machine learning in criminal justice. You are more likely to be a suspect if more people who look like you have been treated as a suspect in the past. Living in an area identified as a high-risk area for crime might mean more police on the street, more stop-and-search and more arrests than a neighbouring area. It is impossible to unpick whether more police leads to more arrests or whether there are more arrests because there is more crime. But if you are a member of a group that is disproportionately targeted by the police, the algorithm, reading the history of bias in the data, will know you are a bad lot before you do anything.

Technology, like expert witnesses, holds a particular weight in justice's scales. We find it hard to see beyond its authority. In one of my last criminal cases, I was instructed to prosecute a young Asian boy accused of armed robbery. The main evidence against him was CCTV footage that showed a boy, probably Asian, about his age and size, wearing a black Puffa jacket and an Arsenal hat. The footage was grainy and unclear, and it was difficult to really see the face clearly enough for a positive ID. So an expert report had been obtained from a 'fashion expert' to say that this combination of clothes, similar to items found at the accused's home, was distinctive. You only had to step outside the court to see that a black Puffa jacket and an Arsenal hat on a teenage boy in London in the 1990s were not distinguishing features. I did not use the report as evidence, as I felt it was unconscionable to produce expert evidence that so clearly defied common sense. The boy was acquitted. But perhaps with the expert evidence the jury might have convicted him. And if expert evidence is presented as being produced by AI, the chances of conviction are even higher.

Technology is often touted as a means of getting rid of human bias and discrimination. But in reality, it just exacerbates it. AI learns from the data. And the data are already irretrievably tarnished before being fed into the machine and amplified. All the AI can do is vomit out prejudiced predictions based on infected information from a sick system. And this type of predictive criminal risk assessment is being used across the world to judge people's inner worlds based on aggregate assessments of the kind of person they are deemed to be. This kind of actuarial risk assessment provides an automated profile of the chances that 'someone like you' would be dangerous to society. But there is no chance to prove that you as an individual will not turn out to be a threat, or to identify opportunities for rehabilitation. Human psychological risk assessments offer a path to personalised risk management; if certain elements of your circumstances increase your risk, they can be addressed. For example, where homelessness is a risk factor, this can be mitigated by organising appropriate housing. But automated actuarial risk assessments condemn people to a life under a suspicion that can never be cast off.

'Pre-crime' is sadly booming. Constant surveillance both online and on streets around the world feeds into an array of algorithms.

The privacy and AI ethics industries have normalised an approach whereby tweaking the algorithm or putting in place an oversight body will cure all problems. But in cases where, essentially, technology is being used to infer a criminal mind before any crime has been committed and to penalise individuals on the basis of what they might be thinking of doing in the future, the concept itself is simply not compatible with human rights and freedom of thought. Predictive policing and morally invasive techniques that claim to be able to get inside our heads are a basic threat to our dignity. There is a very real and pressing need to draw red lines around the kind of tactics and techniques that must never be allowed. We need to consign facecrime, PreCrime and thoughtcrime to the realms of dystopian fiction for good.

CHAPTER 11

———

BODY AND SOUL

As a child, I absolutely hated sports. In summer I dreaded the humiliation of missing every single ball that was sent my way on the tennis court or the rounders pitch, and in winter the trauma of the cross-country run, trudging in incessant loops around a muddy pathway at the back of my windswept school, chilled me to the bone – partly because I usually contrived to miss a couple of circuits by crouching down behind a wall and waiting until the sportier girls came round again. I would do anything I could to get out of PE class. In primary school I feigned hay fever to try to dodge sports day, but my teacher wasn't convinced, even without a lie detector. For most of my teenage years I suffered from a very particular, medically verified knee problem that gave me a free pass out of sports during the week but allowed me to dance all night on a Saturday in heels. Thankfully, I didn't have a Fitbit or a smartwatch or even a phone to give away the guilty secret of my duplicitous step count.

We wear health trackers to help us keep up our daily step count, but what do our steps say about who we are, and how could they be used against us? Maybe in some not-so-distant future, that jog you failed to take will be used to decide whether you are worthy of life-saving healthcare[1] – you clearly don't have the right temperament to merit the costs. Perhaps your heart will murmur to your Fitbit that you should not be eligible for health insurance as you seem to hang around your local McDonald's quite a lot,[2] or your tracker implant will tell your employer you're lazy and you spend too much time in the toilets.[3] Your physical reactions can tell a lot about your mental state – this was the observation that inspired Elizabeth Marston to develop her lie detector test.

Once you have recorded and shared your data, you can't take it back. But millions of people have health wearables and health-related apps, and by wearing them and using them they are constantly and relentlessly giving away information about what they do, how they behave and, crucially, how they think and feel. We have the right to reveal what we think: we do it every day when we open our mouths to speak. But can we really ever be said to be consenting to the wholesale harvesting of our thoughts and emotions if we don't understand what that means and how it works? And what happens when it becomes not a matter of high-end consumer choice, but a compulsory part of the state public health apparatus?

Step by step

Where you are and who you are with can give a crucial insight into what you think. Winston Smith in Orwell's *Nineteen Eighty-Four* remarked that there was 'no rule against walking home by an unusual route: but it was enough to draw attention to you if the Thought Police heard about it'. When Colombia launched its coronavirus tracing app, it asked people to include their personal details as well as information on any mass events they had attended in the previous eight days. Against the backdrop of anti-government protests, it was not only privacy at stake; this information could give a very strong clue as to an individual's opinion of the government.[4] The places you go, the people you meet, the way you travel all provide a detailed picture of who you are, and how and what you think. Access to this data gives access to you, and your mind, in real time.

'Track and trace' apps were at the epicentre of the technological promise to save us from eternal lockdown as the pandemic hit, and they were also one of the fault lines of the constant public debates that pitted privacy against liberty. But the challenges of track and trace are not new – they highlighted a fundamental problem with many health-related apps we walk around with every day. Counting our steps, our heart rate and our movements can reveal much more about us than our health status or geographical location. In 2020, Amazon announced Halo, a new generation of fitness tracker that will not only tell you how many steps you take, but will also track your mood.[5] The band is discreet, but its always-on microphones may be less so as they take read-outs of your speech and tone to assess how you are feeling. For now, at least, Amazon says the recordings will never be uploaded to the cloud, and the analysis takes place on the device so no one else can hear what you are saying. But the step from fitness tracker to mood tracker is an ominous one and may be a sign of what is to come if we do not take steps to limit the ways technology can be used to read our emotions.

Pretty much every part of our lives can be monitored, measured and optimised. Sleep trackers and smart mattresses can measure how sweetly we dream. And you can even connect your sexual experience to an app through a smart vibrator or smart diaphragm. You may want your partner to infer how intense your orgasm was, but do you really want them to be able to verify that with an app? And do you want the guy at We-Vibe to know how often and how hard you come? At the DEF CON hackers' conference in 2016,

New Zealand-based hackers Goldfisk and Follower showed how the smart vibrator We-Vibe 4 Plus not only collected information about a user's temperature and the intensity of their sexual pleasure; it transmitted that information to the manufacturers in real time.[6] They could almost be in the room with you. Surely the intensity of your sexual experience is as intimate a part of your inner life as you can get. Measuring sexual response does not only give a physical read-out; it may also be an indicator of your emotional state. And what does the constant measurement of your sexual experience do for the way you think and feel about sex, or the way others feel or make you feel about you? For women, it's not only their sexual experience that is monitored and quantified; the whole experience of womanhood is under scrutiny and a monthly bleed is a sure sign that women need fixing.

Bleeding data

I remember one morning when I was about 15 making my way downstairs bleary-eyed for a late breakfast, my head aching from the new dental braces that had been fitted in a vain attempt to perfect my smile, the drama of adolescence weighing heavily on my gawky shoulders. As I slumped down in a chair, my mother looked up from the crossword and laughed, 'Oh dear, you're looking a bit spotty! Have you got the curse?' All I could do was cry. Her insight was spot on, her diplomatic handling of her daughter's fragile emotions less so. For many women, their hormonal cycles and the changes they experience throughout their lives have both a physical and an emotional impact. And they also feel the hormonal changes in their bodies in the way society treats them. Fertility is both feared and revered. In the blink of an eye, we move from people asking, 'You're not pregnant, are you?' to 'Why aren't you pregnant?' Menstruation is a curse, pregnancy a blessing, and the menopause a terrifying turbulence after which you can just pull up a rocking chair and knit your way to oblivion. And it's not just about our bodies; it's also about our minds. PMS, baby brain, brain fog, mood swings – if you are a girl or a woman who has ever tried to find out what to expect from any phase of your life, these terms will be familiar even if you have never actually experienced them.

We may have moved on a bit since Henry VIII founded a whole new church so he could marry another woman who might give him a son. And in the West, at least, we generally don't shut women away during their periods because they are 'unclean' or lock them up for being 'hysterical'. But women are still very much defined, dismissed and controlled on the basis of their fertility, their hormonal balance and what that might say about their minds. And women's cycles have been monitored, interpreted and judged for millennia by women themselves and by society at large. The arrival of disposable tampons and other menstrual products in the twentieth century marked a new dawn in the potential for monetising menstruation. But in the twenty-first century, the data economy has opened up a whole other way of cashing in on women's bodies, and also their minds.

When I worked in Silver Moon women's bookshop in the late 1990s, one of the first things I was asked for by a customer was a menstrual calendar. It wasn't something I had ever heard of before, but sure enough, there on the shelves packed with information for and evidence of women's empowerment, I found what they were looking for. A menstrual calendar is designed to let women monitor and understand their own cycles, with all the physical, psychological and emotional shifts and pains that go with them. Owning your own cycle might allow you to manage, if not escape, the curse. Similarly, around that time, fertility monitoring devices like Persona allowed women to check their hormone levels regularly by peeing on a stick that was then read by a portable device to build up a personalised picture of their fertility cycle, identifying ovulation and days when they were more or less likely to get pregnant. However fallible it may have been as a contraceptive method, Persona and similar tools did give women greater insights into their own fertility, at least in principle, to help them make decisions about their lives. It can be useful to understand your cycle whether you are trying to conceive or trying to avoid getting pregnant or not interested in either. And the beauty of both the menstrual calendar and the fertility devices of that time was that they provided insights to the women who wanted them, and only to them. Persona did not broadcast your ovulation day to the neighbourhood, and your menstrual calendar need only be public if you nail it to the door while hanging out the red flags. But if you have a modern 'menstruapp' on your phone, you should assume that the workings of your private parts and all the emotions that may flow from that are anything but private.

In their report *MENSTRUAPPS – How to turn your period into money (for others)*,[7] researchers for the Brazilian digital rights campaign group Coding Rights explained: 'Monitoring your cycle using a menstruapp means telling the app regularly if you went out, drank, smoked, took medication, got horny, had sex, had an orgasm and in what position, what your poop looked like, if you slept well, if your skin is clear, how you feel, and if your vaginal discharge is green, has a strong odor or looks like cottage cheese.' Researchers from Columbia University[8] have estimated that this kind of app is the fourth most popular health app for adults and the second most popular for adolescent girls. Information on women's sex lives, fertility and feelings is very big business.

And just imagine the insights you could glean if you knew not just about the women in your life, but when 150 million women worldwide were feeling grumpy or horny. That is the number of users the Flo app claims to have, and that is just one of hundreds of similar apps, some of which play fast and loose with their users' intimate data. Take Glow, for example, whose marketing strategy is so closely tied to women's fertility goals that it launched with the offer to pay for fertility treatment if you are not pregnant within 10 months of starting on the paid version of the app.[9] While helping you to conceive, they are sharing your data with their partners, including intimate information for targeted advertising so that other companies know who you are and how you're feeling. And your data is so valuable for them, it is not even deleted when you delete the app.[10]

Not only does Glow share information about your monthly highs and lows with strangers, Consumer Reports identified a shocking security breach at the company in 2016 that would allow anyone with your email address to access your data and private conversations. The kind of information you might share with an app like Glow could be very dangerous in the wrong hands. Consumer Reports highlighted information like a history of abortions and low sex drive, which would have been available to stalkers or online bullies without any need for hacking experience. There could be many reasons that you might not want to share this kind of information even with your intimate partner. Following an investigation as a result of this revelation, Glow Inc. reached a settlement with the state of California in 2020, including a $250,000 fine and provisions to improve the privacy and security of their users.[11] Such a fine may be a big deal for you or me, but for a company with the kind of commercial potential that Glow has, it is probably not enough. The fine may have been to do with privacy and security, but the kind of information you could glean from Glow would give you insights into the thoughts and feelings of millions of women. And it could give anyone the keys to individual women's mental and emotional lives that could feed into coercive control offline in the real world too.

But it is not inevitable. Shoshana Zuboff has described how the connected nature of the 'Internet of Things' and the 'smart home' arose out of a design decision. The technology could have been developed as a closed loop. And as a result of Privacy International's campaigning work on menstruapps, four out of the six apps they reported on in 2019 changed their policies on data sharing or launched internal investigations,[12] a clear indication that the models they had used are not the only way they can work. The sharing of our data that reveals our emotional or psychological states could be ring-fenced for our use only, to be shared only with the professionals and people that we need and want it to be. But the closed-loop model is not profitable for the data economy.

And it doesn't stop with your periods. Now that I am heading into my fifties, I am bombarded with information about how I must be turning into an erratic hag suffering from hot flushes, rage, brain fog and insomnia. There are, of course, apps for that too. And according to Facebook, a weighted blanket and a pair of temperature-regulating silk pyjamas are just what I need to face my future in peace. Women are constantly bombarded with messages about how they should look and feel, on the television, in magazines, on billboards, but the 'quantified self' movement and the rise of the 'fitness influencer' powered by personalisation algorithms takes it to new, more dangerous heights.

Your intimate information serves not only to know what you think and where you're at in your life, it can also be used to mould how you think and, in turn, how society thinks about you. Menstruapps don't stop at recording how you are feeling. They also help you to compare yourself against the norm, nudging you towards optimisation or conformity. Glow provides helpful hints for women using the app. A screenshot of the app from the Coding Rights *MENSTRUAPPS* report includes the following insight: 'At age 29 you are part of the overwhelming majority of women having children. One study suggests that the optimum childbearing age of women is late 20s and early 30s. Findings indicate that waiting until this age is associated with greater social advantages and better health outcomes for the mother and infant.' It is no great surprise that the Glow app was founded by 'two male tech entrepreneurs [who] want to help women get pregnant'.[13] But perhaps women don't want, or need, to be told what they should want and when they should want it.

I remember very clearly being 29, in the smoggy heat of Mexico City, looking at myself in the fogged-up bathroom mirror in a moment of panic when my period was late and thinking, 'I just cannot be a mother, no matter what.' Thinking that thought as a married woman in a country where abortion is illegal was bad enough. But thankfully there was no smartphone app back then to reinforce the guilt and push the heteronormative stereotypes of the patriarchy any further down my throat. Women are already bombarded with pressures about how they should be thinking and feeling and what they should be doing with their bodies when, and with whom. When my daughter arrived 10 years later, I was absolutely delighted to be a mother, but equally relieved that I had not gone through the physically and mentally life-changing experience of pregnancy and motherhood when I was 29. This kind of nudging not only affects us as individuals; it affects our whole society, the way it is formed and the place of women and children in the world.

Women's minds are there for moulding, no matter what life stage they are at. Facebook may be a good place to sell stuff to menopausal women, but if you want to reach the younger generation, platforms like Instagram or TikTok are a better bet. Instagram, with its eternal feeds of beautifully filtered bodies, has long been criticised for its impact on young women and teenagers' mental health, but researchers complained that, without the data from Facebook, which owns the platform, they couldn't really assess the extent of the problem.[14] But in 2021, *The Wall Street Journal* reported[15] that internal documents from Facebook showed that the tech giant's own research painted a worrying picture of Instagram's impact on teen girls' mental health. According to the report, in a 2020 internal slide presentation, researchers said: 'Thirty-two per cent of teen girls said that when they felt bad about their bodies, Instagram made them feel worse.' Other slides noted: 'Teens blame Instagram for increases in the rate of anxiety and depression', and 'This reaction was unprompted and consistent across all groups.' *The Wall Street Journal* reports that the features at the heart of Instagram's model and the personalised curation of content are a fundamental part of the problem, with teenagers effectively hooked on the platform being taken on a voyage to increasingly harmful content that can trigger eating disorders, unhealthy body image and depression.

Your soul for sale

The coronavirus pandemic was a salutary reminder of what we cannot entirely control and also what matters most to us – without good health, at both the personal and the public level, we are lost.

And psychiatrists have warned that it is not only our physical health that is affected; we are also facing a mental health crisis like nothing we have seen since the Second World War.[16]

In 2020, as we all found ourselves stranded at home with our demons – anxiety, financial pressure and the absence or constant presence of other people, whether physical or virtual – it seemed that the only way to find help was through our screens. But there are serious risks associated with dealing with our mental health online, as Privacy International highlighted in their 2019 report *Your Mental Health for Sale*.[17] The report showed that the most popular mental health websites in France, Germany and the UK were all collecting and selling on information about visitors searching for resources on depression. While the report focused on a handful of European countries, some of the companies involved are international, and there is no reason to assume that things are any different elsewhere in the world, where data protection is less regulated. They were not only obviously commercial websites either. In the UK they included National Health Service websites[18] and mental health charities, as well as private companies like the Priory. In a follow-up report in early 2020, many of the websites they reported on were still doing it, although the NHS had stopped, and the charity Mind had removed marketing trackers from their site while they reviewed their practices in light of the report. The fact that you, unique identifier number XXX-XXX-XXX, wanted to find out more about depression at 10.45 p.m. on a Monday was for sale on the open data market. They might not know your real-life name, but your unique identifier is as much you as your name or date of birth – it is the key to your mind in the digital world, a label for your online life that can be used to profile and target you.

In some cases, the websites were not only sharing the fact that someone was looking at information about depression; they were even sharing the answers to self-assessment questionnaires. You might want to find out if you could be clinically depressed, but there are plenty of other people who are interested in that information too, not because they care about you, but because of the economic value of real-time access to your state of mind. That online gambling advert full of slim, happy people might look that much more appealing when you are feeling a bit down. Or maybe a bit of porn to fill, or deepen, the void? Human suffering has a price tag attached in the real-time bidding markets of ad tech, and when you are suffering through a connected device, your pain is readily packaged and sold.

The companies who buy your data don't necessarily want to sell you something. A darkened window onto a tortured soul could equally serve to write you off. In the cesspool of big data, you would never know if it was that moment of despair that loaded the dice of life against you so that your loan was turned down or you never got that job. With a black box algorithm, you may never know what data went into the decisions that shape your life, but if mental health data is out there in the global data ecosystem, there's no reason to assume it would not be included. Shouldn't we have the freedom to feel terrible every now and again and keep that inner truth to ourselves while putting a happy face on for the world? Or to look miserable without being told to cheer up because it might never happen? And when we reach out for medical help, we should be confident that, online as offline, our mental health will not be for sale.

While celebrities and politicians encourage us to talk about our mental health, they have done little to make sure that there is a safe space for opening up. That bereavement that hit you hard, those exams you were stressed about, that time your job was getting you down – we all have stressors in our lives and mostly we deal with them, with or without help, more or less effectively. But now, our moods and emotions, our psychological states, however fleeting, common or understandable, can be collected, collated and used against us to profile, target or exclude us in the shadow data economy. I may not mind Facebook trying to sell me a 'Mud Daddy' portable dog washer when I get back from a filthy walk with my black dog, but I don't expect a charity like Mind or a public institution like the NHS to be selling the details of my inner black dog when I reach out for help, or even just peer into their virtual window to see what is on offer on a dark February night.

In 2020, based on its investigation, Privacy International issued a formal complaint[19] to the French data protection authority, the CNIL, against Doctissimo, France's largest health website, highlighting the sale of personal information about psychological states to third parties, including marketing companies like Facebook and Google. If data processing breaches any of our human rights as set out in the European Union's Charter of Fundamental Rights, it will not be lawful. It is difficult to see how the sale of answers to questionnaires on mental illness for targeted advertising could ever meet the standard of free and informed consent required to comply with the rights to freedom of thought and mental integrity protected by the Charter.

Selling mental health data is like auctioning the keys to our minds, and in this case, without our informed consent. It is hawking stolen property when the property in question is human dignity. It cannot be cured by a bigger font on the 'I agree' button. Consent requires understanding and information. And consent requires choice. If even trusted public or charitable organisations are selling my mind, where can I go to get help and information to deal with my demons?

Selling this kind of information is effectively trafficking in mental states. And it puts public mental health at risk when, instead of opening up opportunities for people to get help to address their problems, it exploits and exacerbates them.

The tentacles of health tech are reaching ever further into our minds with the promise of a future human perfected by AI. We can be amplified and augmented, and our problems can be prevented before they become problematic. Health apps have been developed to identify changes in behaviour through your phone that might give early warning of a psychotic episode.[20] And researchers in Michigan are studying ways to use AI to spot early signs of Alzheimer's from conversations.[21] There may be situations where this is useful, but what are the consequences of an early warning of psychosis or dementia? Who is told? What do they do about it? What if the AI is wrong? Could the health app on your phone put you into preventative hospitalisation just in case? And how would you challenge it?

Sharing in some circumstances may help to improve the functionality of health apps, and there is no doubt that some forms of processing and analysing large amounts of health data can help to improve both public and personal health outcomes. But a free-for-all on information about our health and lifestyles is not good for any of us. The decisions about health data need to be made for the good of all, not just the bottom line of health tech companies. It is a choice; not only a personal choice but a policy choice, and one that will dictate our future societies, the human world that our children, if and when we decide to have them, will inhabit.

There are many ways that technology is being harnessed in mental health initiatives, but as Australian legal scholar Piers Gooding has warned, we need new governance models in this field in situations where there is no precedent. But while the scale of change is opaque, it is impossible to know how to give guidance as to 'how the technology should be permitted, how it can be used responsibly, or when it should be discouraged or even forbidden'.[22] We give away traces of our inner lives and the state of our minds already in the technology we wear, talk to and carry in our pockets in ways we don't understand, but what if there was an even more direct channel to read our minds? Luckily, there are some scientific developments that arrive with a fanfare that allows us to really take stock and ask: what could possibly go wrong?

Read my mind

The minds behind the health tech that will make us all better have ambitions way beyond the screens we stare at and the devices we carry around with us. Companies like Elon Musk's Neuralink[23] have their sights on direct access to our brains. Neuralink's technology is based on tiny threads being inserted into the brain to allow a seamless multi-channel interface between man and machine. Facebook also looked into developing brain–computer interfaces (BCIs).[24] But, perhaps recognising the dangers and resistance there could be to invasive mind control, they focused instead on developing non-invasive ways of mind-reading through augmented reality glasses that would pick up your neural activity without you ever having to express yourself out loud. And in 2021, they announced[25] that they were abandoning this line of research altogether. Maybe it was just a bridge too far.

Technology that gives direct access to our brains for mind-reading or manipulative marketing might not sound too appealing, but if you sell it as a useful health technology, what's not to love? Who would object to tech that could help understand and treat brain disorders, and wouldn't we all want to be the best we could possibly be? But who decides what our best selves should be?[26] And how do we meaningfully consent to direct access to our minds? This kind of product could be life-changing for someone with locked-in syndrome, but should it ever be allowed to be a commercial product? In 2020, Musk promised his technology would allow wearers to stream music directly into the brain. As social media commentators noted, he had just invented ears. He also claimed that Neuralink 'could help control hormone levels and use them to our advantage'. It would, he said, enhance our mental abilities and reasoning while helping to relieve anxiety.[27] I'm not sure how it would relieve anxiety; the very idea of it makes me anxious. If you have noticed how your anxiety levels are affected by scrolling through social media and maybe tripping over a tweet with an overinflated futuristic claim, just imagine if you could never, ever switch it off.

If your hormone levels can be used to alter your brain to your advantage, they may also be altered to the advantage of someone else if that was more profitable. You might have to upgrade your brain as often as your phone, those tricky built-in downgrades depleting your battery and clogging up your memory just that bit faster with each new model. What if you had to pay for the ad-free experience to switch off the compulsion to eat doughnuts? And if you couldn't pay, what health provider is going to help you deal with the consequences – they will know that you brought it upon yourself.

In Philip K. Dick's short story 'The Hood Maker', he takes us into a dystopian world where a small group of mutants known as 'teeps' have telepathic powers and can read minds. The only thing that can block them is a hood that renders the wearer's thoughts unreadable. The hood maker of the title is an unknown subversive. Attempting to hide your thoughts is a crime. If you have nothing to hide, you have nothing to fear. Trying to keep your life and your thoughts private becomes suspect.

Research on ways to access our minds directly, bypassing our faculties for communication, brings up profound questions about what our humanity really means. But the truth is that for big tech, humanity is a commodity and BCIs just offer a much quicker and ultimately more efficient way of mining it. When Facebook announced its research, it said it would only be able to read the thoughts we wanted it to, once we decided that we would like to share them. But that is a science fiction fantasy too far. If Alexa can't be trusted to wait for the call, how would Facebook know just when we are ready to share what is going on inside our skulls? And what happens when the technology is out there, complacently accepted as a handy part of everyday life, mandated by the state, and you decide you don't want it? Reading our brain waves, whether through invasive or non-invasive technology, is about as clear an example of an interference with our inner states as a Vulcan mind-meld.

If we allow the development of technology that gives direct access to the brain, your rights are at risk whether it is your brain being hacked or someone else's. The techno-optimist dream of a merger between humanity and technology is the end of freedom of thought as long as others control the technology as they do now. Just as we have extremely tight international and domestic legal controls on atomic energy, we need an urgent clampdown on research and development of technology that could be as devastating for our humanity as the nuclear bomb. It is not only the threat of a functioning direct interface between our brains and computers that is concerning; developments in neuroscience more broadly, like those we have seen in the context of politics and criminal justice, raise new and difficult questions that go beyond the traditional discourse of privacy. And when we are talking about physical access to our minds through our brains, the threat to freedom of thought is no longer metaphysical; it is concrete and it is here now. As the German legal scholar Christoph Bublitz put it in a 2014 article calling for the 'renaissance of a forgotten right', 'in the age of neuroscientific insights and interventions into mind and brain that afford to alter thoughts, the time for the law to define freedom of thought in a way that lives up to its theoretical significance has come'.[28]

Mary Shelley's *Frankenstein* implores us, 'Learn from me, if not by my precepts, at least by my example, how dangerous is the acquirement of knowledge, and how much happier that man is who believes his native town to be his world, than he who aspires to become greater than his nature will allow.' Hers is a cautionary tale about unchecked scientific enquiry and its impact on humanity and dignity against the backdrop of the nineteenth-century Industrial Revolution. But while the language may be archaic, the lessons of *Frankenstein* have never been more relevant than they are today.

Recognising the risks of human enquiry, UNESCO, along with its advisory body, the World Commission on the Ethics of Scientific Knowledge and Technology, developed a working definition of the 'precautionary principle' that is found in many international legal instruments relating to scientific developments, including those that affect our health: 'When human activities may lead to morally unacceptable harm that is scientifically plausible but uncertain, actions shall be taken to avoid or diminish that harm.'[29] Morally unacceptable harm would be harm that is threatening to human life or health, serious and effectively irreversible, inequitable to present or future generations or imposed without adequate consideration of the human rights of those affected. By that definition, the development by private companies of technology that will give widespread access to our minds for profit so obviously risks morally unacceptable harm that it is astounding that governments have not yet taken action to avoid or diminish it. It should be clear that this technology may never be used for financial gain. This is not an issue that requires another ethical code or years of multi-stakeholder consultation. Was there ever a more serious and effectively irreversible threat to human autonomy than direct commercial access to our brains? It is not a covert threat. It is sitting in plain sight on a Twitter thread and a range of YouTube videos (in among the flat-earthers). If there is any truth whatsoever in the medical hype behind brain–computer interfaces, let's ban their use for financial gain and see how far the research goes on pure philanthropy. Europe acted quickly to ban subliminal advertising before it could ever be proved to work. Perhaps some people would have preferred to get their Coke adverts without noticing them, but the pernicious threat of mind manipulation was too grave to risk for someone to have a slightly better user experience at the cinema.

In terms of our rights and freedoms, it doesn't matter if it's snake oil or if it does what it says on the tin. If what it says on the tin destroys our humanity and dignity, we generally have laws to prevent that. And the reason we have not all been buying snake oil as a cure for coronavirus in mainstream online supermarkets is because snake oil sales crashed under effective regulation in the nineteenth century. As individuals, we cannot entirely avoid the ubiquity of surveillance capitalism in the digital world or unpick inflated scientific claims just to be sure, but we can use the law and demand regulation that goes beyond the cosmetic fringes and stops the harm at the heart of it.

Science and technology are a huge part of humanity's future. We all have loved ones we have lost against the hope of a medical breakthrough, and others we hold all the more tightly because their survival would not have been possible just months earlier. But when we listen to the promises of health tech, we need to listen very carefully to the subtext, to the words they are choosing not to say. Could you just pay your way to intelligence for you and your children, like the parents in Kazuo Ishiguro's 2021 dystopian novel *Klara and the Sun*? And if you did, what would that do to your children, or the children of those who can't afford it? If we care about our humanity and our future, we need to protect the integrity of our minds before it is too late. Our children's mental health and our freedom of thought depend on it.

CHAPTER 12

WE DON'T NEED NO
THOUGHT CONTROL ...

Schools form young minds, but educators also form their own opinions of the young minds in their care. In that liminal time after university when I didn't have any idea what to do or where to go, I found myself teaching English as a foreign language to a group of wide-eyed five-year-olds in Asturias, a region in the northwest of Spain I had never even heard of before I got a job there. It was a truly immersive experience for all of us, as I had absolutely no understanding of Spanish when I arrived. By the end of the first lesson, I had worked out that when a child looked nervous or pained and muttered something including the word *baño*, they probably needed to pee. And over the first term, despite the language barrier, I felt that I had grown to know something about their personalities just by observing them in class. There were some children I instinctively liked – the ones who smiled despite my dreadful teaching in particular – and others who always seemed to be complaining incomprehensibly, at whom I struggled not to roll my eyes. I knew it wasn't right, but I had a sudden realisation of the truth that every schoolchild suspects deep down – it's much easier for the teacher to like the pretty, happy children. In the absence of language or anything else to go on, I made inferences about the children's inner lives based exclusively on their appearance, the expressions on their little faces and the tone of their voices. It wouldn't really matter if what they were saying was right; if their voice was whiny, it must surely be wrong.

My teaching experience didn't last long – I was clearly not cut out for it. But I did try. In the run-up to Easter, I set the children a task to make seasonal drawings, which we could then label in English together. As the drawings started to land on my desk, I realised that I had got a lot more than I'd bargained for. Instead of the fluffy-bunny-and-chocolate-egg scenario from the British Easter experience I'd prepped for, these pictures were much, much darker. There was Christ bleeding on the cross or dragging the cross behind him on his stick-man shoulders; there were tears and blood and crowns of thorns; and even more disturbing, there were people in what looked like Ku Klux Klan hoods. 'How do you say *capucha* in English?' asked one earnest little girl, pointing at a hooded figure. 'We don't,' was all I could think to reply. The vocabulary of my concise Spanish–English dictionary did not stretch to Spanish Semana Santa celebrations. When I looked at the first picture, I thought the child must be disturbed, but by the time I had gone through 20, I realised that little lambs, daffodils and Easter bunnies were clearly just not Easter in Spain. Luckily for those children, my prejudice and lack of social context was a fleeting moment in their lives. But for many children today, the automated inferences made about their personalities, moods, prospects and predispositions are based on equally flawed analysis of their inner states, and such inferences can follow them throughout their lives, no matter how skewed they may be.

Mystery eyes

Around the world, the human fallibility of teachers is being replaced, or enhanced, as school surveillance systems are developed to address every possible concern we could have about our children, from academic performance to stranger danger to the risk of self-harm. We don't only want to make sure they are safe; we want to know they feel safe. And to do that, we need to read their minds.

In China, a trial of an intelligent classroom behaviour management system[1] uses facial-recognition CCTV installed in classrooms that scans students' behaviour and expressions every 30 seconds to assess their engagement levels and mood. It registers seven different expressions of emotion – neutral, happy, sad, scared, disappointed, angry and surprised – along with six types of behaviours.[2] Teachers say it drives improvement in their teaching methods, allowing them to adapt and engage better with students. And a student was quoted as saying, 'Previously when I had classes that I didn't like very much, I would be lazy and maybe take a nap on the desk or flick through other textbooks. But I don't dare be distracted since the cameras were installed in the classrooms. It's like a pair of mystery eyes are constantly watching me.' The headmaster of one of the schools in the trial noted that children who focus will be awarded an A, while those whose minds wander will get a B. It seems the student is right to be afraid.[3]

The intrusion into children's mental states in the classroom does not stop with CCTV. In a 2018 trial of technology developed by US company BrainCo in Chinese schools, headbands employing electroencephalography (EEG) sensors to scan students' brains were used on 10,000 students between the ages of 10 and 17 to assess their level of concentration.[4] Teachers were able to track individual concentration levels on an app, and in case that wasn't enough, lights flashing on the headband could alert teachers and shame students who were not focused enough. But the online backlash to the idea of concentration headbands in schools led to the trial being suspended.[5]

Some neuroscientists question the science and the effectiveness of the 'Focus 1' headbands, arguing that any improved results are likely a placebo effect. But from the perspective of children's rights to freedom of thought, that placebo, the chilling effect of feeling that your thoughts can be read, is as much of a problem as the brain scanning itself. Would Anne of Green Gables have spent so much creative time daydreaming as she stared out of the window at the cherry blossom if she had been wearing a brain scanner with a flashing light to tell her teacher when she was distracted? Can you imagine the stress of wondering whether your brain signals were providing enough evidence of concentration to avoid getting into trouble with the teacher? How could you know that your momentary sadness, surprise or distraction would not be used against you? How long until your mood in the classroom is fed into your grades and ultimately the social credit score[6] that will dictate your future life chances?

In the West, we often look at China with a sense of relief that this sort of thing could never happen here. But it is the economic freedom in our societies that allows a US company to develop technology designed to interfere directly with children's right to freedom of thought. Scanning children's brain signals at school must be one of the clearest and most disturbing examples of an attempt to access the inner thoughts of the most vulnerable in society by coercion. Flashing headbands may have been a bridge too far, but the technology for reading students' concentration continues to develop, and BrainCo is still in business, with its products available to buy for educational or stress reduction purposes.[7] And if you dress the justifications up in different clothes, prioritising safeguarding over social credit, we do allow the encroachment of constant surveillance into our children's lives though we may not see the flashing lights.[8]

We want our children to be safe at school. And our fears for the security of our little darlings have given rise to massive systems of surveillance, online and offline in schools around the world. In 2020, Russia announced a new video surveillance system linked to facial recognition capabilities that was to be rolled out in all its schools, reportedly to keep students safe by monitoring their movements and identifying interlopers.[9] In a country where there is no need for sugar-coating surveillance, the programme is called 'Orwell'.[10] But it's not only Russia that has dabbled in the use of facial recognition technology and artificial intelligence in the name of school security. Schools across the United States have explored similar options. New York state introduced the technology in 2018 to protect students from threats such as mass shootings, only to declare a two-year moratorium in 2020 when facial recognition technology came under scrutiny in the wake of the Black Lives Matter protests.[11] Schools in France and Sweden sought to introduce facial recognition technology to identify students coming into school, arguing that it would save time and increase security, but regulators found the systems to be unlawful and a breach of EU data protection law, as well as noting the impact on children's wider human rights and civil liberties.[12] In a series of similar findings against schools for breaches of communications security and collection of pupils' biometric data, European regulators have issued heavy fines while pointing out that the power imbalance between schools and pupils means that schools cannot rely on consent as a justification for the way they collect and use children's data.[13] Of course if you are channelling Orwell's Big Brother outside the reach of EU law, consent is not so much of an issue.

Facial recognition technology monitors our children's physical safety in the offline world, but it can easily be adapted to include AI that interprets their emotions. And their inner worlds are already under online surveillance in schools in the name of safeguarding. Tragic stories of teenage suicide linked to social media make the urge to find ways to protect our children from themselves and others seem ever more urgent. Schools have a duty to take care of their pupils, and in many countries that duty is a legal one. In the drive to deliver on their obligations to keep children safe, schools are understandably looking to AI and technological solutions to help them. And companies such as UK-based Smoothwall are happy to help. On its website, Smoothwall explains how its monitoring services work to safeguard and understand how our children are thinking and feeling. It details how it monitors children, picking up flagged words and phrases typed or viewed that might indicate a risk, even if they are subsequently deleted.[14] Wouldn't it be wonderful if we could pick up every sign of emotional trouble before it became a real problem?

Schools may have a duty of care to look after the welfare of their pupils. But round-the-clock monitoring of children's thinking about sometimes deep and difficult emotions before they can even decide to share their feelings with their friends or parents raises a whole other set of questions about their welfare that could have lasting consequences. The monitoring of even private, offline writing that companies like Smoothwall offer leaves children unable to effectively disown their transient inner thoughts. This is far beyond the kind of empathic intervention we might expect of a school noticing that a child was sad, worried or withdrawn and taking steps to ask what was wrong or offering a shoulder to cry on. If I had been asked to submit my teenage diaries for constant checking, I would have had to stop writing. The alternative would have been to stop feeling.

Campaigners like the UK-based organisation Defend Digital Me are concerned about the scale of online surveillance of children in the name of safeguarding, and the impact it could have on children's future chances.[15] The kind of concerns they are talking about include children being flagged as a suicide risk for looking up 'cliffs' on the internet, or as a potential gang member for searching for information about black rhinos. It is unclear what happens to this kind of information, or the flags, whether real or false positives, once a child leaves school, or how it could affect their future. A 'clean slate' approach would mean that all records collected about children's digital lives in school should be destroyed once they leave education and set out on their adult journey.

As a teenager, I focused on darkness. My clothes, lips and nails were all black and I mined the mobile library that passed through our village for books about obscure corners of the occult. I begged for my bedroom to be painted black, but somehow my mother persuaded me that a Laura Ashley plum and cream theme would serve the same purpose. It didn't. But the darkness still came out in paintings of rotting pigs' heads, sketches of the Kray twins and a passion for the poetry of Sylvia Plath. It wasn't all dark, of course. Like most teenagers, it was essentially all over the place, inexplicable and mainly documented in a carefully hidden diary that revealed how incoherent and rapidly changing my moods really were. By the time I left university, my half-empty glass was half full and I had ditched my black clothes for mostly red, which suits me much better. We all deserve a chance to leave our childhood behind us.

The data economy makes that hard to do, and the way in which schools use technology in education more broadly and their collaborations with private companies also raise serious concerns.[16] The wider impact of a childhood lived through constant surveillance is hard to divine. But the potential chilling effect on creativity and innovation is very real. Imagine the fear of being seen to step out of line, even in the privacy of your own teenage bedroom; the feeling that in a very real sense, your curious childhood questions or your rebellious and difficult adolescent thoughts are being policed as thoroughly as if you had spray-painted them onto the side of a bus shelter. Imagine if you could never, ever dance as though no one's watching.

In a 2021 ground-breaking statement on the ways the digital environment can be used to interfere with children's right to freedom of thought, the UN Committee on the Rights of the Child called on states:

> ... to introduce or update data protection regulation
> and design standards that identify, define and prohibit
> practices that manipulate or interfere with children's
> right to freedom of thought and belief in the digital
> environment, for example by emotional analytics or
> inference. Automated systems may be used to make
> inferences about a child's inner state. They should
> ensure that automated systems or information filtering
> systems are not used to affect or influence children's
> behaviour or emotions or to limit their opportunities or
> development.[17]

The collection, tracking and use of vast troves of data in educational settings interfere with children's rights to keep their thoughts private and free from manipulation. The data trail that children leave today may be used to create detailed avatars of their inner selves that could be used to penalise or manipulate them now and in the future. These 'data daemons' may eventually be fed into algorithms that shape their future access to credit, employment or justice, regardless of the way the child's mind develops and changes over time. Children should not be exposed to the risk that their turbulent inner lives will be used to curtail their chances in adulthood, and we need laws to make that happen.

Moulding minds

In Aldous Huxley's *Brave New World*, children's life chances and future status are dictated by careful control of their biological and educational environments, ensuring that rigid social classes will support community harmony and cohesion. It is a vision of a world without social mobility, where everyone knows their place and their happiness is guaranteed by hyper-sexuality, the pacifying drug soma, and lack of ambition. Children are encouraged to engage in sexual games because this is a way to infantilise and remove the emotional charge from sexual relationships in society at large. This is not the society I want my daughter to grow up in, but it bears some resemblance to the online world that children enter, where Instagram promotes posts that feature bare skin,[18] and a seven-year-old girl's avatar can be gang-raped in a virtual playground in Roblox.[19] I cannot shut her off from outside influence and I can already hear her pleas for TikTok like a loud and insistent preview of her teenage life. But if I want her to be safe there, I know that I will need to actively guide her to find her own opinions of the world in a space that is utterly unfamiliar to me. I may be hopelessly boring and uncool, but I still hope to help her nurture and appreciate her rights and freedoms so that the future will be a better place for all of us.

I was surprised when my daughter suggested fruit machines as a great way for me to earn money halfway through lockdown in 2020. When I asked her where she'd got the idea from, she showed me the adverts she was being bombarded with on a range of seemingly innocuous kids' apps she had downloaded from the Apple app store. Parental controls hadn't stopped the malicious beaming clown faces that popped up at every opportunity on her iPad. A complaint to the Advertising Standards Authority about two of them resulted in a response, six months later, that the gambling companies concerned had promised not to use those apps any more. So, nothing to see here, move on. Complaining made no practical difference, though adding an extra layer of content blockers onto my daughter's devices eventually solved the problem, at least for now. But the problem stretches way beyond my home.

A study from the UK's Gambling Commission in 2018 indicated that 450,000 children aged 11 to 16 in the UK bet regularly. It stated that 39 per cent of the 11–16-year-olds interviewed for the study had spent their own money on gambling over the previous year, and 14 per cent in the previous week.[20] And children's gambling doesn't come out of nowhere. In 2021, researchers from the universities of Plymouth and Wolverhampton established a clear link between online gaming phenomena such as 'loot boxes' and problem gambling.[21] As the Singaporean cyber-security minister put it, 'gaming and gambling is increasingly becoming blurred. What may appear benign today can quickly morph into something a lot more sinister tomorrow.'[22] Keeping our children's eyes fixed to screens is not just a distraction; it is a money-making design feature. In extreme cases, children have racked up thousands of dollars' worth of debt through unsupervised in-app purchases,[23] but all of our children's online games are making money for someone, even if they are paying with their behavioural data rather than with their parents' credit card. We don't need to stop our children from playing online, but we do need careful consideration of how we can make sure that their enjoyment is not being exploited in ways that may ultimately cause them harm.[24]

There is nothing wrong with taking advantage of the wonders of technology to broaden our children's experiences, but we need to be mindful of ends and means, recognising where the traps are and drawing clear lines around what is and what is not acceptable engagement with their minds. It is not just a question of content. The methods used to hook children can also have serious consequences for their freedom and autonomy later on. Technology's impact on children's minds is not only about the data they give up and the information they receive, but also about the psychological buttons that technology picks out and plays with to keep lucrative eyes stuck firmly to their screens.

Every parent knows about the stickiness of the ubiquitous screens and most of us have experienced the raw rage of a child when a blue-lit screen is prised from their hands. We are only just beginning to understand the impact technology has on our mental processes. But already, a clear picture is emerging of the ways in which our reliance on certain types of technology is rewiring our brains.[25] It is one of the reasons we find it so hard to leave our own devices alone, and it is not accidental. Every minute we spend on our shiny screens gives a more detailed picture of how we think and feel and another opportunity to change our thoughts and feelings. Those minutes are money for data harvesters, but what do they cost our children?

The child rights organisation 5Rights described the children's rights issues related to persuasive design in detail in its *Disrupted Childhood* report in 2018, including mental health and developmental impacts. They explain how, 'The culture of excessive sharing, fuelled by persuasive technologies, has resulted in an epidemic of self-doubt, anxiety, low self-esteem and correspondingly aggressive behaviour among the young',while the 'opportunity cost of attracting and keeping children online impacts on their creativity, autonomy, memory, sleep and education'.[26] And they cite academic studies, including a large-scale 2016 survey for *JAMA Pediatrics*, in which academics from King's College, London found that 'Bedtime use of media devices doubles risk of poor sleep in children.'[27] MIT professor Sherry Turkle has noted: 'the capacity for boredom is the single most important development of childhood. The capacity to self-soothe, go into your mind, go into your imagination. Children who are constantly being stimulated by a phone don't learn how to be alone, and if you don't teach a child how to be alone, they will always be lonely.'[28] And while Apple's CEO may extol the need for the 'freedom to be human', two of Apple's major shareholders wrote an open letter to the company in January 2018[29] raising their concerns about the impact of addiction caused by Apple's own persuasive design. Like the fairy-tale Pied Piper of Hamlin, there is no telling where persuasive design could ultimately lead our children.

Down the rabbit hole

The more intuitive the technology, the easier it is for even very small children to navigate their way into dangerous uncharted territory in the digital world. Voice-activated search makes it even easier. As *The Guardian* reported in 2018, any child with a few basic words can launch off on a journey that could take them through Peppa Pig's official online repertoire and into the darker creations of algorithmic content where Peppa drinks bleach and Mickey Mouse is left a blood-spattered corpse after a car accident.[30] Recommender algorithms take the choice of what's in good taste away from both parents and children. According to one report, Alexa decided that a toddler asking for the song 'Digger Digger' was looking for porn and helpfully provided a range of unprintable options.[31] But while that example was caught by parents and any damage limited, we should be really concerned about the cases that we don't hear about and the rise of sexualisation in all the media our children see around them. These are not isolated incidents.

Wired magazine, in a report on the range of bootleg kids' videos available to young children on YouTube, pointed to one example, 'Minnie Mouse Mommy Has Pregnancy Problem & Doctor Treats Episodes!', that had over three million views in one day. That scale of reach is not just a problem for individual children. It moulds our societies. Former YouTube engineer Guillaume Chaslot, who founded AlgoTransparency, a project exploring the impact of algorithms in directing what we see online, explained how recommendations are designed to optimise watch time, not quality. If your kids see something educational on YouTube, it is by coincidence, not design. Chaslot told *Wired*: 'Working at YouTube on recommendations, I felt I was the bad guy in *Pinocchio*: showing kids a colourful and fun world, but actually turning them into donkeys to maximise revenue.'[32]

Revenue is the driver for all our children's online experience, and that revenue mostly comes from digital surveillance that leads to both the recommended content and the advertising children are exposed to over the hours their eyes are glued to the screen. In 2019, YouTube and its parent company Google agreed to pay $170 million to settle allegations by the Federal Trade Commission and the New York attorney general that the YouTube video-sharing service illegally collected personal information from children without their parents' consent.[33] The complaint was about persistent identifiers (or cookies) that were used to track children across the internet. YouTube earned millions of dollars by using these cookies, to deliver targeted ads to viewers of children's channels, according to the complaint. A similar representative claim was brought in the UK by Duncan McCann, a digital rights activist and father of three, to try to stop YouTube tracking children in England and Wales. That claim may have been dropped, due to a technicality of English law, but McCann had his sights set on bigger goals. In a 2021 report for the New Economics Foundation, he called for an outright ban on surveillance advertising, not only for children, but for all of us. A couple of years ago, this might have seemed like a pipe dream, but the tide is turning and it is not only campaigners calling for change. In his 2022 State of the Union Address, US President Joe Biden declared 'It's time to strengthen privacy protections; ban targeted advertising to children; demand tech companies stop collecting personal data on our children.' And in Norway, in 2022, a government appointed committee recommended exploring a total ban on behavioural advertising. A ban on surveillance advertising would mark a fundamental change in our future relationship with technology and with advertising.

As children grow, their capacity for independent critical thought grows with them. But they cannot protect themselves from online risks if they are all around them, just as teaching them about road safety will not protect them if you leave them to play on the central reservation with a box of fireworks.

Making friends

The danger is not only in the screens. Toymakers have not been behind the curve in understanding the lucrative power of normalising children's private friendships with the connected world. My Friend Cayla™ was a talking doll whose bland blonde features provided the kind of deceptive innocent facade beloved of horror movies. Cayla was designed to befriend children and answer their questions by accessing the internet, like a humanoid version of Siri or Alexa intended to be cuddled to sleep. But in 2017, the Norwegian Consumer Council issued a report with several worrying findings about internet-enabled toys, including Cayla. Their list of concerns was every parent's nightmare. Cayla's poor security system meant that anyone could take control of the doll, listen and speak through her with a mobile phone without actually having to touch her. The terms and conditions seemed to sign away all control of personal data so that it could be used for targeted advertising and shared with limitless unidentified third parties. The secrets children told Cayla were automatically shared with a US-based company that specialised in speech recognition and analysis. And Cayla was pre-programmed with endorsements for products and movies thanks to the manufacturer's association with Disney.[34] Unsurprisingly, her favourite movie was *The Little Mermaid*

(Disney version), and in case you hadn't already heard it enough, her favourite song was 'Let It Go' from Disney's *Frozen*. She had an interest in princesses, and she came complete with a hairbrush and mirror. i-Que, on the other hand, was the robot Ken to Cayla's Barbie. He had more 'boyish' interests – he knew all about science. The pair may have looked friendly, but they were about as benign as *Frozen*'s dastardly Prince Hans of the Southern Isles.

Following the Norwegian Consumer Council report, a group of American organisations brought a complaint about My Friend Cayla to the Federal Trade Commission, focusing on the risks to children's data and the recording and sharing of their conversations.[35] And in Europe, the German Federal Network Agency took swift and radical action, ordering parents to destroy the dolls because it said Cayla was a concealed espionage device that was in breach of German telecommunications laws.[36] The German provision used to ban Cayla even meant fines of up to €25,000 for unwitting owners of the doll.[37] Cayla went from award-winning princess to prisoner in a few short years. She is no longer available to buy and now enjoys her own glass cell in the Spy Museum in Berlin.

Using criminal laws designed to combat espionage against a toy may seem heavy-handed. But imagine that Cayla was the man next door sitting in your child's bedroom, recording their conversations to share while using their dreams and fears to exploit them for money – would you not feel that was a matter for the police? The kind of security threats identified could well put children in danger of being targeted by criminals or unscrupulous businesses. But that aside, do you really want your child's sponge-like mind being filled with persuasive arguments for spending more money and staring at themselves in the mirror – all from a piece of plastic tat you bought online for £60?

Cayla may now be little more than a miniature fugitive from justice, but she is not the only anthropomorphic digital device wanting to befriend and mould our children. In 2020, Moxie the robot was launched on the world, billed as a 'revolution in child development'.[38] Originally designed as an educational support tool for children with autism to learn social, cognitive and emotional skills, Moxie's commercial potential was not lost on its creators as the pandemic lockdown left parents desperate for playmates for their traumatised and lonely children.[39] The CEO of Embodied, the company behind the robot, explained, 'We're at a tipping point in the way we will interact with technology. Moxie is a new type of robot that has the ability to understand and express emotions with emotive speech, believable facial expressions and body language, tapping into human psychology and neurology to create deeper bonds.'[40] The developers assured customers that they had fixed the security glitches of other internet-enabled toys like Cayla. There may be clinical settings where Moxie could be a useful aid to children struggling to engage with the world, and having spent lockdown with a tween, I can understand how it might be extremely appealing in a crisis. But do we really want our children to build deeper relationships with a robot than they do with their friends or family?

Moxie offers a chance to outsource our children's emotional development. You can get a read-out on your child's emotional and educational life as they evolve, with the loving help and support of an emotion-enabled robot that uses machine learning to read their expressions and moods. You need never worry about trying to understand your child's complex feelings or answer their difficult questions about life and humanity ever again. Moxie doesn't have the risk of bullying or low self-esteem that you get from social media, or even social life. Presumably it doesn't poo or chew your furniture like a pet might either.

Outsourcing the development of our children's emotional, cognitive and social capacity to a robot, however clever and empathetic, is a dangerous path to take if we believe in a future for human society. The idea of *ren* – that elusive Chinese philosophical concept that has been variously translated as 'conscience', 'humaneness' and 'love' – is one of the foundational qualities that is recognised in the Universal Declaration of Human Rights as making us human. It is the space in which our thoughts, feelings and opinions reach out across the void to understand and engage with others. If we delegate our empathy and love for our children to a robot, how will the next generation know what it means to be human?

Influencing people

In my house, like many others, lockdown forced us to confront our demons and accept compromises that in normal times would have been unthinkable. Like many other parents, understanding that my daughter needed to play with other kids, I cautiously let the online gaming platform Roblox into our lives. Roblox enjoyed a massive expansion in its user base during the pandemic as children who might have played together in their back yard reached out across the void to play in virtual spaces. Through months of isolation, the chance to meet friends across the street, and across borders, in a virtual playground was an absolute lifeline. Rocking the purple hair and cropped tops that they would never have been allowed in the real world, kids played together in the dizzying and sometimes terrifying landscapes of Royal High, Adopt Me, Piggy and Puppet, all with their own extremely irritating and endless soundtracks. Roblox was not only an opportunity for kids to play; it was also a chance for them to create, with endless games options designed by users, some of them children themselves, who made windfalls out of the sudden wave of interest. But boundless creativity can have a dark side.

As the *Sun* newspaper reported in 2018, the Lego-like avatars of Roblox had become a 'haven for Jihadi, Nazi and KKK role play featuring Twin Tower bombings and race-hate murders'.[41] Researchers from Tech Against Terrorism, an organisation that works with the UN to combat online extremism, have found that extremists use platforms like Roblox and Minecraft to recruit young children and teenagers. Users are invited to role-play infamous far-right atrocities like Anders Breivik's 2011 attack on the Norwegian island of Utøya; the 2019 mosque shootings in Christchurch, New Zealand; and the 2019 terrorist attack in El Paso, Texas. And the language of Roblox is used to lure children in through other platforms. For example, comprehensive bomb-making instructions were posted on the app Telegram to a youngster with the message: 'Hey kid, want to make a mailbox bomb for Roblox?' Adam Hadley, director of Tech Against Terrorism, has explained that 'far-right violent extremist and terrorist groups exploit youth culture, not only to evade content moderation, but also to radicalise young people themselves'.[42]

And children are being radicalised at an increasingly young age. In February 2021, the youngest person in the UK to have ever been convicted of a terrorist offence was sentenced. He was just 13 when he downloaded a bomb-making manual from the internet and subsequently became the UK leader of a banned neo-Nazi terrorist group that glorified racist mass murder. These are the extremes. But they show that online and offline we need to know who and what is influencing our children's world views. If we are reticent to let our children go out and play in the street unsupervised, we need to be equally engaged with where they are going and what they are doing through the screen in their bedrooms.

UNICEF's 2017 report on children in the digital world notes how parents in different countries, regions and socio-economic groups vary in their approaches to their children's screen time and online engagement.[43] Some put in place strict rules to restrict time on screens; others have a laissez-faire approach, leaving their children to explore the online world on their own; while some spend time with their children in their online universes, sharing their experiences and talking them through their alternative realities. In 2021, China announced new rules limiting children's access to online games to one hour on Fridays, weekends and public holidays.[44] No doubt the Chinese state will be firmer in policing screen-time limits than I am. But according to the UNICEF report, it is parents' positive engagement with a child's technological life that has the best impact. As child psychologist Sonia Livingstone has discovered, it is not the amount of time on screens that makes the biggest difference to a child's emotional state; it is the strength of their engagement with friends and family that really matters.[45] Just as there is no straightforward answer to parenting in the offline world, managing our children's mental development online is complex and personal. We need to be aware of the dangers, but we mustn't throw the baby out with the bathwater. It is not our children or our parenting skills that need fixing. It is the online environment.

The kids are alright

In the world of Philip Pullman's *His Dark Materials*, a child's daemon changes form as quickly as their mood. It is only with adulthood that the daemon, the animal incarnation of their soul, settles into a permanent form. The resonance of Pullman's imagery lies in the fact that we all recognise, from our own childhood experience and observation of the children around us, the changing daemons of childhood and the malleability of the child's spirit. And it is that fickleness that means our children's freedom of thought requires special protection, particularly in the world of 'surveillance capitalism', where it is 'human futures' that drive the data economy.

Children keep Alexa in their bedroom like a toy, every mistake they make recorded, transported to the cloud, collected and ready to be used and monetised when the time is right. When my daughter asked why she couldn't have an Alexa like her friends, I told her that it is because Alexa steals your dreams and sells them. She hasn't asked for Alexa again. It's important that we stop trying to sugar-coat the surveillance pill, pretending that we can control the data and keep ourselves safe online. The only way to really stop the listening is to get rid of the listening devices, or to take away their profitability.

The data daemons being built up of the inner lives of our children do not only depend on what children say to their devices. Their activity on social media, the swathes of metadata associated with photos and posts and subtle aspects of the way they express themselves reveal much more about their moods and thoughts than they, or we, realise. While they or their parents may have clicked a consent button, could there ever be real informed consent to the boundless consequences of this? We are yet to really understand and internalise the fact that every single engagement our children have in the connected online world is being used to monetise or restrict their futures, to capitalise on their hopes, dreams and deepest fears, and, ultimately, to buy or control their minds. Is this really something we are prepared to accept?

Our children's futures will be defined by their relationships with technology as much as their relationships with each other. For them, the digital world is not a new experience; it is their life, the world around them, part of the wallpaper. And children have a right to play. The UN Committee on the Rights of the Child observed:

> The digital environment promotes children's right to culture, leisure and play, which is essential for their well-being and development. Children of all ages reported that they experienced pleasure, interest and relaxation through engaging with a wide range of digital products and services of their choice, but that they were concerned that adults might not understand the importance of digital play and how it could be shared with friends.

Concerns about the impact of new technologies on children's health and well-being are nothing new. With the dawn of screens in cinemas in the early 1900s came the rising tide of adults' concerns about screen time.[46] And those same worries about the impact of television in my home meant I was one of the few children in my class who did not see J. R. Ewing being shot in 1980. But we need to learn to manage our own fears and to separate myth from reality in terms of the impact on children of their digital interactions. We cannot and should not want to keep our children away from the technology that will shape their world, but we must be able to understand and mitigate the risks they face.

We all want what's best for our own children, and we set digital and informational boundaries with their welfare in mind, as well as the peace and harmony of the household. But how our children grow into the digital world, the ethical codes they learn and the way they process their online experiences will ultimately have a much wider impact. In an interconnected world, we can't isolate our children – their future depends on the futures of all children, no matter how far they may be from our home. And we need to make the online space a safe space accessible to all so our children can go out and shape the world.

There are some things we can't stop completely – there will always be dangers in the world, both online and off. But we can teach our children to recognise the wolf, whether or not it is dressed up as Granny, and how to respond to it. And we can set the rules to improve our children's chances and the protection of their rights in the digital future.

Protecting our children's right to freedom of thought does not mean that a child's mind should be free from influence – that is impossible and undesirable. We are all affected by our surroundings, the things we read, the people we talk to, the world we see around us. Children are hungry for information and experiences to develop their full potential, and keen to reach out and connect with the society around them. And they also need guidance to navigate the world around them as their capacity to understand it evolves. They thrive with good influences. As our children's minds and emotions are increasingly exposed to and affected by technology, we need to ask if we are comfortable with the ways technology touches their minds and what the lasting impact of playing just one more game on the iPad might be. Our children should be able to embrace technology and we should be able to let them do it, confident that the online world gives them the space they need to play and grow in safety. For that to happen, we all need to demand change.

Part 3

THE POSSIBLE

CHAPTER 13

———

THE BACKLASH

We are going to emancipate ourselves from mental
slavery because whilst others might free the body,
none but ourselves can free the mind.

Marcus Garvey

When I was studying law in the late 1990s, it was a boom time
for the human rights movement. The Iron Curtain had fallen
after the blaze of fireworks I'd witnessed at the Berlin Wall in
1989, and former communist states embraced the European
ideals of human rights and democracy. In 1998, four years after
the horrific genocide in Rwanda, the world finally agreed to set
up the International Criminal Court, a permanent global court
to try those responsible for international crimes and the most
serious human rights violations. People who destroyed human
rights could no longer hide behind borders when they could not
or would not be held accountable at home. The Good Friday
Agreement brought an end to the worst violence in Northern
Ireland and set a path to peace based on respect for human rights.
And the UK Human Rights Act rode in on the wave of 'Cool

Britannia' as a new generation of human rights lawyers inspired Bridget Jones to fall for Mark Darcy. African states agreed to set up an African Court on Human and People's Rights that would be able to interpret what international human rights meant from an African perspective. And in December 2000, the European Union finally agreed its Charter of Fundamental Rights, codifying the way human rights in Europe had developed since the 1950s. The Charter included discrete rights to protection of personal data and to mental integrity, developing the concept of privacy and the protection of our inner lives for a new era.

The twenty-first century dawned with a sense of relief – we had survived the twentieth century with the horrors it had brought. Now it was time to lie back and enjoy a new dawn where we could all keep in touch with each other, no matter where we were, through the newly fledged wings of mobile phones, email and the World Wide Web. Europe would finally be reunited. It seemed that the world was healing and we were a long way from the shadows of fascism and the dark days that had inspired the drafters of the UDHR half a century earlier.

But then there was 9/11.

As the world watched in horror, the Big Apple was wounded and shrouded in dust. In cities around the world, workers huddled at screens as the second plane flew, incongruously and incomprehensibly, into the twin towers of the World Trade Center. We watched the smoke gushing out silently, the slow collapse, indecipherable figures flickering at windows, dots falling, the silence. Many of us had seen terrorist attacks before. For me, growing up in Britain and living in London and the Basque country in the early 1990s, it had always been there in the background: bomb scares, burning buses, sudden heavy police presences, the raw grief of public funerals, victims' lives gutted, devastated communities and miscarriages of justice. But this was something different: the scale, the audacity, the mind-bending horror of mass murder in the heart of Manhattan. It was not only the economic centre of the American dream that had been hit, but also the home of global diplomacy with the UN headquarters. Offices filtered out, people walked home; everyone wondered what would come next. Everything changed.

Hearts and minds

Suddenly we needed to understand the terrorist mind. How could anyone think themselves into a state where they would take their own life and thousands of others with them in the name of an ideology? What made them do it? How did they conceive of something so extreme it was beyond even the imagination of the most melodramatic disaster movie director? New York was just the beginning. Madrid, London, Bali, Paris, Barcelona, Kampala and so many other cities were devastated by the incomprehensible and deadly hatred that was spreading around the world. Somehow the vicious violence and depravity dressed up in the religious clothing of organisations like al-Qaeda and the Islamic State continued to have a magnetic pull on the minds of thousands of people. Something had to be done.

Abhorrent ideas do not deserve the oxygen of a public platform. The right to freedom of expression does not protect speech that destroys the rights of others. Limiting the spread of those ideas is key to protecting human rights more broadly, particularly where they are used to manipulate other minds. But we need to be very cautious about crossing the line between criminalising deeds, or even words, and criminalising thoughts. As states and international organisations have attempted to stop terrorism in its tracks, the policy debates have moved steadily backwards from the point of punishing terrorist attacks, to preventing terrorism, then to preventing the more nebulous idea of violent extremism, and finally to preventing extremist ideology, whatever and wherever that might be. If you step back from acts of violence or incitement to violence, the thing you are trying to prevent becomes a chimera. The shift from preventing terrorism to preventing 'extremist ideology' pulls the focus from preventing actions and behaviour to trying to prevent thoughts, beliefs and opinions.

The fight against global terrorism was not a battle for territory; it was a battle for 'hearts and minds'. And the search for signs of minds that needed changing, like the McCarthyite hunts for 'reds under the beds' that US legal scholar Zechariah Chafee experienced, left no stone unturned. In countries like the UK, spotting the first shoots of radicalisation became not only a job for security services and police; it pulled in teachers, doctors, anyone in a position of trust. This 'whole of society' approach to extremist thought has been heavily criticised. The UN Special Rapporteur on human rights while countering terrorism has pointed out that 'the perception that a government can authorize or control the way that individuals think or what they believe through targeted ideological or theological interventions or what authorized thoughts or beliefs are has no place in societies governed by the rule of law and respect for human dignity'.[1]

There is nothing wrong with engaging in an open battle of ideas – the whole point of freedom of opinion and expression is to inform, understand, influence and persuade through open, rational debate. Preventing the growth of hatred and violence in society is clearly a goal that is synonymous with protecting and promoting human rights for all, but the way this has developed since 2001 shows the grave danger of the Machiavellian approach of letting the ends justify the means.

There is intense academic debate about the predictive connection between radicalisation and terrorism, and there are serious concerns about the validity of risk assessment models that tell us whether people are disposed towards violent acts.[2] But the technological and political steamroller of the battle against extremism continues to drive the development of techniques to get inside the human mind and pick up the first sign of 'evil' thoughts before they can do any damage. Preventing terrorism has to be a good thing, but the techniques used to detect extremists or to de-radicalise them are not only used on potential terrorists; they can be harnessed by the terrorists themselves. And there are always opportunities for them to be used more broadly to make us all 'good' citizens or 'good' consumers, or simply to divide and rule in our own back yard and around the world.

Terrorism changes all of us and has always been used as an excuse for a clampdown on liberties and a justification for stripping away rights. As well as the drive to get inside the terrorist mind and change it, this trend in the security and counter-terrorism sphere has given a degree of licence to governments around the world to penalise people just for holding ideas, beliefs or ideologies that are disruptive of the status quo.[3] In China, the Muslim Uighur population has borne the brunt of this, being rounded up and forced into 're-education camps'. But it is happening everywhere and it is something we should all be worried about. By 2020, ill-defined ideas about preventing 'extremism' reached their inevitable conclusion when counter-terror police in the UK listed the environmental protest group Extinction Rebellion as an organisation promoting extremist ideology.[4] The desire to save the planet had become thoughtcrime. In our rush to stop bad people doing bad things, we must never forget that human rights are for all of us.

Monstering human rights[5]

If you are a good citizen, you may think you don't need human rights. Across the world, the media and politicians have spent the past two decades trivialising human rights with myths and scaremongering.[6] The International Criminal Court could undermine American sovereignty and due process,[7] an Australian Human Rights Act would let judges bully politicians into changing the law,[8] an 'illegal' immigrant has a right to family life because he has a cat so can't be deported,[9] the idea of voting rights for prisoners makes the UK prime minister feel 'physically sick'.[10] The pernicious idea that outsiders, criminals and misfits are the only people to benefit from human rights is corrosive and false. Migrants characterised as 'swarms'[11] lose their humanity so that keeping people out by building walls or keeping them on islands and floating detention centres has become so familiar we barely notice it at all.

Hyperbole, distortion, misinformation – these are the strategies that have been used to undermine support for human rights and to hijack the idea of freedom to justify destroying the rights of others. They are the same tools of radicalisation used by the extremist. An atmosphere where rights are seen as nothing more than a get-out-of-jail-free card for recalcitrant sinners has built up like a sudden sea fog around us. We can't see beyond our own ship. It is the kind of fog they call a 'haar' in Scotland, the kind that lends itself to myth-building and temporary blindness. As we have become oblivious to our need for human rights, they are slowly slipping away.

In the wake of 9/11, just as the terrorism was international and irrational, so was the backlash against human rights. And it was fuelled by other global factors too. A rise in populist politics drove countries in the West that were traditionally associated with the international defence of human rights into an inward-looking spiral of hatred and division. China consolidated its geopolitical power, giving financial support and infrastructure to developing countries around the world without the requirement of human rights that has traditionally been the price of development aid. At home, the Chinese state was left to develop its repressive technological capabilities almost entirely unchecked as it justified its crackdown on the Uighur minority as a counter-extremism effort, guaranteeing blind eyes around the world. And Russia has shown that borders are no object to the state intent on violating human rights, murdering opponents seeking sanctuary in countries like the UK without apparent fear of retribution.[12] In a speech in September 2016, the then UN High Commissioner for Human Rights, the Jordanian Zeid Ra'ad Al Hussein, made the direct link between fear, the appeal of the populist and the manipulative potential of new information delivery methods in the digital age:

> Populists use half-truths and oversimplification – the two scalpels of the arch propagandist, and here the internet and social media are a perfect rail for them, by reducing thought into the smallest packages: sound-bites; tweets. Paint half a picture in the mind of an anxious individual, exposed as they may be to economic hardship and through the media to the horrors of terrorism. Prop this picture up by some half-truth here and there and allow the natural prejudice

of people to fill in the rest. Add drama, emphasizing
it's all the fault of a clear-cut group, so the speakers
lobbing this verbal artillery, and their followers, can feel
somehow blameless.

The formula is therefore simple: make people,
already nervous, feel terrible, and then emphasize it's all
because of a group, lying within, foreign and menacing.
Then make your target audience feel good by offering
up what is a fantasy to them, but a horrendous injustice
to others. Inflame and quench, repeat many times over,
until anxiety has been hardened into hatred.[13]

After four years in office, taking on major powers like the United
States, China and Russia over their human rights records, Zeid
announced in December 2017 that he would not seek a second
term, because 'to do so, in the current geopolitical context, might
involve bending a knee in supplication'.[14]

How have we come to a place where even the UN, founded on
the principles of human rights, feels it is struggling to find support
for those very values? What is it that has shifted public opinion on
human rights globally to the point that politicians feel they can
openly deride and dismiss rights and still win elections in Western
liberal democracies? Are our democracies shifting to become simply
the tyranny of the masses? J. S. Mill said: 'Bad men need nothing
more to compass their ends, than that good men should look on
and do nothing.' But why are so many good people doing nothing
today? Are we afraid of the social media pile-on, or government
disapproval if we rise to defend human rights? Or are we too busy
scrolling, numbly, through post upon post of like-minded moaning
or therapeutic cat videos to notice or take a stand?

Hackable humans

Part of the problem is the way we see ourselves, driven by our new digital age. In the digital world, we are no longer the rational free humans who determine our own futures that Mill imagined. We are just consumers to be nudged and manipulated into doing the bidding of multinational corporations or governments seeking to influence their citizens. We are 'the product'.[15] Ideas of transhumanism that look to a future when humanity and technology may be fused together, and ethical debates about 'robot rights', take the focus away from the inherent dignity of the human being. When humanity is reduced to being just another machine, the logic of human rights is lost.

The Israeli historian Yuval Noah Harari, in his book *21 Lessons for the 21st Century*, warns of a near future when humans will be hackable. As he explained in an interview with Al Jazeera, 'When you combine our increasing understanding of biology, especially brain science, with the enormous computing power that machine learning and AI is giving us, what you get from that combination is the ability to hack humans, which means to predict their choices, to understand their feelings, to manipulate them and also to replace them. If you can hack something you can also replace it.'[16] The people selling technological products and services that claim to understand our minds and mould them might even believe that future is already here. The drive for technologists to get inside our minds is premised on the idea that by accessing our minds, our behaviour can be predicted, or changed. And the reason why so many are rushing to do this is the extremely lucrative market in what Shoshana Zuboff calls 'human futures', selling access to our future choices, decisions and life chances.

Two theories underpin these technological developments: determinism, 'the theory that all events, including moral choices, are completely determined by previously existing causes';[17] and behaviourism, 'the theory that human behaviour is based on conditioning (mental training and the influence of habit), rather than being explained by thoughts and feelings'.[18] In the twenty-first century, these two theories have taken on the mantle of science. But in previous generations, they propped up the work of the astrologer, the magician and the priest, who all pushed the idea that our futures were not in our own hands. Whether it is couched in terms of God's will or just science, determinism seals our fates and sets our future in stone. The determinist's argument reduces us to nothing more than complex machines, driven by code imprinted on a chunk of animated meat.

Hannah Arendt noted, 'the trouble with modern theories of behaviorism is not that they are wrong but that they could become true, that they actually are the best possible conceptualization of certain obvious trends in modern society. It is quite conceivable that the modern age – which began with such an unprecedented and promising outburst of human activity – may end in the deadliest, most sterile passivity history has ever known.'[19]

These theories may sound appealing if you like science fiction, or if you are in the AI business. But they fail to take on the human part in the deterministic equation. In a series of studies,[20] psychologists in the United States have demonstrated that when people lose their belief in free will, their work and academic performance drops, and they have a lower sense of life's meaningfulness and a greater tendency to stress and anxiety. It seems that whether or not we have free will as a scientific fact, a belief in free will helps us as individuals and societies because it saves us from the apathy of fatalism, imbues us with agency and empathy and generally makes us nicer and more productive. In the same way that in previous centuries questioning God was a sign of madness and a threat to the status quo, questioning science can be hard to do. If scientists say we have no free will, surely they must be right? But scientific knowledge, like humanity and human rights law, evolves. And the suggestion that science has proven that free will is a myth is itself in serious scientific doubt. Recent neuroscientific research seems to indicate that human fallibility may have skewed the interpretation of scientific fact. There is hope for free will after all.[21]

The freedom to choose is not only an esoteric idea; it is a practical prerequisite for peaceful co-existence, happiness and human development. We are hard-wired for freedom because freedom is what makes us human, in our selves and in our connections with each other. And it is not just a philosophical nicety; it is a natural right and one that is so important to our humanity that it is protected in the strongest terms in international law. International human rights law was born as a defence to the risks associated with unchecked determinism dressed up in the spurious science of eugenics in the 1930s. If humanity is 'hackable', as Yuval Noah Harari claims,[22] human rights law gives us the framework to protect us from the hackers. It has no substitute and we urgently need to recognise its crucial relevance.

Changing the language

As a teenager, I always seemed to be talking the wrong way. As I moved from the Isle of Man to southern England and then up to Edinburgh, my accent and the words I used always marked me out as the wrong kind of person. But in my third year, I escaped the

English language for a year in France. In French, the world finally worked for me and I felt free. Nobody tried to guess what school I'd gone to or who my parents might be, to decide how I must think. I made friends who really had run away with the circus, learned to be creative in the kitchen, and fell in love with someone good who loved me back, at least for a while. Changing the language shifts your perspective, and that changes everything.

In the twenty-first century, it is the language of ethics rather than human rights that is being used to describe the landscape and define the boundaries of acceptability in the technology sphere. There are a plethora of regional and international ethical frameworks blossoming around the world. The digital rights NGO AlgorithmWatch has created a global inventory[23] of ethical frameworks for AI. By April 2020, it had listed 173 of them; by the time you read this book, there will be many more. I'm sure they are all carefully thought out and no doubt provide useful prisms for considering the future of technology. Many of them consider issues like human autonomy and agency that are central to freedom of thought. But while ethics may inform understanding of and need for law and regulation, it should never be used to sideline the law. You don't need to be much of a cynic to see why ethical guidelines may be more palatable to big tech than actual regulation. Ethics are optional. They can be a good marketing tool, but you are never going to find yourself in court over a purely ethical dispute. Human rights law is ethics with teeth. We need to move the discussion back to the law, specifically human rights law, and we must make it work for us.

Privacy and data protection have been the primary language of human rights in the sphere of technology over the past two decades, but the language of data protection never really opened up the problem for me. It felt cold and distant. I spent many years writing papers that talked about personal data and its fundamental importance to our human rights, but it was always abstract, a technicality.[24]

By focusing on data, we are looking at the techniques companies use to get inside our heads, not the impact of it. When I started to think about digital rights in terms of freedom of thought, it suddenly felt acutely personal, fundamental and clear. If you look at regulating our relationship with technology from the perspective of protecting our minds rather than protecting our data, the solutions become simpler, but also more radical. The question of regulation shifts to purpose and potential impact rather than the technicalities.

If a company is selling privileged, personalised access to our minds for political marketing purposes and manipulation of voters, we don't need to look at the details in the data or even at evidence of whether their product actually works to know that it is wrong. They are selling unlawful interference with our right to freedom of thought, which has serious consequences for our individual freedom, our democracies and the societies we all live in. Governments have an obligation to prevent that. If your criminal justice system is using AI to predict whether someone may become a criminal, they are penalising that person based on inferences about their mental state. This is a violation of the absolute right not to be penalised for your thoughts or inferences about your thoughts alone. Whether or not any of it works does not matter from a human rights perspective – your rights may be violated even if, in reality, your mind is not. The obligation to protect involves prevention, not just cure.

What does our acquiescence to the ubiquity of technology and mass surveillance in our lives mean for freedom of thought? Could it be said that, according to the principle that human rights are 'living instruments', the right to freedom of thought has lost its relevance and resonance in modern society? Are we consenting to the loss of freedom of thought? Does the backlash against human rights mean genuine freedom has gone out of fashion? I believe that such a view would be a betrayal of the earlier generations who fought for our rights and the future generations who rely on us to protect theirs. Although we may be rather late to wake up to the issue, we should view the living tree doctrine as a route to recognising the new threats to our fundamental right to freedom of thought, whatever guise they may come in, and establishing the scope of the right clearly in this new context. This requires an understanding of the way technology currently interacts with our thoughts and thought processes. This book is, hopefully, a starting point.

The philosopher David Hume said that reason was nothing but a slave of the passions. Moral psychologist Jonathan Haidt, in his book *The Righteous Mind*, comes to a similar conclusion, describing the link between emotion and reason as resembling the relationship between an elephant and its rider. The elephant represents our automatic responses and intuitions, and the rider helps to guide the elephant with an overlay of rational thought. According to Haidt, it is the elephant that is the driving force for our moral judgement and our ability to relate to others. Freedom of thought gives time for the rider and the elephant to discuss their respective positions. It gives them the space to plot a course that will not result in the disastrous consequences of the elephant stampeding through a village. Freedom of thought is the seat of human morality, not because it allows for high-minded reasoning, but because it makes us responsible for our words and actions. Manipulation takes control of the elephant by distracting the rider.

The role of Facebook in driving genocidal violence against the Rohingya Muslim population in Myanmar shows the devastating potential for social media to control our elephants to spread hate. WhatsApp groups driving mob lynchings and hate crimes in India provide more evidence of the way digital communications give deadly impetus to vicious rumour. And the use of surveillance technology to identify potential critics and wipe out the Uighur population in China is a stark example of the very real threat of automated reading and condemnation of human beings. What we think informs what we do, and manipulation of our minds can lead us to do unthinkable things. But the daily threat to our rights is not elsewhere. It is not someone else's problem. It is in our homes, in our pockets and in our heads; in the messages we receive and the information about our inner lives we unwittingly give away. Yet what if we just say no? What if we demand another way, a future where technology is harnessed to enhance our rights and those of others across the world? What if we could make a connected world that fulfils its promise of promoting freedom of thought and allows each and every one of us the potential to become the people we want to be, online and off?

The foundation of the future must be human dignity and freedom, not corporate libertarianism or state totalitarianism. We need to reclaim the idea of freedom and ground it firmly in human rights, not robot rights, corporate interests or individualism. And we need to move beyond the narrow scope of privacy to a space where we can guarantee all rights – civil and political, economic, social and cultural, for all people, everywhere. Freedom of thought and opinion are the keys to unlocking that space, and we must all be prepared to use them or lose them. Freedom is not about doing whatever we want and to hell with the consequences. As the philosopher Jean-Jacques Rousseau observed, 'the mere impulse of appetite is slavery, while obedience to a law which we prescribe to ourselves is liberty'. Seventy years ago, the world gave us human rights that are universal, indivisible and inalienable. Now we need to make sure we have the laws to protect them.

CHAPTER 14

FREEING OUR MINDS

Unless someone like you cares a whole awful lot,
nothing is going to get better, it's not.

Dr Seuss, *The Lorax*

When Apple CEO Tim Cook gave his commencement speech at Stanford in 2019, he delivered a stark warning about the current direction of travel of technology:

> If we accept as normal and unavoidable that everything in our lives can be aggregated, sold, or even leaked in the event of a hack, then we lose so much more than data.
>
> We lose the freedom to be human.
>
> Think about what's at stake. Everything you write, everything you say, every topic of curiosity, every stray thought, every impulsive purchase, every moment of frustration or weakness, every gripe or complaint, every secret shared in confidence.

In a world without digital privacy, even if you have done nothing wrong other than think differently, you begin to censor yourself. Not entirely at first. Just a little, bit by bit. To risk less, to hope less, to imagine less, to dare less, to create less, to try less, to talk less, to think less. The chilling effect of digital surveillance is profound, and it touches everything.[1]

Science and technology have played a crucial role in improving public health to support human development. Engineering allowed for sewage systems that permitted the exponential growth of cities needed to power the industrial age. Vaccinations dramatically reduced childhood mortality, and contraceptives decoupled sex and pregnancy, meaning women no longer needed to spend their entire adult lives pregnant and could enter the workforce with the hope that one day they might have gender equality. Technological innovation can make us happier and healthier, but just as cigarettes turned out to be not as good for respiratory illness as their manufacturers once claimed, and psychiatrists like Ewen Cameron may not all have had their patients' well-being at heart, not all technology is as good for us as it seems.

In *Nineteen Eighty-Four*, George Orwell describes 'the scientist of today' as 'a mixture of psychologist and inquisitor, studying with extraordinary minuteness the meaning of facial expressions, gestures and tones of voice and testing the truth producing effects of drugs, shock therapy, hypnosis and physical torture'.[2] Ultimately, in Orwell's dystopian state of Oceania, science and technological development stalled in part because 'progress depended on the empirical habit of thought, which could not survive in a strictly regimented society'.[3] Without guaranteeing the right to freedom of thought, technological innovation will eat itself.

As Cook recognised in his Stanford address, if we did not have this 'freedom to be human' that freedom of thought gives us:

> Silicon Valley would have been stopped in its tracks
> before it had even gotten started … If we believe that
> freedom means an environment where great ideas
> can take root, where they can grow and be nurtured
> without fear of irrational restrictions or burdens, then
> it's our duty to change course, because your generation
> ought to have the same freedom to shape the future as
> the generation that came before.[4]

We don't need new rights to protect our inner freedoms; the drafters of the International Bill of Rights did a fantastic job establishing strong parameters for our freedoms to think, believe and form opinions with space to grow. Tim Cook's freedom to be human is our right to freedom of thought. But we do need new legal frameworks at the national and regional levels where consensus may be possible, to ensure a protective space around our rights to mental autonomy and integrity that the absolute rights to freedom of thought and opinion entail. And this is starting to happen. Since I started working on freedom of thought in 2017, interest in the practical application of the right has grown. Regulating to protect the right to freedom of thought doesn't necessarily need to refer to the right directly; it's what it does, not what it is called that matters. Laws and regulations that limit the ability of technology to interfere with our minds, whether they regulate electoral law, personal data use, advertising or criminal evidence all help to provide effective protection to our freedom to think for ourselves.

To begin with, we might not know where the limits of absolute protection in human rights law should be, but a good rule of thumb is that if it feels wrong, it probably is. Reading our metadata to understand when we are most vulnerable to a sale; using insights about our anxieties and our potential for addiction or criminality to manipulate or judge us; looking into our brains to know how we might vote or how guilty we feel; judging our political or sexual preferences based on our faces – all of these developments feel very, very wrong.

The creepy lines

Former Google CEO Eric Schmidt famously said, 'the Google policy on a lot of things is to get right up to the creepy line and not cross it.' The legal line we need to draw around our inner freedom *is* that creepy line. Right now, Google and every other company whose business model relies on 'surveillance capitalism' is blurring the line into oblivion. We need to bring it into focus urgently. But it is not necessarily a single, unbroken line; it is more of a series of contour lines that map out the core of what it means to have the freedom to think. To define freedom of thought and opinion in the twenty-first century we must highlight the creepy lines so no one can claim they didn't see them coming.

Firstly, we need to draw a line around our inner life, with its absolute protection. At what point does thought spill out as expression, where it may legitimately be analysed, managed and judged? When I see my daughter's face crumple, it is not a breach of her inner freedom to interpret her expression as disappointment or upset and to respond by trying to make her feel better or to understand what the problem is. We all make inferences about the feelings and thoughts of people around us, based on a range of different cues filtered through our own character, experience and biases. This is part of the glue that binds society together and is essential to human communication and empathy. Reading each other is a normal, if flawed, part of human interaction.

But a human response to human cues is very different to an automated analysis. If I am managing my daughter's emotions through a computer read-out from a device she is wearing day and night that she can't remove, we have sprinted past the creepy line. When the analysis of our mental and emotional landscape from outer cues is automated, unavoidable and cannot be challenged, it becomes a violation of the right to freedom of thought.

We need grey areas too, the spaces where we work out what we think through external exploration, gathering evidence, testing out a theory, a sketch or a calculation and rubbing it out when it proves to be wrong. David Kaye, the former UN Special Rapporteur on freedom of opinion and expression, explored the boundaries of the inner realm in the digital context in his reports on surveillance[5] and human rights and artistic expression,[6] highlighting the problem of thinking, planning and even doodling in a connected world where our mental workings are recorded on a scale barely even imagined by George Orwell.

When we are talking about boundaries between our inner lives and the outer world, we need to talk about consent. The line between what I think and what I express is an informed and uncoerced decision to share. When I tell you my secrets, I have decided that I want you to know them. Not because you have read my secret diary or put me in thumbscrews, but because I have consented to sharing with you. When I decide to sit in the hypnotherapist's chair to overcome my addiction, I am consenting to a degree of influence over my mind that without my consent would clearly be unlawful manipulation. But genuine consent does not sit in a yellow button at the bottom of a long set of terms and conditions. Informed consent requires a comprehensive understanding of what it is that we are consenting to, now and in the future. It also requires choice and the realistic possibility of saying no.

We need to think more carefully about the consequences of our trade-off with big tech if we are to find the right threshold for personal data use that we can reasonably be allowed or expected to consent to. We cannot sell our absolute rights. Just as it will never be lawful to sell ourselves into slavery or to consent to torture, we cannot effectively consent to the deprivation of our right to freedom of thought, now or for the future. And that must be clear in the laws that constrain technology and the ways they are applied.

When we look at the future of technology in our world, it will be defined by the legal lines we draw to protect our mental freedom. If we really want to live in societies with respect for human dignity and freedom, there are certain things we need effective laws to stop. Some may be in discrete areas that underpin our democratic societies, like elections, children's rights, criminal justice and access to work and basic services. Others may go to the underlying problems in the online world that are inherent to the current business model and the social, economic, cultural and political drivers behind technology that gets inside our minds. The scale and complexity of the issues are reflected in the burgeoning field of law and regulation that is seeking to tackle the threats and the harms we are already experiencing: draft laws on neuro-ethics in Chile, online safety in the UK, the regulation of AI in the European Union and digital rights in Nigeria are just a snapshot of some of the legal developments on the table at the time of writing. The details will dictate whether or not these laws are successful. But beyond the legislative detail, there are some fundamental things that absolutely must change if we want to reset our technological future and plot a course to guarantee our freedom to think.

Surveillance advertising is the fuel that drives surveillance capitalism. Big tech companies like Google, Facebook and Amazon are where they are not because of their capacity for innovation, but because of their capacity to harness our minds en masse for advertising. Perhaps the most potent way to protect our freedom of thought is to take away the economic imperative for looking into and changing our minds. A ban on surveillance advertising would be a revolutionary step towards mental freedom, and a much healthier one than Edward Bernays' 'torches of freedom'. It would not stop online advertising; it would just send it in a direction that respects our mental space. We could still be served adverts for tents when searching for a camping holiday. But advertising would focus on the context, not the individual. A ban on surveillance advertising would also cut the profitability of hacking our minds for online sales.

Personalisation is driven by the economic imperative of surveillance capitalism and can have devastating consequences for our freedom to access information and form our opinions freely. It can also be used to make it harder for us to switch off. If you want to read news or even watch movies that are tailored to you specifically, this should always be on an opt-in basis, and you must be told, in clear language, what information is used to personalise your experience, with regular opportunities to change your mind. We need to have real control over the direction our minds are taken in. The way we receive information has a fundamental impact on what we think. Algorithms that decide for us who we are and what we like should never be the default in our search for information. We must learn from the horrors of the last century that social control, amplified by communication technology, can have devastating consequences for whole populations. And experimentation with social control through information feeds like Facebook's emotional contagion experiment should never, ever be permitted.

Persuasive design is the glue that keeps us stuck to our devices. It is the 'stickiness' in your phone that makes it hard to look into the eyes of the person across the table, the dopamine rush of the likes that keeps your kids online and makes them scream at you when you try to prise them off. The dark patterns[7] that trick us into doing things against our interests, like buying things we don't need at prices we can't afford, or constantly upgrading our hardware, are not accidental side effects of a pleasant user experience; they are based on design decisions. Regulation needs to draw a clear line between making something attractive and making it addictive. And the difference between fair competition in an open marketplace and trickery should be set in stone. If we want to have freedom of thought, we need the freedom to let go and put our technology down. If Tim Cook really values the freedom to be human, he must also be ready to embrace the possibility of less profit as we all wake up from the torpor of the poisoned apple.

Developing technology to read brains directly is a dangerous track to go down. Once you have that technology, how do you prevent it being used coercively to oblige people to reveal their thoughts? We need to hit pause on the technologists' dreams of total mental access. There may be medical uses for brain–computer interfaces that justify their use in a way that doesn't threaten our inner freedom. But just as subliminal advertising was banned before it got out of testing, we need to prohibit the use of brain–computer interfaces outside of medical settings before it is too late. Similarly, reading brains to assess political opinions or guilt in criminal trials is so clearly problematic for the individuals who may be subjected to it, and to the foundations of democracy and justice, that it should never be permitted. Taking away the commercial or political potential would mean that any research in this field of neuroscience is clearly targeted at liberating minds rather than controlling them.

Emotion recognition technology that claims to read our feelings in real time through biometric information like video, voice or gait analysis or with the data exhaust we leave in our digital lives invades our inner freedom and puts us at risk of being penalised for inferences made about our thoughts. Emotion analysis technology in general should be categorised as high risk and should never be allowed in public spaces, criminal justice or security settings, or as a basis for decisions that affect our life chances. Similarly, lie detector tests – whatever technology they use – should have no place in courts or any other context where the results of the test will change the course of a person's life. Modern-day variations on physiognomy or phrenology that take our biometric information as an indicator of our inner lives should be prohibited by law. Automated assessments of criminality, political opinion or sexual orientation or other mental characteristics based on biometric information pose a fundamental threat to our freedom of thought. Judging our minds and our futures through our bodies should not be allowed. To be fully human, there must be parts of ourselves that should be simply unknowable.

Freedom of thought and opinion includes the right to change and evolve. We need to make sure that any profiles drawn from our data about who we are and how we think can be challenged and erased. Decisions on our finances, education or life chances must be explainable and must not be based on shadowy risk assessments of our minds drawn from big data. It's not about the data itself; it's the story it tells of our lives and the assumptions it creates about other lives. This is particularly important for children. Any inferences made from tracking and monitoring children must not be allowed to follow them into their adult lives. The infinite potential of our minds should never be condemned by our data trails.

Freedom in the global village

When 71-year-old Georgeta Stoicescu was attacked by a pack of stray dogs in Bucharest in 2000, the European Court of Human Rights found that Romania had violated her human rights because it had not done enough to deal with the dangerous dogs problem on its streets. There was enough information in the public domain for the government to know that packs of dogs were a threat to life and limb. Failing to address the problem was a failure to protect Mrs Stoicescu's physical integrity.[8] Human rights law works by stopping our public bodies from trampling over our rights. But it also puts an obligation on them to protect us from other threats to our rights. Negative obligations tell the state what it cannot do; positive obligations tell it what it must do to protect the rights of people under its jurisdiction or control.

Governments have an obligation to protect our human rights from obvious threats, whether those come from a virus, a pack of wild dogs or an out-of-control tech industry. If our governments were previously unaware of the risks of the kinds of activities described in Part 2 of this book, they can no longer feign ignorance. We know the dangers. In the twentieth century, Camel's advertisements claimed that 'More Doctors Smoke Camel' as they pushed the supposed health benefits of their deadly products. Jaron Lanier is a pioneer of virtual reality and sometimes referred to as 'the conscience of Silicon

Valley'. He has described social media as 'worse than cigarettes in that cigarettes don't degrade you. They kill you, but you're still you.'[9] It is time for governments to call the big tech dogs off our inner freedom.

You may have heard the argument that the internet is a global phenomenon that cannot be tamed by domestic legislation. Somehow we have been conned into believing that there is something magical about it, that we can't touch it and therefore we can't really control it; that the onward march of the Internet of Things and of surveillance capitalism is as inevitable as the word of God. But law governs our relationships between ourselves, with our governments and between our states. Law evolves to meet human needs, and human rights law develops where it is needed to protect our humanity. National borders may pose political challenges, but they are not a fundamental barrier to addressing global problems. Global business can be curtailed and even broken up if it undermines our humanity and our human rights, including our economic, social and cultural rights. The toxic effects of corruption and modern slavery are reflected in laws that criminalise those things beyond our borders, so that you cannot pick and choose your ethical and legal frameworks as you change country. Cross-border frameworks and laws that reach beyond national frontiers exist in many areas that affect human rights. The European Union has been at the forefront of creating legal protections for personal data in cyberspace that transcend physical borders. And the European Court of Human Rights has held states accountable for the human rights violations they commit outside their national frontiers.[10] The problem is not legal, it is political. So where will we find the political will for change?

Ethics must inform but not supplant the harder realities of law. The increasing use of human rights law to challenge algorithmic injustice around the world not only changes the specific policies it targets, but also triggers a broader shift as public bodies and tech companies start to quietly review their use of tech before they have to face court proceedings or, perhaps even worse, the court of public opinion. Carly Kind, the director of the Ada Lovelace Institute, an independent research body looking at AI and society, has described this as the 'third wave of AI ethics', which is moving from tweaking philosophical principles to real change on the ground.[11] The concrete difference is that it involves law – human rights law – not just ethical frameworks, and when organisations know that they will lose in court, they start to rethink what they are doing before they have to get there. What is more, despite threats by Google to pull out of Australia[12] or Facebook from Europe[13] in the face of legal challenges, they may in fact be more inclined to clean up their act everywhere than to give up access to a lucrative market anywhere.

At the international level, the conversation is changing as the real problem we have with tech is coming into focus. In September 2021, UN High Commissioner for Human Rights Michele Bachelet included the right to freedom of thought in her report on the urgent threats posed by AI to our human rights, in which she called on states to 'expressly ban AI applications that cannot be operated in compliance with international human rights law and impose moratoriums on the sale and use of AI systems that carry a high risk for the enjoyment of human rights, unless and until adequate safeguards to protect human rights are in place'.[14] The UN Committee on the Rights of the Child made the first official statement on the way that technology might interfere with the right to freedom of thought in its 2021 General Comment on the rights of the child in the digital environment. And the UN Secretary-General's High-level Panel on Digital Cooperation note:

We are delegating more and more decisions to
intelligent systems, from how to get to work to what
to eat for dinner. This can improve our lives, by freeing
up time for activities we find more important. But it is
also forcing us to rethink our understandings of human
dignity and agency, as algorithms are increasingly
sophisticated at manipulating our choices – for
example, to keep our attention glued to a screen.[15]

UN Special Rapporteurs on freedom of religion or belief, freedom of opinion and expression, human rights while countering terrorism, and extreme poverty, among others, have also flagged up the risks of AI and other technological developments for inner freedom in recent years. The recognition of the importance of the right to freedom of thought in facing our future is growing. In the first UN report focusing explicitly on the right to freedom of thought,[16] in October 2021, Ahmed Shaheed, the UN Special Rapporteur on freedom of religion or belief, called for the UN Human Rights Committee to explore the practical application and interpretation of the right through a new General Comment, noting that despite its limited use in the past, the right 'stands ready to rise to the complex challenges of the 21st century and beyond'.[17]

In 2019, the Council of Europe's Committee of Ministers issued a declaration on the manipulative capabilities of algorithmic processes, which recognised that 'fine grained, sub-conscious and personalised levels of algorithmic persuasion may have significant effects on the cognitive autonomy of individuals and their right to form opinions and take independent decisions'.[18] In the same declaration, the Council of Ministers recognised that this potential should not be underestimated and could 'lead to the corrosion of the very foundations of the Council of Europe': human rights and democracy. As I write, the European Union is considering its legal framework for the future of AI on the continent, including the potential to ban high-risk uses of AI that try to get inside our minds. In the UK, the Age Appropriate Design Code, introduced to protect children online, has had an impact on the way big tech operates for everyone well beyond British borders.[19] And in Chile, legislators are looking at new laws to govern the future of neuroscience. There are too many developments to mention here. And by the time you read this, some of the solutions highlighted earlier in this chapter, unthinkable five years ago, may already have made their way into national or international statutes.

Our world is a work in progress and the way it looks today will be very far from the way it will look to our grandchildren. People often argue that the enormous economic interests bolstered by the apparently infinite reach of technology companies like Google and Amazon into our lives make it impossible to change things. The all-pervasive power of what Amnesty International calls 'the Surveillance Giants' may feel immutable today. But in the eighteenth century, the economic and political might of the East India Company, which employed J. S. Mill, propped up by the magnanimity of British global colonial coercive power, no doubt seemed just as inevitable. In time, the tech giants that employ the ethicists of today will be consigned to history too.

We are often presented with two alternatives for a digital future – the authoritarian surveillance model of China, or the capitalist libertarian surveillance model of the United States. Europe's development of privacy and data protection law sometimes looks like a possible way out, but the real third way for the future of humanity could come from anywhere. Perhaps it will emerge from a place that values happiness over profit, like Bhutan, with its Gross National Happiness index; or from a culture built on collectives. Chile's draft laws on neuroscience may become a global template or an opportunity for the rest of the world to learn and perfect. Maybe it will be a feminist society like Iceland that will save our souls. Or perhaps, like Zera Yacob's ideas on freedom and equality, the way forward may emerge from East African perspectives, no matter how oppressive government policies may be.[20] The former head of AI Ethics at Google and co-founder of the organisation Black in AI, Ethiopian-born Eritrean–American Timnit Gebru, has explained how her experience having to seek asylum, fleeing war as a political refugee at the age of 15, informs her work because she understands viscerally how division works.[21] And trail-blazing Ethiopian behavioural scientist Abeba Birhane advocates a new approach to AI and technology in Africa, 'creating programmes and databases that serve various local communities and not blindly importing Western AI systems founded upon individualistic and capitalist drives'.[22] Kebene Wodajo, an Ethiopian researcher in law and business ethics at the University of St Gallen, is exploring legal means to address structural injustice in technology, focusing on the societal rather than the individual harms of technology and the responses we need to protect our communities.[23] Just because the solutions are not in Silicon Valley or Brussels does not mean there are no solutions; we just have to be open to where we look for them. If you believe that your human rights are important, you need to start somewhere to protect them.

In the small places

In our lives and our homes, we must wake up to the threats to our inner freedom and think about our choices, talk to our children, and devise our own strategies to protect ourselves and those around us. The tech industry thrives on surveillance capitalism because we have allowed it to, and we feed it the information it needs to exploit us. We need to stop and think – demand choices and stop accepting unconscionable interferences with our rights. To make money, technology needs consumers; as consumers, we have the power to decide how we want to engage with technology and, more importantly, how we want it to engage with us. Wherever you are and whoever you are, you can start making a difference today.

We make daily choices about how we spend our time, money and attention. While technology has been harnessed to manipulate the way we direct all three, the coup is not yet complete, and 'surveillance capitalism' is still in its adolescence. There is time to take back control of our own minds as long as we refuse to give in to the impression that it is all too complicated, overwhelming and inevitable so we should just accept it and relax with another mindfulness app.

The first step to dealing with the problem on an individual level is to make it personal. Start looking and asking questions about the information you share and receive (consciously and unconsciously), and what it might say about you and how it could affect the way you think. In the first lockdown, like many others, I found myself joining several local WhatsApp groups that would help us to help each other without sharing the same virus-laden air. It wasn't long before I received my first piece of disinformation, a long video message about draft legislation that would make all vaccines obligatory. Those legislative clauses, like the vaccine at that time, did not exist. If you made it through 2020 and 2021 without receiving fake news about compulsory vaccinations, 5G or the coronavirus hoax on social media then you were an exception. But you don't have to be part of the problem. Before you share, stop, have a cup of tea, check the source, verify the information and decide whether it really is a good idea.[24] Freedom of thought is about the space to think before you share.

Addictions are hard to admit to and harder to beat. But it is our dependence on our devices that feeds the beast of surveillance capitalism. That is why persuasive design is so lucrative. The more time and attention we give to our devices, the more information they get about our rhythms, behaviours and personality and the more influence they have on our minds. Take a close look at how dependent you are on your devices, what information you are leaking, and how it could conceivably be used against you or others.

Twitter can feel like a sinkhole, with hours lost scrolling through reams of despair and ire to find the occasional useful nugget. When I installed adversarybot, a bot designed by the organisation Privacy International to show how the information in your Twitter feed can be used to interpret your frame of mind so that it can be exploited, the granularity of my shifting moods shocked me. Cambridge University Psychometrics Centre's Apply Magic Sauce[25] demo has also been a revelation. Apparently on Twitter I could pass for a 30–39-year-old man; perhaps I have more gravitas in 280 characters.

You can request a download of all the information Facebook holds on you, which might be a happy trip down memory lane or a cringe-inducing reminder of the banality of a life lived on social media. Apparently my Facebook persona's main interests are Jean-Claude Juncker, Justin Bieber and wool. One out of three isn't bad, though I did wonder how they'd got hold of my primary school wool project, and it did explain the large numbers of regional farm-animal videos that appeared inexplicably in my feed. And if you don't like the way social media views you, you can start looking for ways to trip up the algorithm, like teenager Samantha Mosley and her friends, who created an elaborate technique of cooperative obfuscation to confuse Instagram so it couldn't track and target them.[26]

Understanding how to respond when social media presses your buttons is also crucial. If you feel under attack or overwhelmed whenever you check your feed, the organisation Glitch,[27] set up by campaigner Seyi Akiwowo in response to her own experience of online abuse, can provide you with vital advice and tools for digital self-care.

If you want to know how much of your precious time on this mortal coil you are wasting on your device, there are apps for that too. I was shocked by the hours of productive time I lost every day when I tracked my use, and at times it has been a struggle writing this book with the constant urge to just check my email. But I found freedom from my phone with the aptly named Freedom[28] app, which locks me out even when my fingers are itching. And science journalist Catherine Price's book *How to Break Up With Your Phone* offers a wealth of tips for managing your relationship with the tech in your pocket. The market for apps, hardware and other resources that are designed to let you take back control of your mind is booming. And if we use them, perhaps the market in protecting our autonomy will expand.

There are more and more resources that will help you to reduce your data trail, limit the information you are sharing on your devices and understand how to manage, digest and analyse the information you get online. You can choose products that are shifting the economic model away from profiling and targeting based on data to embed privacy by design. Search with DuckDuckGo instead of Google, install Brave as your browser, downgrade to a new-generation dumb phone ... By the time you read this, there will be many more options, and every time you make a conscious choice away from the surveillance capitalism economy, an alternative economic model that protects freedom of thought becomes a more viable possibility.

When Apple launched a new iOS update in May 2021, requiring users to opt in rather than opt out of sharing their data with apps, 95 per cent of users in the United States and 87 per cent worldwide said no thanks.[29] It turns out that, when asked clearly if they want to offer up their souls through their data, most people refuse. This is perhaps the clearest signal yet that we really can say no to the surveillance capitalism business model if alternatives are available. As a result, we will no doubt see new innovation and entrepreneurs rushing to fill the gap and change our future relationship with technology. When they do that, we need to be sure that the new direction is one that will help foster freedom of thought and opinion, one that will see the value in social justice and human dignity over the lure of quick cash.

If your picture appears online, or if you ever have to use a photo as part of an application process, you may want to know what AI tools think about people like you. In late 2019, researcher Kate Crawford teamed up with artist Trevor Paglen to create ImageNet Roulette, part selfie app, part art installation, part political statement. ImageNet Roulette allowed you to upload a photo of yourself to get a read-out from a massive database of photos scraped from the net and labelled to teach AI what to think about people. One photo of me on the beach in a winter coat was labelled as a 'nun'; another, of me up a mountain in Rwanda, came back with 'maenad' – though I wasn't sure whether that was me or the mountain gorilla sitting behind me. My results may reveal the misogynistic sidelining of women of a certain age, but others who used the app, like *Guardian* journalist Julia Carrie Wong, had even more disturbing results, seeing their photos being marked up with racial slurs.[30] And MIT researcher Dr Joy Buolamwini found, when she started working on facial recognition technology, that it could not even recognise her as human until she put on a white mask.

What you find when you look into the personal data oracle may be so off-beam that you feel there is nothing to worry about. But remember that the inferences made about you can be used to decide how you will be treated, whether they are right or wrong. And they may also be used to fuel disadvantage for others, with potentially devastating consequences. It is the scale of the operation to get inside our heads and to sell the contents that matters, not necessarily the accuracy of the findings. ImageNet Roulette was not just another selfie app craze. Its creators said they wanted to 'shed light on what happens when technical systems are trained on problematic training data. AI classifications of people are rarely made visible to the people being classified. ImageNet Roulette provides a glimpse into that process – and to show the ways things can go wrong.' As a result of the media furore their work sparked, ImageNet announced that it was going to delete more than half of the 1.2 million pictures of humans in the dataset.[31] Artists provoke change. So can we.

Organising for change

As a result of her personal experience of bias in machine learning, Dr Joy Buolamwini founded the Algorithmic Justice League[32] and has been at the forefront of the drive to change tech policy and design in the United States and around the world. To bring about widespread change, we need to organise. What is happening to our human rights in the digital world is not just personal, it is political, and for those old enough to vote, putting human rights at the heart of our political choices and our political demands is one way to push for wider reform and demand our politicians take responsibility to respect and protect our rights. Depending on where you are, you can run the browser extension Who Targets Me[33] to get a picture of how political parties are profiling and reaching you through social media. Even if they are parties you are politically aligned with, you may not like what you see and you may want to tell the politicians who hope to represent you what you think about it. Voting is vitally important to bring about change. As an individual it is perhaps the single most powerful tool that you have. But if politicians really want voter engagement, they should be prepared to listen to what voters think about their campaign tactics and to change them. Your vote may be the first step to improving the protection of human rights in your country, and around the world, online and offline.

Online we have unprecedented opportunity to reach out and connect to other people and their different ways of thinking. Finding and sharing information opens up new avenues of thought, lighting up different perspectives on the world. Access to technology and the connected world is increasingly recognised as a human right in itself.[34] It is a luxury our ancestors never dreamed of. It is a chance to grow our own minds and to touch others so we can all glow like a string of fairy lights twinkling around the globe. Connectivity has helped drive massive social movements and allowed human rights defenders in repressive states to get messages out to the world that their governments fight hard to suppress. Socrates would no doubt have been in his element. There are dangers with the direction of travel, but we must not lose sight of the incredible opportunities that technology offers to transport us to even better realms of inner freedom and to organise for change. The internet is a superhighway of connection and information that has huge potential to support the development of beliefs and opinions that will guide us to a better future.

We can each play our part, but it is not enough for us to act alone. Change comes when we work together, sometimes faster than you could ever imagine. There are human rights organisations all over the world challenging the impact of new technology on our minds and harnessing the power of technology to promote human rights.

Big organisations like the online activist network Avaaz campaign to combat online disinformation, and Amnesty International took up the call for companies like Google and Facebook to respect our right to freedom of opinion along with other human rights. Privacy International started out small in an era when no one was really talking about privacy and data protection, but the scope of their work now recognises that privacy is a gateway to other human rights and freedoms, including the right to freedom of thought and opinion. Article 19's focus on freedom of expression has expanded to explore concrete ways to protect freedom of opinion in the digital age too. You will find many more organisations working in this space throughout this book. And wherever you are, you will find NGOs, small groups and individual activists who are advocating, organising and demonstrating for change in the digital world. The digital rights organisation Access Now has been hosting an annual digital rights conference, RightsCon, which moved online in 2020 with over 7,600 participants from 158 countries. Geography is no longer a barrier to getting involved. And if you can't find an organisation dealing with the issues you care about where you are, you can always start one yourself.

One of the most powerful tools for driving change is information and challenge. In many countries data protection law gives you the right to request details of all the information held on you through subject access requests (SARs) and to complain if it is inaccurate or being used in ways that do not protect your rights. Freedom of information (FOI) requests allow you to ask public bodies for information on their activities, including their policies on human rights, technology and data protection. National human rights institutions, ombudsman schemes and regulatory authorities offer a chance to raise your concerns about human rights issues or the way public institutions or private companies are affecting your rights. Complaining may not sound like an exciting way to a better future, but by making something you think is wrong a problem for someone else, you may also help to force organisations, companies and countries to change course, if only because they prefer the path of least resistance.

Max Schrems was an Austrian PhD student studying in the United States when he experienced a creeping horror at the way Facebook and other American companies were exploiting personal data and abusing their informational power, not only in the United States, but all over the world. Most people stare into the abyss and do nothing, but not Schrems. When he returned to Europe, he decided to test the limits of European data protection law – in the days before the General Data Protection Regulation (GDPR) – and complained about Facebook's European subsidiary based in Dublin to the Irish Data Protection Commission. When his case was referred to the Court of Justice of the European Union in Luxembourg in 2015, the court found that European human rights provisions meant that the Safe Harbor agreement between the European Union and the United States that allowed data to be shipped across the Atlantic was invalid, because it didn't provide enough protection to data once it was shared outside the European Union. Neither the European Union nor the United States was particularly happy about the decision, but at least for now, in Europe, human rights law trumps political and economic expediency. He may not have stopped the flow of data across the Atlantic entirely, but Max Schrems has had a profound impact on the free-for-all of big tech over our data and the protection of digital rights worldwide. And he did it, essentially, by complaining.

If you don't feel like complaining yourself, there are increasing numbers of group claims and class actions challenging the impact of technology on our minds, and NGOs are using strategic litigation to tackle these issues more and more. Legal challenges can be creative, tackling fast-moving developments that affect us all in a way that allows the law to flex and respond to the new human rights issues raised by technology while policy makers may be slow to catch up with new regulations. Even losing a case can help to clarify and expand the scope of the law as it applies to technology. Digital rights organisations across Europe[35] are starting to test the existing protections through the courts, with live cases challenging the legality of real-time bidding under the European Union's GDPR, bulk state surveillance and many other practices that have serious implications for our collective freedom of thought. This kind of case may well shape the way the law and technology work in the future while policymakers are still wringing their hands about which way to go. So far, the legal challenges to online fundamental rights threats have focused on privacy and protection of personal data. But as the technology increasingly reaches its tendrils inside our heads, it is time to consider how the GDPR should be viewed as a tool to protect not only our data, but our rights to freedom of thought, opinion and mental integrity.

Things change, and often they change because people, individuals, groups, movements and countries make them change. Sometimes the shift seems to come almost overnight, like the magic of the crumbling wall in Berlin in 1989. Sometimes it takes years, decades or even centuries of pushing to change things, with millions of people around the world playing their part in small shifts or grumbling movements, until the tectonic plates grind against each other, provoking a tsunami of action. Votes for women and equal pay; racial equality and Black Lives Matter; the rise and fall of the tobacco industry; the environmental movement and the fight against man-made climate change: all these issues have changed our world, sometimes slowly and sometimes in an overwhelming rush. All have seemed – and may still seem at times – insurmountable, but generations of people have dedicated themselves in great or small ways to making change happen, even if their work is not yet done. Some have put themselves in physical or moral danger, facing threats from the state, their neighbours or the economic interests they challenge. But many, many millions more have contributed by quietly donating small sums of money, changing their shopping habits or voting for change at the ballot box. We cannot do it alone. You don't have to be an activist to contribute to change, and if we want the freedom to think for ourselves, we all have to take responsibility for it by reclaiming our digital rights and demanding respect for human rights around the world, online and off. Your part may be big or small, but whether you are a technologist, a lawyer, a politician, a civil servant, an investor, a teacher, a concerned parent or a consumer of technology, you could make a difference for all our futures.

The freedom to think for ourselves is what makes us human. Once we lose it, we may never get it back. It is not too late to change course, to harness technology to liberate rather than to subjugate our minds. But the time for change is now; we cannot afford to wait.

ACKNOWLEDGEMENTS

———

I am immensely grateful for the time and support so many people have contributed to make this book what it is. My agent Charlie Brotherstone and my editor Mike Harpley, for believing in my vision while helping to make it much, much better. My dear friend E. J. Flynn, for being a diligent, constructive and enthusiastic first reader. So many others, for taking the time to read and give feedback and suggestions on early chapters, including Brennan Jacoby, Frances Sheahan, Sonia Kalsi, Evelyn Aswad, Michelle Gilman, Jemma Best, James Ross, Dennis Van Der Veur, David Diaz-Jogeix, Desiree Artesi, Illona Aylmer, Clare Mortimer, Richard Bolton, James McDonald and Wafaa El Antari. For research assistance I would like to thank Basanti Mardemootoo and Tanmeet Singh. And for their insights in formulating my ideas around freedom of thought and the issues covered in this book, I am grateful to Iris Urazov, Lorna Woods, Alice Thwaite, Elspeth Guild, Baroness Helena Kennedy, Darren Schreiber, Simon Cox, Lisa Bolton, Simon McCarthy Jones, Jorge Abril Sanchez, Samantha Mosley, Russell Mosley, Alice Moloney, Robbie Scarff, Kate Jones, Baroness Beeban Kidron, Aaron Schull and Jim Balsillie. Finally, it is in large part due to the encouragement of my dear friend the late Jonathan Cooper

OBE that the ideas in this book became anything more than a fleeting thought. There are many others who have provided moral support, challenge and perspective over the years it has taken to bring this book together, and I feel blessed that I do still live in a world where I have access to the information, people and time I need to have the freedom to think.

ENDNOTES

Introduction: The Best of All Possible Worlds

1 Grassegger, H., and Krogerus, M., 'The Data That Turned the World Upside Down', *Vice*, 2017, https://www.vice.com/en_us/article/mg9vvn/how-our-likes-helped-trump-win.

2 Under the 30-year rule.

3 See Vermeulen, B., 'Article 9', in P. van Dijk et al. (eds), *Theory and Practice of the European Convention on Human Rights*, 4th edn, Cambridge, Intersentia Press, 2006, p.752.

4 Zhang, S., 'Your DNA Is Not Your Culture', *The Atlantic*, 2018, https://www.theatlantic.com/science/archive/2018/09/your-dna-is-not-your-culture/571150/.

5 Berners-Lee, T., '30 years on, what's next #ForTheWeb?', Web Foundation, speech broadcast in 2019, https://webfoundation.org/2019/03/web-birthday-30/.

Chapter 1: Inner Freedom

1 *Abrams v. United States* (1919), 250 US 616.

2 Irons, P., '"Fighting Fair": Zechariah Chafee, Jr., the Department of Justice, And The "Trial At The Harvard Club"', *Harvard Law Review*, vol. 94, no. 6, 1981, p.1205.

3 United States of America State Subcommittee Hearing, 1952.

4 Chafee, Z., *An Inquiring Mind*, New York, Harcourt Brace & Co., 1928.

5 The Declaration of Independence, 1776.

6 American Bill of Rights, 1787.

7 Silence Dogood letters, No. 8, 9 July 1722, US Government Archives, https://founders.archives.gov/documents/Franklin/01-01-02-0015.

8 *Whitney v. California* (1927), 274 US 357.

9 Declaration of the Rights of Man drafted by the French National Constituent Assembly, 1789.

10 Arendt, H., *The Origins of Totalitarianism*, Berlin, Schocken Books, 1951.

11 Cokely, C., 'Declaration of the Rights of Woman and of the Female Citizen, work by de Gouges', *Britannica*, https://www.britannica.com/topic/Declaration-of-the-Rights-of-Woman-and-of-the-Female-Citizen.

12 Just 12 years after the publication of J. S. Mill and Harriet Taylor's ideas on women's equality in *The Subjection of Women* (1869).

13 Drafting Committee of the Universal Declaration of Human Rights, UN Library, https://research.un.org/en/undhr/draftingcommittee.

14 Malik, C., 'What Are Human Rights', *The Rotarian*, 1948.

15 Lindkvist, L., 'Freedom of Thought and Conscience', in *Religious Freedom and the Universal Declaration of Human Rights*, Cambridge University Press, 2017.

16 United Nations Economic and Social Council, 'Commission on Human Rights: Summary Record of the Fourteenth Meeting', E/CN.4/SR.14, 1947, pp.3–4; Humphrey, J., *Human Rights and the United Nations*, Transnational Publishers Inc., 1983, p.25.

17 United Nations Economic and Social Council, 'Commission on Human Rights: Summary Record of the Fourteenth Meeting', E/CN.4/SR.14, 1947, p.7.

18 For an exploration of the meaning of *ren* in English, see Homer, D., 'The Development of Altruism in Confucianism', *Philosophy East and West*, vol. 1, 1951, pp.48–55.

19 For further explanations of *ren* in the context of human rights, see de Bary, T., and Weiming, T., *Confucianism and Human Rights*, Columbia University Press, 1999.

20 Chu, R. G., 'Rites and Rights in Ming China', in *Confucianism and Human Rights*, Columbia University Press, 1999.

21 Belorussian Soviet Socialist Republic (SSR), Czechoslovakia, Poland, Saudi Arabia, South Africa, the Soviet Union, the Ukrainian SSR and Yugoslavia.

22 This meant that the ICCPR and the ICESCR, while having large numbers of signatories, have not been signed up to by all members of the United Nations. Although the United States signed the ICESCR, it has yet to ratify it. Latest signatures and ratifications can be found at https://indicators.ohchr.org/.

23 United Nations, 'Hundred and Twenty-Seventh Meeting: Draft International Declaration of Human Rights E/800 (continued), A/C.3/SR.127, 1948, p.391.

24 Schabas, William, *The Universal Declaration of Human Rights: The Travaux Préparatoires*, 2013, cited in S. Lighart, 'Freedom of thought in Europe: do advances in "brain-reading" technology call for revision?', *Journal of Law and the Biosciences*, vol. 7, no. 1, January–June 2020, lsaa048, https://doi.org/10.1093/jlb/lsaa048.

25 For example, Chile and Belgium.

26 United Nations Economic and Social Council, 'Commission on Human Rights: Summary Record of the One Hundredth and Sixty-Fourth Meeting', E/CN.4/SR.164, 1950.

27 Ibid.

28 Aswad, E., 'Losing the Freedom to Be Human', *Columbia Human Rights Law Review*, vol. 52, 2020.

29 Scheinin, M., 'Article 18', in *The Universal Declaration of Human Rights:*

A Commentary, Oxford University Press, 1992, pp.264–6.

30 Case of *Nolan and K v. Russia*, ECtHR Application no. 2512/04, 2009, para 61.

31 As reported in Scheinin, M., 'Article 18', in *The Universal Declaration of Human Rights: A Commentary*, Oxford University Press, 1992, p.266.

32 The European Convention on Human Rights includes these rights in a similar formulation to the UN instruments, separating thought, conscience and belief from opinion and expression, while the Inter American Convention on Human Rights distinguishes 'freedom of thought and expression' from religion, conscience and belief and makes no reference to 'freedom of opinion'. The African Charter on Human and Peoples' Rights includes freedom of conscience but is silent on the broader range of inner freedoms described in the UDHR.

33 When Finnish parents decided to name their child 'The One and Only Marjaana', the Finnish state wouldn't let them, so they took their case to the European Commission of Human Rights in Strasbourg. Although the case was decided on other grounds, in a rare example of jurisprudence touching on freedom of thought, the European Commission of Human Rights found

that, given the 'comprehensiveness of the concept of thought', a parent's wish to name their child in a certain way would come within the scope of the right to freedom of thought.

34 UN Human Rights Committee, 'CCPR General Comment No. 22: Article 18 (Freedom of Thought, Conscience or Religion)', CCPR/C/21/Rev.1/Add.4, 1993.

35 UN Human Rights Committee, 'CCPR General Comment No. 34: Article 19 (Freedoms of Opinion and Expression), CCPR/C/GC/34, 2011.

36 Article 20(2) of the ICCPR: 'Any advocacy of national, racial or religious hatred that constitutes incitement to discrimination, hostility or violence shall be prohibited by law.'

37 Nowak, M., *UN Covenant on Civil and Political Rights*, CCPR Commentary, 1993, pp.442.

38 See Aswad, E., 'Losing the Freedom to Be Human', *Columbia Human Rights Law Review*, vol. 52, 2020, for a detailed analysis of the drafting of Article 19(1) of the ICCPR – the right to hold opinions without interference.

39 UN Human Rights Committee, 'CCPR General Comment No. 34: Article 19 (Freedoms of opinion and expression)', CCPR/C/GC/34, 2011.

40 Ibid.

Chapter 2: Of Gods and Men

1 See Carr, N., *The Shallows: How the Internet Is Changing the Way We Think, Read and Remember*, Atlantic Books, 2011.

2 Mill, J. S., *On Liberty*, London, 1859.

3 Hyman, I., 'The Menace of Memes', *Psychology Today*, 2019, https://www.psychologytoday.com/intl/blog/

mental-mishaps/201910/the-menace-memes.

4 https://twitter.com/ivankatrump/status/1052155198519558144?lang=en.

5 Moran, L., 'Ivanka Trump's Motivational "Socrates" Tweet Goes Hilariously Awry', *Huffington Post*,

2018, https://www.huffingtonpost.co.uk/entry/ivanka-trump-socrates-quote_n_5bc5bfc3e4b055bc9479dce2?ri18n=true&guccounter=1&guce_referrer=aHR0cHM6Ly9kdWNrZHVja2dvLmNvbS8&guce_referrer_sig=AQAAAKqUYqrh0FPPSHVfT0jMuEgOZsUVFcSSm2DEii6AUIsiFbYgmltCSdjfHcuXZceLFg9QRji8uzXSXMc6HuqqB3pzXZsrjMjk2VX4N2id2aQB9_2Hm_F96SXowLbabZ56g6RueUwTgDa20te8OZOgIvomoKTSVKbOTWealMeagkeA.

6   LaCapria, K., 'Did Socrates Say "When Debate is Lost, Slander Becomes the Tool of the Losers"?' *Truth or Fiction*, 2019, https://www.truthorfiction.com/did-socrates-say-when-debate-is-lost-slander-becomes-the-tool-of-the-losers/.

7   Duignan, B., 'Plato and Aristotle: How Do They Differ?' *Britannica*, https://www.britannica.com/story/plato-and-aristotle-how-do-they-differ.

8   Staff Writer, 'Socrates was guilty as charged', *University of Cambridge News*, 2009, https://www.cam.ac.uk/news/socrates-was-guilty-as-charged.

9   See Mill, J. S., *On Liberty*, London, 1859.

10   Voltaire, 'Freedom of Thought', in *Philosophical Dictionary*, 3rd edn, Amsterdam, 1765.

11   Einstein, A., *Ideas and Opinions*, trans. S. Bargmann, London, Crown Publishers, 1954, p.271.

12   Heilbron, J. L., *Galileo*, New York, Oxford University Press, 2010, p.218.

13   Sharratt, M., *Galileo: Decisive Innovator*, Cambridge, Cambridge University Press, 1994, pp.171–5.

14   Fantoli, A., 'The Disputed Injunction and Its Role in Galileo's Trial', in E. McMullin (ed.), *The Church and Galileo*, University of Notre Dame Press, 2005, pp.117–49.

15   Numbers, R. L., *Galileo Goes to Jail and other myths about science and religion*, Harvard University Press, 2009, p.77.

16   Drake, S., *Galileo At Work*, Chicago, University of Chicago Press, 1978, pp.356–7.

17   Orwell, G., *Nineteen Eighty-Four*, London, Secker & Warburg, 1949.

18   Paul, L., *FLAT EARTH: To The Edge And Back (Official Movie)*, YouTube, 2019, https://www.youtube.com/watch?v=vpljiOgd9RQ.

19   El Rincón de Mayriel, 'Las brujas de Zugarramurdi', Wordpress, 2013, https://elrincondemayriel.wordpress.com/tag/maria-ximilegui/.

20   Idoate, F., *Un documento de la Inquisición sobre brujería en Navarra*, Pamplona, 1972, p.29.

21   Doward, J., 'Why Europe's wars of religion put 40,000 "witches" to a terrible death', *The Guardian*, 2018, https://www.theguardian.com/society/2018/jan/07/witchcraft-economics-reformation-catholic-protestant-market-share.

22   Ibid.

23   Wikipedia, 'Helen Duncan', https://en.wikipedia.org/wiki/Helen_Duncan

24   Abera, T., 'Rationality and Ethics in Zara Yacob's "Hatata"', *Imperial Journal of Interdisciplinary Research*, vol. 2, no. 2, 2016.

25   Sumner, C., *Classical Ethiopian Philosophy*, Commercial Printing Press, 1985.

26   Herbjørnsrud, D., 'The African Enlightenment', *AEON*, 2016, https://aeon.co/essays/yacob-and-amo-africas-precursors-to-locke-hume-and-kant.

27   Ibid.

28 Steinberg, J., 'Spinoza's Political Philosophy', *The Stanford Encyclopedia of Philosophy*, 2019.

29 See Nadler, S., *Spinoza: A Life*, Cambridge, Cambridge University Press, 2001; and Goldstein, R., *Betraying Spinoza: The Renegade Jew Who Gave Us Modernity*, New York, Schocken Books, 2006.

30 Benedict de Spinoza, writing a reply in December 1675 to Albert Burgh, in de Spinoza, B., *Correspondence of Spinoza*, trans. A. Wolf, Montana, Kessinger Publishing, 2003, p.354.

31 de Spinoza, B., *The Chief Works of Benedict de Spinoza*, trans. R. H. M. Elwes, vol. 1, London, George Bell and Sons, 1891.

32 Ibid.

33 Ibid.

34 Ibid.

35 Mill, J. S., *On Liberty*, London, 1859.

36 See Capaldi, N., *John Stuart Mill: A Biography*, Cambridge, Cambridge University Press, 2004.

37 Mill, J. S., *On Liberty*, London, 1859.

38 United States Commission on International Religious Freedom, 'Violating Rights: Enforcing the World's Blasphemy Laws', 2020.

Chapter 3: Inside Your Head

1 *Jones v. Opelika* (1942), 316 US 584, p.618.

2 In the 1942 Supreme Court judgment in *Jones v. Opelika*, a case about the legality of licensing and tax requirements on the distribution of religious tracts.

3 Foucault, M., *History of Madness*, Routledge, 2009.

4 Ibid.

5 See Seeman, M. V., 'Psychiatry in the Nazi Era', *The Canadian Journal of Psychiatry*, vol. 50, no. 4, 2005.

6 Raz, M., *The Lobotomy Letters: The making of American psychosurgery*, University of Rochester Press, 2013.

7 Partridge, M., *Pre-frontal Leucotomy*, Oxford, Blackwell Scientific Publications, 1950.

8 El-Hai, J., 'Race and Gender in the Selection of Patients for Lobotomy', *Wonders and Marvels*, 2016, https://www.wondersandmarvels.com/2016/12/race-gender-selection-patients-lobotomy.html.

9 Peace + AI Research (PAIR), 'Whiteboard sketching, Waterfall of Meaning', Barbican Centre, 2019, https://artsandculture.google.com/asset/whiteboard-sketching-waterfall-of-meaning-people-ai-reseach-pair/zAGR_q9tsV--aA.

10 Van Wyhe, J., 'The History of Phrenology on the Web', http://www.historyofphrenology.org.uk.

11 Hatfield, W., 'Handwritten Phrenological Character Analysis of Miss M. J. A. Percival', *History of Phrenology*, 1912, http://www.historyofphrenology.org.uk/hatfield.html

12 Noted in his autobiography, *The Life and Letters of Charles Darwin*.

13 The Victorian 'scientists' of race were epitomised in the character of Dr Thomas Potter in *English Passengers*, Matthew Kneale's wide-ranging novel about religion, race, genocide and the search for a lost Eden in the 19th century. Like Potter, many of those developing theories of race

at the time sought to stigmatise anyone who was not like them with arguments dressed up in science. Potter's assessment of 'the Celtic race', based on his observations of the ship's crew (who originated from the Isle of Man), would no doubt have served to exclude me from the job market of the time: 'Typically the forehead is sloping, showing evidence of the "snout" characteristic, noted by Pearson as an indication of inferior intelligence. The skull is marked by deep eye sockets, expressing tendencies of servitude. Cranial type: G. As to his general character, the Celt is wanting in the industriousness and nobility of spirit of his Saxon neighbour, his dominating characteristic being indolence … the moral qualities of the Celt are poor, being characterized by idleness and resignation …' While Kneale deals with Potter's theories with humour and a wry nod to his own Manx roots, the dangerous, dehumanising and potentially genocidal impact of those ideas is never far from the surface.

14 Beddoe, J., *The Races of Britain; A contribution to the anthropology of Western Europe*, Bristol Arrowsmith, 1885.

15 Saini, A., *Superior: The Return of Race Science*, London, Fourth Estate, 2019.

16 Lombroso, C., *L'uomo Delinquente*, 1876.

17 Jenkinson, J., 'Face Facts: A History of Physiognomy from Ancient Mesopotamia to the End of the Nineteenth Century', *Journal of Biocommunication*, vol. 24, no. 3, 1997.

18 See Part 2.

19 Ibid.

20 Lamb, M., *Who Was Wonder Woman? Long-ago LAW alumna Elizabeth Marston was the muse who gave us a superheroine*, Boston University, 2001.

21 Recent research indicates that some people lie more than others, with 5% of people responsible for almost half the lies. See Serota, K., 'The Prevalence of Lying in America: Three Studies of Self-Reported Lies', *Human Communication Research*, 2010.

22 *R v. Warne* (1980), 2 Cr. App.R. (S.) 42, Chapman, J.

23 White, M., '11 April 1995: Jonathan Aitken unsheathes his sword of truth', *The Guardian* research department, 2011, https://www.theguardian.com/theguardian/from-the-archive-blog/2011/jun/06/newspapers-national-newspapers.

24 Asif, N., 'An introduction to sharia law and the death penalty', Oxford University School of Law, 2021, https://www.law.ox.ac.uk/research-and-subject-groups/death-penalty-research-unit/blog/2021/01/introduction-sharia-law-and.

25 Kamieński, K., 'Drugs', in *The International Encyclopedia of the First World War*, 2019, https://encyclopedia.1914-1918-online.net/article/drugs.

26 History.com Editors, 'MK-Ultra', History.com, 2017, https://www.history.com/topics/us-government/history-of-mk-ultra.

27 Kinzer, S., 'From mind control to murder? How a deadly fall revealed the CIA's darkest secrets', *The Guardian*, 2019, https://www.theguardian.com/us-news/2019/sep/06/from-mind-control-to-murder-how-a-deadly-fall-revealed-the-cias-darkest-secrets.

28 Cavanaugh, D., 'The CIA's Operation "Midnight Climax" Was Exactly What it Sounded Like', *Medium*, 2016, https://medium.com/war-is-boring/

the-cias-operation-midnight-climax-was-exactly-what-it-sounded-like-fa63f84ad015.

29 Wikipedia, 'Nuremberg Trials', on the Donald Ewen Cameron page, https://en.wikipedia.org/wiki/Donald_Ewen_Cameron#Nuremberg_trials. See also BBC Scotland, *Eminent Monsters*, 2020.

30 CBC/Radio Canada, 'MK Ultra', broadcast 1980, https://www.cbc.ca/fifth/episodes/40-years-of-the-fifth-estate/mk-ultra.

31 CBC/Radio Canada, 'Brainwashed: The Secret CIA Experiments in Canada', broadcast 2017, https://www.cbc.ca/fifth/m_episodes/2017-2018/brainwashed-the-secret-cia-experiments-in-canada.

32 Cashore, H., et al., 'Trudeau Government Gag Order in CIA Brainwashing Case Silences Victims, Lawyer Says', CBC/Radio Canada, 2017, https://www.cbc.ca/news/canada/canadian-government-gag-order-mk-ultra-1.4448933.

33 CBC/Radio Canada, 'MK Ultra', broadcast 1980, https://www.cbc.ca/fifth/episodes/40-years-of-the-fifth-estate/mk-ultra.

Chapter 4: The Politics of Persuasion

1 Cohen, J., and Shear, M. D., 'Poll Shows More Americans Think Obama is a Muslim', *The Washington Post*, 2010, http://www.washingtonpost.com/wp-dyn/content/article/2010/08/18/ar2010081806913.html.

2 As BBC journalist Anne Soy put it in 2020, 'They remain ostracised and impoverished even now because of colonial propaganda – a lesser-known legacy of colonialism', https://www.bbc.co.uk/news/av/world-africa-53514916/legacy-of-kenyan-clan-branded-evil-by-colonialists.

3 Taylor, P. M., *The Projection of Britain*, Cambridge University Press, 1981. See also Wu, T., *The Attention Merchants: The Epic Scramble to Get Inside Our Heads*, New York, Knopf Publishing Group, 2018, Ch. 3, footnote 6.

4 Wu, T., *The Attention Merchants: The Epic Scramble to Get Inside Our Heads*, New York, Knopf Publishing Group, 2018, Ch. 3.

5 In conversation with Emma Briant, https://emma-briant.co.uk/.

6 Posetti, J., and Matthews, A., *A Short Guide to the History of 'Fake News' and Disinformation*, International Center for Journalists, 2018.

7 Neander, J., and Marlin, R., 'Media and Propaganda: The Northcliffe Press and the Corpse Factory Story of World War I', *Global Media Journal* (Canadian edn), vol. 3, no. 2, pp.67–82.

8 Bernays, E. L., *Propaganda*, 1928.

9 The Institute for Propaganda Analysis was set up in the US (1937–42) as a response to concerns in America about the threat of propaganda for democratic values, 'to teach people how to think, not what to think'.

10 See Wu, T., *The Attention Merchants: The Epic Scramble to Get Inside Our Heads*, New York, Knopf Publishing Group, 2018.

11 See Young, J., *The History of Tobacco and Its Growth Throughout the World*, Stanford University Press.

12 Although there was a brief ban in New York City.

13 See Brandt, A. M., *The Cigarette Century: The Rise, Fall and Deadly Persistence of the Product that Defined America*, New York, Basic Books, 2007. See also Wu, T., *The Attention Merchants: The Epic Scramble to Get Inside Our Heads*, New York, Knopf Publishing Group, 2018, Ch.5, footnote 11.

14 Mougel, N., *Module 1-0 – Explanatory Notes – World War I Casualties*, trans. Centre Européen Robert Schuman, 2011, http://www.centre-robert-schuman.org/userfiles/files/REPERES%20%E2%80%93%20module%201-1-1%20-%20explanatory%20notes%20%E2%80%93%20World%20War%20I%20casualties%20%E2%80%93%20EN.pdf.

15 https://www.who.int/news-room/fact-sheets/detail/tobacco.

16 Huxley, A., *Brave New World Revisited*, 1958.

17 As Aldous Huxley noted, we can all respond to reason and truth. But we can also respond to unreason and falsehood – 'particularly in those cases where the falsehood evokes some enjoyable emotion, or where the appeal to unreason strikes some answering chord in the primitive, subhuman depths of our being', Huxley, A., *Brave New World Revisited*, 1958.

18 See Haidt, J., *The Righteous Mind: Why Good People Are Divided by Politics and Religion*, Penguin Books Ltd, 2012.

19 Huxley, A., *Brave New World Revisited*, 1958.

20 Ibid.

21 Bergerson, A. S., 'Listening to the Radio in Hildesheim, 1923–53', *German Studies Review*, vol. 24, no. 1, 2001, pp.83–113.

22 Arendt, H., *The Origins of Totalitarianism*, Berlin, Schocken Books, 1951.

23 Palthe, A., 'Verdict Albert Speer', *Traces of War*, 2019, https://www.tracesofwar.com/articles/4574/Verdict-Albert-Speer.htm.

24 Palthe, A., 'Final statement Albert Speer', *Traces of War*, 2019, https://www.tracesofwar.com/articles/4573/Final-statement-Albert-Speer.htm.

25 Wu, T., *The Attention Merchants: The Epic Struggle To Get Inside Our Heads*, Atlantic Books, 2017

26 Huxley's disturbing views on eugenics are a feature of this collection, as they are in his novel. Like many of the thinkers cited, some of his views are extremely damaging to human rights and would be considered morally unacceptable today. While he provides valuable insights into the ways in which our minds can be manipulated, which are prescient and useful for understanding the challenges we face to protect our freedom of thought today, citing his work is in no way an endorsement of his views on eugenics.

27 Huxley, A., *Brave New World Revisited*, 1958.

28 Wu, T., *The Attention Merchants: The Epic Struggle To Get Inside Our Heads*, Atlantic Books, 2017

29 Harris, T., 'About', Tristan Harris website, www.tristanharris.com (accessed 23 May 2021).

30 A 1990s TV advert for Tampax Compaq with plastic applicator featured a woman on roller skates being pulled along by dogs as an image of freedom.

Chapter 5: The Power of Human Rights

1   MacIntyre, A., *After Virtue*, University of Notre Dame Press, 1981.

2   Nietzsche, F., *Beyond Good and Evil*, Germany, 1886.

3   See judgment of 26 July 1994, BGHS 40. 218; judgment of 3 November 1992, BGHS 39. 1; and judgment of 20 March 1995, NJW 1995. 2732 (5 StR 378/94).

4   See Cashore, H., et al., 'Trudeau Government Gag Order in CIA Brainwashing Case Silences Victims, Lawyer Says', CBC/Radio Canada, 2017, https://www.cbc.ca/news/canada/canadian-government-gag-order-mk-ultra-1.4448933.

5   The prison closed in 2018 with various reports that the site would be turned into luxury flats, a museum and, in 2021 a Catholic church.

6   The US State Department's report on human rights in the country in 2007 noted that prison conditions were 'harsh' due to the high numbers of inmates: https://2001-2009.state.gov/g/drl/rls/hrrpt/2007/100499.htm.

7   *The Prosecutor v. Ferdinand Nahimana, Jean-Bosco Barayagwiza, Hassan Ngeze* (2003) Case No. ICTR-99-52-T.

8   Ibid.

9   Ibid.

10 Ibid.

11 Ibid.

12 Ibid.

13 *Ferdinand Nahimana, Jean-Bosco Barayagwiza, Hassan Ngeze (Appellants) v. The Prosecutor (Respondent)* (2007), Case No. ICTR-99-52-A.

14 Article 6(3) of the Statute of the International Criminal Tribunal for the Prosecution of Persons Responsible for Genocide and Other Serious Violations of International Humanitarian Law Committed in the Territory of Rwanda and Rwandan Citizens Responsible for Genocide and Other Such Violations Committed in the Territory of Neighbouring States, 1994.

15 For example, see Article 20 of the International Covenant on Civil and Political Rights, and Human Rights Committee General Comment No. 11: 'For Article 20 to become fully effective there ought to be a law making it clear that propaganda and advocacy as described therein are contrary to public policy and providing for an appropriate sanction in case of violation', UN Human Rights Committee, 'CCPR General Comment No. 11: Article 20 (Prohibition of propaganda for war and inciting national, racial or religious hatred)', CCPR/GEC/4720/E, 1983.

16 See Wambua-Soi, C., 'Remembering Rwanda's genocide', Aljazeera English, 2012, https://www.aljazeera.com/features/2012/7/1/remembering-rwandas-genocide.

17 For example, the UK, Canada and Australia.

18 See Directive (EU) 2018/1808 of the European Parliament and of the Council of 14 November 2018 amending Directive 2010/13/EU on the coordination of certain provisions laid down by law, regulation or administrative action in Member States concerning the provision of Audiovisual Media Services (Audiovisual Media Services Directive) in view of changing market realities, p.84.

19 'Does subliminal advertising actually work?', BBC News, https://www.bbc.co.uk/news/magazine-30878843.

20 Moore, T. E., 'Scientific Consensus and Expert Testimony: Lessons from the Judas Priest Trial', *Skeptical Inquirer*, vol. 20, no. 6, 1996.

21 Ibid.

22 Daus, M. W., 'Subliminal Messages in Music: Free Speech or Invasion of Privacy?', *University of Miami Entertainment & Sports Law Review*, vol. 10-1, 1992.

23 See *Malone v. United Kingdom* (1984), 7 EHRR 14, and *Zakharov v. Russia* (2015), ECtHR 47143/06.

24 For example, bulk powers under the UK Investigatory Powers Act 2016.

25 Cited in Mesaki, S., 'Witchcraft and the Law in Tanzania', *International Journal of Sociology and Anthropology*, vol. 1, no. 8, 2009, pp.132–8.

26 Jacobs, R., 'When Governments Go After Witches', *The Atlantic*, 2013, https://www.theatlantic.com/international/archive/2013/10/when-governments-go-after-witches/280856/.

27 Levinson-King, R., 'Canada's Last Witch Trials: Women accused of fake witchcraft', BBC News, 2018, https://www.bbc.co.uk/news/world-us-canada-45983540.

28 Jacobs, R., 'Saudi Arabia's War on Witchcraft', *The Atlantic*, 2013, https://www.theatlantic.com/international/archive/2013/08/saudi-arabias-war-on-witchcraft/278701/; https://www.jpost.com/Middle-East/Saudi-Arabias-Anti-Witchcraft-Unit-breaks-another-spell.

29 Kent, C., 'The UN Will Hold Its First Meeting to Discuss Witchcraft-Related Violence', *Vice*, 2017, https://www.vice.com/en_asia/article/wjxney/the-un-will-hold-its-first-meeting-to-discuss-witchcraft-related-violence. See also Gary Foxcroft, Director of the Witchcraft and Human Rights Information Network, www.whrin.org.

30 Africans Unite Against Child Abuse (AFRUCA), 'What is Witchcraft Abuse? Safeguarding African Children in the UK Series 5', 2017.

31 A. Crawford and T Smith, "The Torso in the Thames: A 20 year mystery", in BBC News, 21st September 2021. https://www.bbc.co.uk/news/uk-58415046

32 See L. van der Putten, KidsRights Report, "No Small Sacrifice - Child Sacrifice in Uganda, in a Global Context of Cultural Violence" 2014. The Ugandan Prevention and Prohibition of Human Sacrifice Act was passed in May 2021 aimed at tackling the growing problem of child sacrifice in the country.

33 A/HRC/47/L.9, accessible at https://undocs.org/A/HRC/47/L.9.

34 Hogg, P. W., *Constitutional Law of Canada*, Ontario, Thomson Carswell, 2007.

Chapter 6: Facebook Knows You Better

1 'Artificial Intelligence Risks to Privacy Demand Urgent Action', Bachelet Press Release UN OHCHR, 15 September 2021, https://www.ohchr.org/EN/NewsEvents/Pages/DisplayNews.aspx?NewsID=27469.

2 Johnson, B., 'Privacy No Longer a Social Norm, Says Facebook Founder', *The Guardian*, 11 January

2010, https://www.theguardian.com/technology/2010/jan/11/facebook-privacy.

3 https://en.wikipedia.org/wiki/John_Darwin_disappearance_case.

4 Schaposnik, Laura P., and Unwin, James, 'The Phone Walkers: A study of human dependence on inactive mobile devices', *Behaviour*, 31 May 2018, https://brill.com/view/journals/beh/155/5/article-p389_4.xml.

5 Knapton, Sarah, 'Facebook Knows You Better Than Your Members of Your Own Family', *Daily Telegraph*, 12 January 2015, http://www.telegraph.co.uk/news/science/science-news/11340166/Facebook-knows-you-better-than-your-members-of-your-own-family.html.

6 Kosinski, Michal, et al., 'Private Traits and Attributes Are Predictable From Digital Records of Human Behaviour', *PNAS*, 12 February 2013, https://www.pnas.org/content/pnas/110/15/5802.full.pdf.

7 Ibid.

8 Weir, Kirsten, 'The Pain of Social Rejection', *Monitor on Psychology* 2012, vol. 43, no. 4, https://www.apa.org/monitor/2012/04/rejection.

9 DeWall, C. Nathan, et al., *Acetaminophen Reduces Social Pain: Behavioral and Neural Evidence*, Association for Psychological Science Research report, 2010, https://www.semel.ucla.edu/sites/default/files/publications/July%202010%20-%20Tylenol%20reduces%20social%20pain.pdf.

10 Stachl, Clemens, et al., 'Predicting Personality From Patterns of Behaviour Collected with Smartphones', *PNAS*, 18 June 2020, https://www.pnas.org/content/pnas/117/30/17680.full.pdf.

11 'Why Freedom of Thought Requires Free Media and Why Free Media Require Free Technology', Professor Eben Moglen's speech at re:publica, Berlin, 2012, https://re-publica.com/en/file/republica-2012-eben-moglen-freedom-thought-requires-free-media-0.

12 Kaye, David, *Research Report on Artistic Freedom of Expression*, 24 July 2020, https://undocs.org/en/A/HRC/44/49/Add.2.

13 Zuboff, S. *The Age of Surveillance Capitalism: The Fight for a Human Future at the New Frontier of Power*, London, Profile Books, 2019.

14 Madrigal, Alexis C., 'Reading the Privacy Policies You Encounter in a Year Would Take 76 Work Days', *The Atlantic*, 1 March 2012, https://www.theatlantic.com/technology/archive/2012/03/reading-the-privacy-policies-you-encounter-in-a-year-would-take-76-work-days/253851/.

15 Williams, James, *Stand Out of Our Light*, Cambridge University Press, 2018, http://dx.doi.org/10.1017/9781108453004 (online version published under Creative Commons Licence).

16 Kramer, Adam D. I., et al., 'Experimental Evidence of Massive-scale Emotional Contagion through Social Networks', *PNAS*, 2 June 2014, https://www.pnas.org/content/111/24/8788; 'Facebook Admits Failings over Emotion Manipulation Study', BBC, 3 October 2014, https://www.bbc.co.uk/news/technology-29475019.

17 Rushe, Dominic, 'Facebook Sorry – Almost – For Secret Psychological Experiment on Users', *The Guardian*, 2 October 2014, https://www.theguardian.com/technology/

2014/oct/02/facebook-sorry-secret-psychological-experiment-users.

18 'In re: Facebook (Psychological Study)', https://epic.org/privacy/internet/ftc/facebook/psycho/.

19 '30 Achievements in Women's Health in 30 Years (1984–2014): Decrease in teen pregnancy', Office on Women's Health, https://www.womenshealth.gov/30-achievements/09; Hill, Amelia, 'How the UK Halved Its Teenage Pregnancy Rate', *The Guardian*, 18 July 2016, https://www.theguardian.com/society/2016/jul/18/how-uk-halved-teenage-pregnancy-rate-public-health-strategy#:~:text=Last%20week%2C%20the%20Office%20for,all%20age%20groups%20under%2025; '"Dramatic" Drop in Teenage Alcohol Consumption in Scotland', BBC, 26 September 2018, https://www.bbc.co.uk/news/uk-scotland-45645295; Klass, Perri, 'Binge Drinking Drops Among Teenagers', *The New York Times*, 31 July 2017, https://www.nytimes.com/2017/07/31/well/family/binge-drinking-drops-among-teenagers.html; 'Adolescents Drink Less, Although Levels of Alcohol Consumption Are Still Dangerously High', WHO press release, 26 September 2018, https://www.euro.who.int/en/media-centre/sections/press-releases/2018/adolescents-drink-less,-although-levels-of-alcohol-consumption-are-still-dangerously-high.

20 Levin, Sam, 'Facebook Told Advertisers It Can Identify Teens Feeling "Insecure" and "Worthless"', *The Guardian*, 1 May 2017, https://www.theguardian.com/technology/2017/may/01/facebook-advertising-data-insecure-teens.

21 Horton, Alex, 'Channeling "The Social Network," lawmaker grills Zuckerberg on his notorious beginnings', *The Washington Post*, 11 April 2018, https://www.washingtonpost.com/news/the-switch/wp/2018/04/11/channeling-the-social-network-lawmaker-grills-zuckerberg-on-his-notorious-beginnings/.

22 https://about.fb.com//news/h/comments-on-research-and-ad-targeting/.

23 'Real Time Bidding: The auction for your attention', EDRi, 4 July 2019, https://edri.org/our-work/real-time-bidding-the-auction-for-your-attention/.

24 'Profiling Children for Advertising: Facebook's Monetisation of Young People's Personal Data', Reset Australia policy briefing, https://au.reset.tech/uploads/resettechaustralia_profiling-children-for-advertising-1.pdf.

25 McCann, D., and Hall, M., 'Blocking the Data Stalkers', New Economics Foundation, 2018, https://neweconomics.org/uploads/files/NEF_Blocking_Data_Stalkers.pdf.

26 Ibid.

27 Fagan, C., and Wright, L., 'Ad Tech Fuels Disinformation Sites in Europe: The numbers and the players', Global Disinformation Index, 2020, https://disinformationindex.org/wp-content/uploads/2020/03/GDI_Adtech_EU.pdf.

28 Griffin, Andrew, 'Twitter is watching how you use your phone – but it can be stopped', *The Independent*, 27 November 2014, http://www.independent.co.uk/life-style/gadgets-and-tech/twitter-is-watching-how-you-use-your-phone-but-it-can-be-stopped-9886456.html.

29 As Harvard law professor Eben Moglen points out, 'In the twentieth century, people were tortured to reveal their thoughts and inform on their friends and family but in the twenty-first century you just build social networks and everyone informs on everyone else': 'Why Freedom of Thought Requires Free Media and Why Free Media Require Free Technology', Professor Eben Moglen's speech at re:publica, Berlin, 2012, https://re-publica.com/en/file/republica-2012-eben-moglen-freedom-thought-requires-free-media-0.

30 See, for example, Jenkin, Matthew, 'Tablets Out, Imagination In: The schools that shun technology', *The Guardian*, 2 December 2015, https://www.theguardian.com/teacher-network/2015/dec/02/schools-that-ban-tablets-traditional-education-silicon-valley-london; Retter, Emily, 'Billionaire Tech Mogul Bill Gates Reveals He Banned His Children From Mobile Phones Until They Turned 14', *Daily Mirror*, 21 April 2017, https://www.mirror.co.uk/tech/billionaire-tech-mogul-bill-gates-10265298; Bilton, Nick, 'Steve Jobs Was a Low-Tech Parent', *The New York Times*, 10 September 2014, https://www.nytimes.com/2014/09/11/fashion/steve-jobs-apple-was-a-low-tech-parent.html.

31 O'Connell, Mark, 'Why Silicon Valley Billionaires Are Prepping for the Apocalypse in New Zealand' *The Guardian*, 15 February 2018, https://www.theguardian.com/news/2018/feb/15/why-silicon-valley-billionaires-are-prepping-for-the-apocalypse-in-new-zealand.

Chapter 7: The Ministry of Truth

1 Galli, Giulia, et al., 'Brain Indices of Disagreement With One's Social Values Predict EU Referendum Voting Behavior', *Social Cognitive and Affective Neuroscience*, vol. 12, no. 11, November 2017, pp.1758–65, https://doi.org/10.1093/scan/nsx105https://academic.oup.com/scan/article/12/11/1758/4111142.

2 Kanai, R., et al., 'Political Orientations Are Correlated with Brain Structure in Young Adults', *Current Biology*, vol. 21, 2011, pp.677–80.

3 Schreiber, D., et al., 'Red Brain, Blue Brain: Evaluative Processes Differ in Democrats and Republicans', *PLoS ONE*, vol. 8, no. 2, 2013, e52970, doi:10.1371/journal.pone.0052970.

4 Kosinski, M., 'Facial Recognition Technology Can Expose Political Orientation From Naturalistic Facial Images', *Scientific Reports*, vol. 11, 2021, p.100, https://doi.org/10.1038/s41598-020-79310-1 https://www.nature.com/articles/s41598-020-79310-1.

5 Schreiber, D., et al., 'Red Brain, Blue Brain: Evaluative Processes Differ in Democrats and Republicans', *PLoS ONE*, vol. 8, no. 2, 2013, e52970, doi:10.1371/journal.pone.0052970.

6 Randall, K., 'Neuropolitics, Where Campaigns Try to Read Your Mind', *The New York Times*, 4 November 2015, https://www.nytimes.com/2015/11/04/world/americas/neuropolitics-where-campaigns-try-to-read-your-mind.html.

7   Malkin, E., and Randall, K., 'Mexico's Governing Party Vows to Stop Using Neuromarketing to Study Voters', *The New York Times*, 11 November 2015, https://www.nytimes.com/2015/11/12/world/americas/mexicos-governing-party-vows-to-stop-using-neuromarketing-to-study-voters.html.

8   Halpern, Sue, 'The Neuroscience of Picking a Presidential Candidate', *The New Yorker*, 3 February 2020, https://www.newyorker.com/tech/annals-of-technology/the-neuroscience-of-picking-a-presidential-candidate.

9   See Chapter 6.

10 Ibid.

11 Cambridge Analytica website – no longer available since the company closed down.

12 Confessore, Nicholas, and Hakim, Danny, 'Data Firm Says "Secret Sauce" Aided Trump; Many Scoff', *The New York Times*, 6 March 2017, https://www.nytimes.com/2017/03/06/us/politics/cambridge-analytica.html?_r=0.

13 Cadwalladr, Carole, and Graham-Harrison, Emma, 'Revealed: 50 Million Facebook Profiles Harvested for Cambridge Analytica in Major Data Breach', *The Guardian*, 17 March 2018, https://www.theguardian.com/news/2018/mar/17/cambridge-analytica-facebook-influence-us-election; https://www.orwellfoundation.com/journalist/carole-cadwalladr-2/.

14 Wayne, Leslie, 'Democrats Take Page From Their Rival's Playbook', *The New York Times*, 31 October 2008, https://www.nytimes.com/2008/11/01/us/politics/01target.html.

15 Oakes, Omar, 'IPA Calls for Suspension of Micro-targeted Political Ads', *Campaign*, 20 April 2018, https://www.campaignlive.co.uk/article/ipa-calls-suspension-micro-targeted-political-ads/1462598.

16 *Democracy Disrupted? Personal information and political influence?*, ICO report, 11 July 2018, https://ico.org.uk/media/action-weve-taken/2259369/democracy-disrupted-110718.pdf.

17 'La posibilidad, o más bien la certeza, como acredita el todavía reciente asunto de Cambridge Analytica, de la utilización de técnicas de big data para modular, cuando no manipular, opiniones políticas evidencia la necesidad de que las garantías normativas y las limitaciones legales sean contundentes, precisas y efectivas en lo que se refiere a la recopilación y tratamiento de los datos personales relativos a las opiniones políticas que puedan llevar a cabo los partidos políticos en el marco de sus actividades electorales': Gálvez, J. J., 'El Constitucional tumba la ley que permite a los partidos recopilar datos para crear perfiles ideológicos', *El País*, 22 May 2019, https://elpais.com/politica/2019/05/22/actualidad/1558530147_953979.html.

18 SENTENCIA 76/2019, de 22 de mayo (BOE Official State Gazette), no. 151, 25 June 2019, https://hj.tribunalconstitucional.es/en/Resolucion/Show/25942.

19 See, for example, Broderick, Ryan, and Darmanin, Jules, 'The "Yellow Vest" Riots In France Are What Happens When Facebook Gets Involved With Local News', BuzzFeed, 5 December 2018, https://www.buzzfeednews.com/article/ryanhatesthis/france-paris-yellow-jackets-facebook.

20 Manavis, Sarah, 'How Celebrities Became the Biggest Peddlers of 5G Coronavirus Conspiracy Theories',

New Statesman, 6 April 2020, https://www.newstatesman.com/science-tech/social-media/2020/04/how-celebrities-became-biggest-peddlers-5g-conspiracy-theory-coronavirus-covid-19.

21 Satariano, Adam, and Alba, Davey, 'Burning Cell Towers, Out of Baseless Fear They Spread the Virus', *The New York Times*, 10 April 2020, https://www.nytimes.com/2020/04/10/technology/coronavirus-5g-uk.html.

22 Report of the independent international fact-finding mission on Myanmar, A/HRC/39/64, 12

September 2018, https://www.ohchr.org/Documents/HRBodies/HRCouncil/FFM-Myanmar/A_HRC_39_64.pdf.

23 Ibid., para. 32.

24 Ibid., para. 38.

25 Ibid., para. 74.

26 'UN: Facebook has turned into a beast in Myanmar', BBC, 13 March 2018, https://www.bbc.co.uk/news/technology-43385677.

27 Avaaz and Guns Down Campaign – Survivors of Social Media Harm, https://secure.avaaz.org/campaign/en/facebook_survivors/.

Chapter 8: Consenting Adults

1 Shashkevich, A., 'Meeting Online Has Become the Most Popular Way US Couples Connect, Stanford Sociologist Finds', *Stanford News*, 2019, https://news.stanford.edu/2019/08/21/online-dating-popular-way-u-s-couples-meet/.

2 'Finding Love Online: More than half of couples set to meet via the internet', Sky News, 2019, https://news.sky.com/story/finding-love-online-more-than-half-of-couples-set-to-meet-via-the-internet-11871341.

3 Aldous Huxley, *Brave New World*, 1932, Chapter 5.

4 See Chapter 7.

5 Office of the Privacy Commissioner of Canada, Joint Investigation of Clearview AI, Inc. by the Office of the Privacy Commissioner of Canada, the Commission d'Accès à l'Information du Québec, the Information and Privacy Commissioner for British Columbia, and the Information Privacy Commissioner of Alberta, 2021, https://www.priv.gc.ca/en/opc-actions-and-decisions/investigations/

investigations-into-businesses/2021/pipeda-2021-001/.

6 According to the Yogakarta Principles, which reflect the current status of international human rights law in relation to issues of sexual orientation and gender identity, 'Sexual orientation is understood to refer to each person's capacity for profound emotional, affectional and sexual attraction to, and intimate and sexual relations with, individuals of a different gender or the same gender or more than one gender; gender identity is understood to refer to each person's deeply felt internal and individual experience of gender, which may or may not correspond with the sex assigned at birth, including the personal sense of the body (which may involve, if freely chosen, modification of bodily appearance or function by medical, surgical or other means) and other expressions of gender, including dress, speech and mannerisms': International Commission of Jurists, Yogyakarta Principles – Principles

on the application of international human rights law in relation to sexual orientation and gender identity, Yogyakarta Principles, 2007.

7 Wang, Y., and Kosinski, M., 'Deep Neural Networks Are More Accurate Than Humans at Detecting Sexual Orientation From Facial Images', *PsyArXiv*, 2017, p.2, https://psyarxiv.com/hv28a//.

8 Quach, K., 'The Infamous AI Gaydar Study Was Repeated – and, no, code can't tell if you're straight or not just from your face', *The Register*, 2019, https://www.theregister.co.uk/2019/03/05/ai_gaydar/.

9 *The Precautionary Principle (UNESCO)*, World Commission on the Ethics of Scientific Knowledge and Technology (COMEST) report, 2005.

10 www.humandignitytrust.org.

11 Este, J., 'Tracing homophobia in South Korea's coronavirus surveillance program', *The Conversation*, 2020, https://theconversation.com/tracing-homophobia-in-south-koreas-coronavirus-surveillance-program-139428.

12 'Gay People', in 'Nazi Persecution: 1933–1945', Holocaust Memorial Day Trust, https://www.hmd.org.uk/learn-about-the-holocaust-and-genocides/nazi-persecution/gay-people/.

13 Many other countries are doing the same: Rainbow Europe (rainbow-europe.org); ILGA Europe, 'Bodily integrity – Annual Review of the Human Rights Situation of Lesbian, Gay, Bisexual, Trans, and Intersex People Covering the Period of January to December 2020', Rainbow Europe, 2021.

14 'Out of Control: How consumers are exploited by the online advertising industry', Forbrukerrådet, 2020, https://fil.forbrukerradet.no/wp-content/uploads/2020/01/2020-01-14-out-of-control-final-version.pdf.

15 Singer, N., and Krolik, A., 'Grindr And OkCupid Spread Personal Details, Study Says', *The New York Times*, 2020, https://www.nytimes.com/2020/01/13/technology/grindr-apps-dating-data-tracking.html.

16 Hern, A., 'Grindr Fined £8.6M in Norway over Sharing Personal Information', *The Guardian*, 2021, https://www.theguardian.com/technology/2021/jan/26/grindr-fined-norway-sharing-personal-information.

17 'Apps and Traps: Dating Apps Must Do More to Protect LGBTQ Communities in Middle East and North Africa', Article 19, 2018, https://www.article19.org/resources/apps-traps-dating-apps-must-protect-communities-middle-east-north-africa/.

18 'There's Something Seriously Wrong with Dating Apps', *Medium*, 2019, https://medium.com/read-write-participate/theres-something-seriously-wrong-with-dating-apps-f41db8af1e82.

19 McMullan, T., 'Are the Algorithms That Power Dating Apps Racially Biased?', *Wired* UK, 2019, https://www.wired.co.uk/article/racial-bias-dating-apps/; Kleinman, A., 'Black People and Asian Men Have a Much Harder Time Dating on OkCupid', *Huffington Post* UK, 2017, https://www.huffingtonpost.co.uk/entry/okcupid-race_n_5811840.

20 Dent, S., 'Tinder Ditches Its Hidden Desirability Scores', *Engadget*, 2019, https://www.engadget.com/2019-03-18-tinder-dumps-desirability-scores.html.

21 Ibid.

22 Sharma, M., 'The Biases We Feed to Tinder Algorithms: How a Machine-Learning Algorithm Holds Up a Mirror to Society', *Diggit*, 2019, https://www.diggitmagazine.com/articles/biases-we-feed-tinder-algorithms.

23 See Chapter 6.

24 Sharma, M., 'The Biases We Feed to Tinder Algorithms: How a Machine-Learning Algorithm Holds Up a Mirror to Society', *Diggit*, 2019, https://www.diggitmagazine.com/articles/biases-we-feed-tinder-algorithms.

25 Gay, E., 'The Complete Evidence in the Grace Millane Murder Trial: Inside the Case That Gripped a Nation', *Stuff*, 2020, https://www.stuff.co.nz/national/crime/117623648/the-complete-evidence-the-grace-millane-murder-trial-heard-inside-the-case-that-gripped-a-nation.

26 https://wecantconsenttothis.uk/.

27 Moore, A., and Khan, C., 'The Fatal, Hateful Rise of Choking During Sex', *The Guardian*, 2019, https://www.theguardian.com/society/2019/jul/25/fatal-hateful-rise-of-choking-during-sex.

28 Ibid.

29 Ibid.

30 Ibid.

31 European Union: European Parliament, *Report on Eliminating Gender Stereotypes in the EU*, OJ (2012/2116 INI), 2012, https://www.europarl.europa.eu/doceo/document/A-7-2012-0401_EN.html?redirect#title2.

32 For a discussion on this issue, see, for example, Langton, Rae, 'Is Pornography Like the Law?' and McGowan, Mary Kate, 'On Multiple Types of Silencing', in Mari Mikkola (ed.), *Beyond Speech: Pornography and Analytic Feminist Philosophy*, Oxford University Press, 2017.

33 Kühn, S., and Gallinat, J., 'Brain Structure and Functional Connectivity Associated with Pornography Consumption: The Brain on Porn', *JAMA Psychiatry*, vol. 71, no. 7, 2014, pp.827–34, https://jamanetwork.com/journals/jamapsychiatry/fullarticle/1874574.

34 Pinto, R. A., et al., 'Open Letter to Ögmundur Jónasson, Icelandic Minister of Interior, regarding Internet censorship', Stjornarradid, undated, https://www.stjornarradid.is/media/innanrikisraduneyti-media/media/frettir-2013/bref-til-radherra-28.-februar.pdf.

35 ICCPR, Article 19(3).

36 Heiðar- og Ómarsdóttir, B., 'ICELAND: To ban or not to ban? Debating pornography in Iceland', in Alan Finlay (ed.), *Global Information Society Watch 2015 Sexual Rights and the Internet*, APC and Hivos, 2015, https://www.giswatch.org/en/country-report/internet-rights/iceland#sdfootnote4sym.

37 *Hynes v. Mayor of Oradell*, 425 US 610, 619 (1976).

38 *Kovacs v. Cooper*, 336 US 77 (1949).

39 *Kokkinakis v. Greece*, 17 EHRR 397, para 48 (1994): 'First of all, a distinction has to be made between bearing Christian witness and improper proselytism. The former corresponds to true evangelism, which a report drawn up in 1956 under the auspices of the World Council of Churches describes as an essential mission and a responsibility of every Christian and every Church. The latter represents a corruption or deformation of it. It may, according to the same report, take the form of activities offering material or social

advantages with a view to gaining new members for a Church or exerting improper pressure on people in distress or in need; it may even entail the use of violence or brainwashing; more generally, it is not compatible with respect for freedom of thought, conscience and religion of others.'

40 In Srinivasan, A., *The Right to Sex*, Bloomsbury, 2021.

41 Emerging Technology from the arXiv, 'First Evidence That Online Dating Is Changing the Nature of Society', *MIT Technology Review*, 2017, https://www.technologyreview.com/2017/10/10/148701/first-evidence-that-online-dating-is-changing-the-nature-of-society/.

Chapter 9: Social Credit

1 See Gilman, Michele, 'Poverty Lawgorithms', including the following example: Rutkin, Aviva, 'People Will Follow a Robot in an Emergency – Even if It's Wrong', *New Scientist*, 29 February 2016, https://www.newscientist.com/article/2078945-people-will-follow-a-robot-in-an-emergency-even-if-its-wrong.

2 Kuo, Lily, 'China Bans 23m From Buying Travel Tickets as Part of "Social Credit" System', *The Guardian*, 1 March 2019, https://www.theguardian.com/world/2019/mar/01/china-bans-23m-discredited-citizens-from-buying-travel-tickets-social-credit-system.

3 Human Rights Watch Report, *China's Algorithms of Repression: Reverse Engineering a Xinjiang Police Mass Surveillance App*, 1 May 2019, https://www.hrw.org/report/2019/05/01/chinas-algorithms-repression/reverse-engineering-xinjiang-police-mass.

4 Grauer, Yael, 'Revealed: Massive Chinese Police Database', *The Intercept*, 29 January 2021, https://theintercept.com/2021/01/29/china-uyghur-muslim-surveillance-police/.

5 Matsakis, Louise, 'How the West Got China's Social Credit System Wrong', *Wired*, 29 July 2019, https://www.wired.com/story/china-social-credit-score-system/.

6 Blue, V., 'Your Online Activity Is Now Effectively a Social "Credit Score"', *Engadget*, 17 January 2020, https://www.engadget.com/2020-01-17-your-online-activity-effectively-social-credit-score-airbnb.html?guccounter=1&guce_referrer=aHR0cHM6Ly9kdWNrZHVja2dvLmNvbS8_cT1haXJibmircGF0ZW50O50K3NleCt3b3JrZWVlZXMmdD1uZXdleHQmYXRiPXYyMzUtMXJrJmlhPXdlYg&guce_referrer_sig=AQAAAEp9SF94kLHnBy9HTT-LZkgCIX1Gfb1pUhJX2qVxtHTb_vuBrBYCYG-6-QCkgHwBzMIm68wupCLzNPF6bLVzpKQv_GL6Cpiy1_6yIYb_wxQvqQymaQTCOLQsGim0X8Rol7uuum7bWZ0IzkjTbI9WlYZpmvuxoDyJziUHXGavRriJ.

7 Martin, Henry, 'Miriam Margolyes' Dover cottage was used as secret helicopter drop-off point for millions of pounds of cocaine after drugs gang rented it as part of their plot to fly Class A into Britain', *Daily Mail*, 26 July 2019, https://www.dailymail.co.uk/news/article-7290259/Miriam-Margoyles-cottage-used-secret-helicopter-drop-point-millions-pounds-cocaine.html.

8   Korff, Douwe, 'Passenger Name Records, Data Mining and Data Protection: The need for strong safeguards', Council of Europe, The Consultative Committee of the Convention for the Protection of Individuals With Regard to Automatic Processing of Personal Data (T-PD), 15 June 2015, https://rm.coe.int/16806a601b.

9   Opinion 1/15: see Court of Justice of the European Union Press Release 84/17, https://curia.europa.eu/jcms/upload/docs/application/pdf/2017-07/cp170084en.pdf .

10 'We Won! Home Office to stop using racist visa algorithm', Joint Council for the Welfare of Immigrants, https://www.jcwi.org.uk/news/we-won-home-office-to-stop-using-racist-visa-algorithm.

11 *Report of the Events Relating to Maher Arar, Factual Background Volume 1*, Commission of Inquiry into the Actions of Canadian Officials in Relation to Maher Arar, http://www.sirc-csars.gc.ca/pdfs/cm_arar_bgv1-eng.pdf.

12 Solon, Olivia, 'US Border Agents Are Doing "Digital Strip Searches". Here's how to protect yourself', *The Guardian*, 31 March 2017, https://www.theguardian.com/us-news/2017/mar/31/us-border-phone-computer-searches-how-to-protect.

13 Lomas, Natasha, '"Orwellian" AI Lie Detector Project Challenged in EU Court', TechCrunch, 5 February 2021, https://techcrunch.com/2021/02/05/orwellian-ai-lie-detector-project-challenged-in-eu-court/?guc counter=1&guce_referrer=aHR0c HM6Ly9kdWNrZHVja2dvLmNv bS8&guce_referrer_sig=AQAAAG fVwt7LsJdddcbb6tn5bxi6n39QvTwR zgpyd0jOCgp0s7gVczei-SYifidAi4z

7PHn1aKiUJplk--9O4M91cbpZ0qU gVD15ZQI8FYTmiE2RZ9PAm-dqJZchgKJgOpWO2EruTbsHSzA T0FacLgoiYmpEe8tLz4hfNfEsS8z BICyt.

14 Feathers, Todd, and Rose, Janus, 'An Insurance Startup Bragged It Uses AI to Detect Fraud. It Didn't Go Well', *Vice*, 26 May 2021, https://www.vice.com/en/article/z3x47y/an-insurance-startup-bragged-it-uses-ai-to-detect-fraud-it-didnt-go-well.

15 See Fry, H., *Hello World: How to Be Human in the Age of the Machine*, Doubleday, 2018.

16 Association Belge des Consommateurs Test-Achats ASBL and others, Case C-236/09.

17 Leo, Ben, 'MO COMPARE Motorists fork out £1,000 more to insure their cars if their name is Mohammed', *The Sun*, 22 January 2018, https://www.thesun.co.uk/motors/5393978/insurance-race-row-john-mohammed/.

18 See Chapter 1. Mill was horrified that only those professing a faith were allowed to give evidence in court while an atheist's word was not acceptable testimony.

19 Ruddick, Graham, 'Facebook Forces Admiral to Pull Plan to Price Car Insurance Based on Posts', *The Guardian*, 2 November 2016, https://www.theguardian.com/money/2016/nov/02/facebook-admiral-car-insurance-privacy-data.

20 Ibid.

21 Shoshana Zuboff coined this term in her book *The Age of Surveillance Capitalism*.

22 Uncovering the Hidden Data Ecosystem campaign, https://www.privacyinternational.org/campaigns/data-brokers.

23 Ram, Aliya, and Murgia, Madhumita, 'Data Brokers: Regulators try to rein

in the "privacy deathstars"', *Financial Times*, 8 January 2019, https://www.ft.com/content/f1590694-fe68-11e8-aebf-99e208d3e521.

24 Ibid.

25 Dazio, Stefanie, 'Weather Channel App to Change Practices After LA Lawsuit', *AP News*, 19 August 2020, https://apnews.com/article/virus-outbreak-technology-us-news-los-angeles-ca-state-wire-f6a83c0b8e0a65563e4c76955c37c0ab.

26 Ibid.

27 Du, Lisa, and Maki, Ayaka, 'These Cameras Can Spot Shoplifters Even Before They Steal', *Bloomberg*, 4 March 2019, https://www.bloomberg.com/news/articles/2019-03-04/the-ai-cameras-that-can-spot-shoplifters-even-before-they-steal.

28 The ombudsman decides whether a consumer's treatment was 'fair and reasonable' in all the circumstances.

29 https://undocs.org/A/74/493.

30 Gilman, Michele, 'AI Algorithms Intended to Root Out Welfare Fraud Often End Up Punishing the Poor Instead', *The Conversation*, 14 February 2020, https://theconversation.com/ai-algorithms-intended-to-root-out-welfare-fraud-often-end-up-punishing-the-poor-instead-131625.

31 The Dutch Section of the International Commission of Jurists (Nederlands Juristen Comité voor de Mensenrechten – NJCM) is an organisation involved in the protection and strengthening of human rights and fundamental freedoms. The Civil Rights Protection Platform (Platform Bescherming Burgerrechten) focuses on the protection of traditional civil rights. Privacy First aims to preserve and promote the right to privacy. The

Umbrella Organisation of DBC-Free Practices (Koepel van DBC-Vrije praktijken) is committed to the protection of the right to privacy of clients of psychotherapists.

32 https://privacyinternational.org/news-analysis/3363/syri-case-landmark-ruling-benefits-claimants-around-world. Judgment in English here: https://uitspraken.rechtspraak.nl/inziendocument?id=ECLI:NL:RBDHA:2020:1878.

33 Gilman, Michele, 'Poverty Lawgorithms', accessible here: https://datasociety.net/wp-content/uploads/2020/09/Poverty-Lawgorithms-20200915.pdf.

34 Zimmermann, Annette, 'The A-level Results Injustice Shows Why Algorithms Are Never Neutral', *New Statesman*, 14 August 2020, https://www.newstatesman.com/politics/education/2020/08/level-results-injustice-shows-why-algorithms-are-never-neutral.

35 Kuchler, Hannah, 'Men Only? Facebook, "dark ads" and discrimination', *Financial Times*, 3 October 2018, https://www.ft.com/content/bfd60c3c-c5d0-11e8-8167-bea19d5dd52e.

36 Scheiber, Noah, 'Facebook Accused of Allowing Bias Against Women in Job Ads', *The New York Times*, 18 September 2018, https://www.nytimes.com/2018/09/18/business/economy/facebook-job-ads.html.

37 Murphy, Hannah, 'Facebook Settles With Civil Rights Groups in Discrimination Case', *Financial Times*, 19 February 2019, https://www.ft.com/content/f4ed1984-4a04-11e9-8b7f-d49067e0f50d.

38 Kendall, Marisa, 'Facebook Sued Over Alleged Housing Discrimination', *The Mercury News*, 19 August 2019,

https://www.mercurynews.com/2019/08/19/facebook-sued-again-alleged-housing-discrimination/.

39 Noble, Safiya U., *Algorithms of Oppression: How Search Engines Reinforce Racism*, New York University Press, 2018.

40 Ibid., p.3.

41 Krugman, Paul, 'Sex, Money and Gravitas', *The New York Times*, 1 August 2013, https://www.nytimes.com/2013/08/02/opinion/krugman-sex-money-and-gravitas.html.

42 Booth, Robert, 'Unilever Saves on Recruiters by Using AI to Assess Job Interviews', *The Guardian*, https://www.theguardian.com/technology/2019/oct/25/unilever-saves-on-recruiters-by-using-ai-to-assess-job-interviews.

43 https://www.reuters.com/article/us-amazon-com-jobs-automation-insight-idUSKCN1MK08G.

44 Chen, Angela, and Hao, Karen, 'Emotion AI Researchers Say Overblown Claims Give Their Work a Bad Name', *Technology Review*, 14 February 2020, https://www.technologyreview.com/2020/02/14/844765/ai-emotion-recognition-affective-computing-hirevue-regulation-ethics/.

45 For example, the US Employee Polygraph Protection Act, https://www.dol.gov/agencies/whd/fact-sheets/36-eppa.

46 Orwell, George, *Nineteen Eighty-Four*, Penguin Modern Classics, 2000, p.7.

47 Sun, Nikki, 'China's Tech Workers Pushed to Their Limits by Surveillance Software', *Financial Times*, 15 June 2021, https://www.ft.com/content/b74b6ad6-3b8d-4cd8-9dd6-3b49754aa1c7.

Chapter 10: Pre-Crime and Punishment

1 Satel, Sally, and Lilienfeld, Scott O., *Brainwashed: The Seductive Appeal of Mindless Neuroscience*, Basic Books, 2013, Chapter 4, 'The Telltale Brain'.

2 Giridharadas, Anand, 'India's Novel Use of Brain Scans in Courts Is Debated', *The New York Times*, 14 September 2008, https://www.nytimes.com/2008/09/15/world/asia/15brainscan.html?_r=3&pagewanted=2&oref=login.

3 *State of Maharashtra v. Aditi Baldev Sharma and Pravin Premswarup Khandelwal*, Sessions Case No. 508/07 (2008).

4 Ibid.

5 See Satel, Sally, and Lilienfeld, Scott O., *Brainwashed: The Seductive Appeal of Mindless Neuroscience*, Basic Books, 2013, Chapter 4, 'The Telltale Brain'.

6 In the Supreme Court of India Criminal Appeal No. 1267 of 2004, *Smt Selvi and Others v. State of Karnataka*, https://www.thehindu.com/migration_catalog/article16297234.ece/BINARY/Supreme%20Court%20judgement%20on%20narco-analysis%20test%20(833%20Kb)#page=6&zoom=auto,-262,188.

7 Ibid., paragraphs 192 and 193.

8 384 US 757 (1966), p.764.

9 *Smt Selvi and Others v. State of Karnataka*, paragraph 92.

10 Rutbeck-Goldman, Ariela, 'An "Unfair and Cruel Weapon": Consequences of Modern-Day Polygraph Use in

Federal Pre-Employment Screening', *UC Irvine Law Review*, vol. 7, no. 3, article 9, https://scholarship.law. uci.edu/cgi/viewcontent.cgi?article= 1301&context=ucilr.

11 UK government policy paper: Mandatory polygraph tests factsheet, updated 28 July 2021, https://www. gov.uk/government/publications/ domestic-abuse-bill-2020-factsheets/ mandatory-polygraph-tests-factsheet#can-offenders-be-recalled-to-custody-for-failing-a-polygraph-examination.

12 Grierson, Jamie, 'Lie-detector Tests Planned for Convicted Terrorists Freed on Licence', *The Guardian*, 21 January 2020, https://www. theguardian.com/politics/2020/jan/ 21/lie-detector-tests-planned-for-convicted-terrorists-freed-on-licence.

13 *Smt Selvi and Others v. State of Karnataka*.

14 See, for example, a 2010 study of 1,000 adults in the US: Serota, Kim B., et al., 'The Prevalence of Lying in America: Three Studies of Self-Reported Lies', *Human Communication Research*, vol. 36, no. 1, 1 January 2010, pp.2–25, https://doi.org/10.1111/j.1468-2958.2009.01366.x.

15 'How South Yorkshire Police Is Using Lie Detector Tests to Identify Sex Offenders', *Yorkshire Post*, 22 January 2018, https://www.yorkshirepost. co.uk/news/crime/how-south-yorkshire-police-using-lie-detector-tests-identify-sex-offenders-1764532/.

16 See Gender Shades: https://www. youtube.com/watch?v=TWWsW1w-BVo&feature=youtu.be / https://www. ajlunited.org/.

17 https://reclaimyourface.eu/the-problem/.

18 http://www.faception.com/.

19 Rees, Jenny, 'Facial Recognition Use by South Wales Police Ruled Unlawful', BBC, 11 August 2020, https://www.bbc.co.uk/news/uk-wales-53734716.

20 'Facial Recognition to "Predict Criminals" Sparks Row Over AI Bias', BBC, 24 June 2020, https://www. bbc.com/news/amp/technology-53165286?.

21 Rue, Lauren, 'Racial Influence on Automated Perceptions of Emotions', 7 December 2018, https://papers.ssrn. com/sol3/papers.cfm?abstract_id= 3281765.

22 'Rayshard Brooks: What happened before police shot him dead?', BBC, 18 June 2020, https://www.bbc.co.uk/ news/world-us-canada-53052077.

23 Ryan-Mosley, Tate, and Strong, Jennifer, 'The Activist Dismantling Racist Police Algorithms', *Technology Review*, 5 June 2020, https://www. technologyreview.com/2020/06/05/ 1002709/the-activist-dismantling-racist-police-algorithms/.

24 Ibid.

25 See a range of examples from across the EU, in Algorithmwatch 2019 report, https://algorithmwatch. org/wp-content/uploads/2019/01/ Automating_Society_Report_2019. pdf.

26 Lammy Review Final Report 2017, https://www.gov.uk/government/ organisations/lammy-review.

27 Report of the Stephen Lawrence Inquiry 1999, https://www.gov.uk/ government/publications/the-stephen-lawrence-inquiry.

28 Cork, Tristan, 'Black People Eight Times More Likely to Be Fined for Breaching Coronavirus Lockdown Rules', *Bristol Post*, 4 August 2020, https://www.bristolpost.co.uk/news/ bristol-news/black-people-eight-times-more-4394625.

Chapter 11: Body and Soul

1 Phelan, S. M., et al., 'Stigma and Bias About Lifestyle Choices and Obesity Have Been Shown to Affect Access to Healthcare: Impact of weight bias and stigma on quality of care and outcomes for patients with obesity', *Obesity Reviews*, April 2015, vol. 16, no. 4, pp.319–26, doi: 10.1111/obr.12266 /.

2 The rewards offered by some health insurance companies connected to activity tracking are not altruistic; your activity can be used to assess your risk.

3 Saner, Emine, 'Employers Are Monitoring Computers, Toilet Breaks – Even Emotions. Is your boss watching you?', *The Guardian*, 14 May 2018, https://www.theguardian.com/world/2018/may/14/is-your-boss-secretly-or-not-so-secretly-watching-you.

4 See Privacy International.

5 Hern, Alex, 'Amazon's Halo Wristband: The fitness tracker that listens to your mood', *The Guardian*, 28 August 2020, https://www.theguardian.com/technology/2020/aug/28/amazons-halo-wristband-the-fitness-tracker-that-listens-to-your-mood.

6 Hern, Alex, 'Someone Made a Smart Vibrator, So Of Course It Got Hacked', *The Guardian*, 10 August 2016, https://www.theguardian.com/technology/2016/aug/10/vibrator-phone-app-we-vibe-4-plus-bluetooth-hack.

7 Felizi, Natasha, and Varon, Joana, *MENSTRUAPPS – How to turn your period into money (for others)*, https://chupadados.codingrights.org/en/menstruapps-como-transformar-sua-menstruacao-em-dinheiro-para-os-outros/.

8 Moglia, Michelle, et al., 'Evaluation of Smartphone Menstrual Cycle Tracking Applications Using an Adapted APPLICATIONS Scoring System', *Obstetrics & Gynecology*, vol. 127, no. 6, June 2016, pp.1153–60, doi: 10.1097/AOG.0000000000001444; https://journals.lww.com/greenjournal/Fulltext/2016/06000/Evaluation_of_Smartphone_Menstrual_Cycle_Tracking.24.aspx.

9 Stern, Joanna, 'Fertility App Will Pay For Fertility Treatments If You Can't Get Pregnant', ABC News, 8 August 2013, https://abcnews.go.com/Technology/glow-fertility-app-pregnant-give-money/story?id=19901626.

10 For analysis of the Glow app and others, see Felizi, Natasha, and Varon, Joana, *MENSTRUAPPS – How to turn your period into money (for others)*, https://chupadados.codingrights.org/en/menstruapps-como-transformar-sua-menstruacao-em-dinheiro-para-os-outros/.

11 Bellinson, Jerry, 'Glow Pregnancy App Exposed Women to Privacy Threats, Consumer Reports Finds', *Consumer Reports*, updated 17 September 2020, https://www.consumerreports.org/mobile-security-software/glow-pregnancy-app-exposed-women-to-privacy-threats/.

12 'No Body's Business But Mine: How Menstruation Apps Are Sharing Your Data', Privacy International.

13 As ABC News put it when the app launched in 2013: see Stern, Joanna, 'Fertility App Will Pay For Fertility Treatments If You Can't Get Pregnant', ABC News, 8 August 2013,

https://abcnews.go.com/Technology/glow-fertility-app-pregnant-give-money/story?id=19901626.

14 McQuater, Katie, 'Psychiatrists Call for Social Networks to Hand Over Data for Online Harms Research', *Research Live*, 17 January 2020, https://www.research-live.com/article/news/psychiatrists_call_for_social_networks_to_hand_over_data_for_online_harms_research/id/5063972.

15 Wells, Georgia, et al., 'Facebook Knows Instagram Is Toxic for Teen Girls, Company Documents Show', *The Wall Street Journal*, 14 September 2021, https://www.wsj.com/articles/facebook-knows-instagram-is-toxic-for-teen-girls-company-documents-show-11631620739.

16 Sample, Ian, 'Covid Poses "Greatest Threat to Mental Health Since Second World War"', *The Guardian*, 27 December 2020, https://www.theguardian.com/society/2020/dec/27/covid-poses-greatest-threat-to-mental-health-since-second-world-war.

17 https://www.privacyinternational.org/campaigns/your-mental-health-sale.

18 The NHS stopped this practice, apparently in response to the Privacy International report.

19 https://www.privacyinternational.org/news-analysis/3986/mental-health-site-sharing-your-personal-data-were-going-after-them.

20 Hui, C. L., et al., 'ReMind, a Smartphone Application for Psychotic Relapse Prediction: A longitudinal study protocol', *Early Intervention in Psychiatry*, Wiley Online Library.

21 'Developing AI Technology to Detect Early Signs of Alzheimer's Disease', news-medical.net.

22 Gooding, Piers, 'Mapping the Rise of Digital Mental Health Technologies: Emerging issues for law and society', https://doi.org/10.1016/j.ijlp.2019.101498.

23 https://www.neuralink.com/.

24 https://tech.fb.com/imagining-a-new-interface-hands-free-communication-without-saying-a-word/.

25 tech.fb.com.

26 Australian independent legal scholar Fleur Beaupert notes, 'An analysis of freedom of opinion and expression from the perspective of psychosocial disability and madness illuminates the "symbolic violence" that is perpetrated by psychiatry and the mental health paradigm and reified by mental health laws', in her article 'Freedom of Opinion and Expression: From the Perspective of Psychosocial Disability and Madness', https://www.mdpi.com/2075-471X/7/1/3.

27 Cuthbertson, Anthony, 'Elon Musk Claims His Neuralink Chip Will Allow You to Stream Music Directly to Your Brain', *The Independent*, 21 July 2020, https://www.independent.co.uk/life-style/gadgets-and-tech/news/elon-musk-neuralink-brain-computer-chip-music-stream-a9627686.html.

28 Bublitz, Jan Christoph, 'Freedom of Thought in the Age of Neuroscience: A Plea and a Proposal for the Renaissance of a Forgotten Fundamental Right', ARSP Band 100, Heft 1, 2014.

29 'The Precautionary Principle', World Commission on the Ethics of Scientific Knowledge and Technology (COMEST), UNESCO, 2005.

Chapter 12: We Don't Need No Thought Control ...

1   Li, Pei, and Jourdan, Adam, 'Sleepy Pupils in the Picture at High-Tech Chinese School', Reuters, 17 May 2018, https://uk.reuters.com/article/uk-china-surveillance-education/sleepy-pupils-in-the-picture-at-high-tech-chinese-school-idUKKCN1II128.

2   Hardy, Rich, 'AI in Schools: China's massive and unprecedented education experiment', *New Atlas*, 28 May 2018, https://newatlas.com/china-ai-education-schools-facial-recognition/54786/.

3   England, Rachel, 'Chinese School Uses Facial Recognition to Make Kids Pay Attention', *Engadget*, 17 May 2018, https://www.engadget.com/2018-05-17-chinese-school-facial-recognition-kids-attention.html.

4   Baynes, Chris, 'Chinese Schools Scanning Children's Brains to See If They Are Concentrating', *The Independent*, 15 January 2019, https://www.independent.co.uk/news/world/asia/china-schools-scan-brains-concentration-headbands-children-brainco-focus-a8728951.html; Ye, Yvaine, 'Brain-reading Headsets Trialled on 10,000 Schoolchildren in China', *New Scientist*, 14 January 2019, https://www.newscientist.com/article/2190670-brain-reading-headsets-trialled-on-10000-schoolchildren-in-china/#Echobox=1547505185.

5   Jiangnan, Xian, 'AI Headbands Tracking Student Attention Levels Suspended Amidst Online Controversy', *People's Daily*, 1 November 2019, http://en.people.cn/n3/2019/1101/c90000-9628768.html.

6   See Chapter 9.

7   https://www.brainco.tech/.

8   5Rights Foundation, *Digital Times*, Winter 2019, https://5rightsfoundation.com/uploads/digital-times-pink-for-online-distribution-compressed.pdf.

9   'Russia to Install "Orwell" Facial Recognition Tech in Every School – Vedomosti', *The Moscow Times*, 16 June 2020, https://www.themoscowtimes.com/2020/06/16/russia-to-install-orwell-facial-recognition-tech-in-every-school-vedomosti-a70585.

10 Luxmoore, Matthew, 'Yes, Big Brother IS Watching: Russian Schools Getting Surveillance Systems Called "Orwell"', RFERL, 17 June 2020, https://www.rferl.org/a/russian-schools-getting-surveillance-systems-called-orwell-/30676184.html.

11 Ryan-Mosley, Tate, 'Why 2020 Was a Pivotal, Contradictory Year for Facial Recognition', *Technology Review*, 29 December 2020, https://www.technologyreview.com/2020/12/29/1015563/why-2020-was-a-pivotal-contradictory-year-for-facial-recognition/.

12 Pascu, Luana, 'French Privacy Regulator Finds Facial Recognition Gates in Schools Illegal', *Biometric Update*, 30 October 2019, https://www.biometricupdate.com/201910/french-privacy-regulator-finds-facial-recognition-gates-in-schools-illegal.

13 Reventlow, Nani Jansen, 'Protecting Children's Digital Rights in Schools', Digital Freedom Fund, 30 July 2020, https://digitalfreedomfund.org/protecting-childrens-digital-rights-in-schools.

14 https://www.smoothwall.com/education/monitor/.

15 See their report, *The State of Data 2020*, https://defenddigitalme.org/wp-content/uploads/2020/11/The-state-of-data-2020-v2.2-1.pdf.

16 In February 2020, the New Mexico attorney general launched a case against Google, which it accused of using free Chromebooks distributed to schools around the world as a back door for illegal gathering of children's data, including their surfing habits, passwords and geolocation. Google disputed the claim and the case was later dismissed by a Federal Judge. See: Staff, Nick, 'Google Sued by New Mexico Attorney General for Collecting Student Data Through Chromebooks', *The Verge*, 20 February 2020, https://www.theverge.com/2020/2/20/21145698/google-student-privacy-lawsuit-education-schools-chromebooks-new-mexico-balderas. Algernon, 'Federal Judge Dismisses New Mexico's Lawsuit Claiming Google Gathered Data on Children' September 2020, Las Cruces Sun-News https://eu.lcsun-news.com/story/news/2020/09/28/google-lawsuit-new-mexico-dismissed-gathering-data-children/3562072001/.

17 UN Committee on the Rights of the Child, General Comment No. 25 (2021) on children's rights in relation to the digital environment (21 March 2021).

18 Richard, Édouard, et al., 'Undress or Fail: Instagram's algorithm strong-arms users into showing skin', European Data Journalism Network, https://algorithmwatch.org/en/story/instagram-algorithm-nudity/.

19 The mother of a seven-year-old girl from North Carolina was horrified when she saw her daughter's avatar being raped by two male characters on the platform. Roblox blamed the incident on hackers: 'Roblox Blames "Gang Rape" on Hacker Adding Code to Game', BBC, 18 July 2018, https://www.bbc.co.uk/news/technology-44875920.

20 'Number of Child Gamblers Quadruples in Just Two Years', BBC, 21 November 2018, https://www.bbc.co.uk/news/business-46286945/ ; *Young People & Gambling 2018, A research study among 11-16 year olds in Great Britain*, Gambling Commission, November 2018, https://www.gamblingcommission.gov.uk/news/article/gambling-commission-publishes-new-report-on-children-and-gambling-trends.

21 'Loot Boxes Linked to Problem Gambling in New Research', BBC, 2 April 2021, https://www.bbc.co.uk/news/technology-56614281.

22 Republic of Singapore, Remote Gambling Bill: Second Reading (2014), cited in Close, James, and Lloyd, Joanne, *Lifting the Lid on Loot-Boxes: Chance-Based Purchases in Video Games and the Convergence of Gaming and Gambling*, March 2021, https://www.begambleaware.org/sites/default/files/2021-03/Gaming_and_Gambling_Report_Final.pdf.

23 Chen, Brian X., 'Are Your Children Racking Up Charges From Mobile Games? Here's How to Fight Back', *The New York Times*, 6 February 2019, https://www.nytimes.com/2019/02/06/technology/personaltech/children-charges-mobile-games.html.

24 Close, James, and Lloyd, Joanne, *Lifting the Lid on Loot-Boxes: Chance-Based Purchases in Video Games and the Convergence of Gaming and Gambling*, March 2021, https://www.begambleaware.org/sites/default/files/

2021-03/Gaming_and_Gambling_
Report_Final.pdf, note 22.

25 See, for example, Carr, N., *The
Shallows: How the Internet Is
Changing the Way We Think, Read and
Remember*, Atlantic Books, 2011.

26 Kidron, Baroness, et al., *Disrupted
Childhood: The Cost of Persuasive
Design*, https://5rightsfoundation.
com/static/5Rights-Disrupted-
Childhood.pdf.

27 Carter, B., et al., 'Association Between
Portable Screen-based Media Device
Access or Use and Sleep Outcomes',
JAMA Pediatrics, vol. 170, no. 12,
2016, pp.1202–8. Cited in https://
5rightsfoundation.com/static/5Rights-
Disrupted-Childhood.pdf, fn129.

28 Cited in https://5rightsfoundation.
com/static/5Rights-Disrupted-
Childhood.pdf, fn126.

29 OPEN LETTER FROM JANA
PARTNERS AND CALSTRS
TO APPLE INC., https://
thinkdifferentlyaboutkids.com/letter/.

30 Bridle, James, 'How Peppa Pig
Became a Video Nightmare for
Children', *The Observer*, 17 June
2018, https://www.theguardian.com/
technology/2018/jun/17/peppa-pig-
youtube-weird-algorithms-automated-
content.

31 'Toddler Asks Amazon's Alexa to Play
Song But Gets Porn Instead', *New
York Post*, 30 December 2016, https://
nypost.com/2016/12/30/toddler-asks-
amazons-alexa-to-play-song-but-gets-
porn-instead/.

32 Orphanides, K. G., 'Children's
YouTube Is Still Churning Out Blood,
Suicide and Cannibalism', *Wired*,
23 March 2018, https://www.wired.
co.uk/article/youtube-for-kids-videos-
problems-algorithm-recommend.

33 'Google and YouTube Will Pay Record
$170 Million for Alleged Violations

of Children's Privacy Law', FTC, 4
September 2019, https://www.ftc.gov/
news-events/press-releases/2019/09/
google-youtube-will-pay-record-170-
million-alleged-violations.

34 'Connected Toys Violate European
Consumer Law', 6 December 2016,
https://www.forbrukerradet.no/
siste-nytt/connected-toys-violate-
consumer-laws/.

35 https://epic.org/privacy/kids/EPIC-
IPR-FTC-Genesis-Complaint.
pdf. The organisations included the
Electronic Privacy and Information
Centre, the Campaign for a
Commercial Free Childhood, the
Centre for Digital Democracy, the
Institute for Public Representation
and the Consumers' Union.

36 'German Parents Told to Destroy
Cayla Dolls Over Hacking Fears',
BBC, 17 February 2017, https://
www.bbc.co.uk/news/world-europe-
39002142.

37 'German Doll Ban Illustrates Flaws
in Product Safety Regulation',
17 February 2017, https://www.
forbrukerradet.no/siste-nytt/german-
doll-ban-illustrates-flaws-in-product-
safety-regulation/.

38 https://embodied.com/.

39 Jargon, Julie, 'Pandemic Tantrums?
Enter the Robot Playmate for Kids',
The Wall Street Journal, 4 August
2020, https://www.wsj.com/articles/
pandemic-tantrums-enter-the-robot-
playmate-for-kids-11596542401.

40 Gottsegen, Gordon, 'Embodied
Unveils Moxie, a Robot That Teaches
Kids How to Relate to Humans', 28
April 2020, https://www.builtinla.
com/2020/04/28/embodied-unveils-
moxie.

41 Keach, Sean, 'PURE EVIL: Roblox
kids' game haven for Jihadi, Nazi and
KKK roleplay featuring Twin Tower

bombings and race-hate murders', *The Sun*, 6 July 2018, https://www.thesun.co.uk/tech/6710158/roblox-game-racist-jihad-nazi-kkk-racism-twin-towers-children/.

42 Townsend, Mark, 'How Far Right Uses Video Games and Tech to Lure and Radicalise Teenage Recruits', *The Observer*, 14 February 2021, https://www.theguardian.com/world/2021/feb/14/how-far-right-uses-video-games-tech-lure-radicalise-teenage-recruits-white-supremacists.

43 UNICEF, *The State of the World's Children 2017, Children in a Digital World*, https://www.unicef.org/media/48601/file.

44 Ni, Vincent, 'China Cuts Amount of Time Minors Can Spend Playing

Online Video Games', *The Guardian*, 30 August 2021, https://www.theguardian.com/world/2021/aug/30/china-cuts-amount-of-time-minors-can-spend-playing-video-games.

45 Livingstone, Sonia, and Blu-Ross, Alicia, *Parenting for a Digital Future: How Hopes and Fears about Technology Shape Children's Lives*, Oxford University Press, 2020.

46 https://www.unicef-irc.org/publications/pdf/Children-digital-technology-wellbeing.pdf, p.8, citing Chas Critcher, in Drotner, K., and Livingstone, S. (eds.), *The International Handbook of Children, Media and Culture*, London, Sage, 2008.

Chapter 13: The Backlash

1 See *Report of the Special Rapporteur on the promotion and protection of human rights and fundamental freedoms while countering terrorism*, 21 February 2020.

2 Ibid.

3 Ibid. The UN Special Rapporteur on the promotion and protection of human rights and fundamental freedoms while countering terrorism raised her profound concerns 'about the increased regulatory focus on thought and action in the so-called "pre-criminal" or, more accurately, "pre-terrorist" space'.

4 Dodd, Vikram, and Grierson, Jamie, 'Terrorism Police List Extinction Rebellion as Extremist Ideology', *The Guardian*, 10 January 2020, https://www.theguardian.com/uk-news/2020/jan/10/xr-extinction-rebellion-listed-extremist-ideology-police-prevent-scheme-guidance.

5 See the work of human rights barrister Adam Wagner on human rights reporting in the UK media, https://ukhumanrightsblog.com/category/blog-posts/poor-reporting/.

6 Ibid.

7 Human Rights Watch, *Myths and Facts About the International Criminal Court*, https://www.hrw.org/legacy/campaigns/icc/facts.htm.

8 Castan Centre for Human Rights Law, Monash University, 'Human Rights Act Myth Busters. Myth 3: Judges would use a Human Rights Act to bully politicians into changing laws to comply with human rights', https://www.monash.edu/law/research/centres/castancentre/our-areas-of-work/education/myth-busters/myth-3.

9 Wagner, Adam, 'Catgate: Another myth used to trash human rights', *The Guardian*, 4 October 2011, https://

www.theguardian.com/law/2011/oct/04/theresa-may-wrong-cat-deportation.

10 Aldridge, Alex, 'Can "Physically Ill" David Cameron Find a Cure for his European Law Allergyy?', *The Guardian*, 6 May 2011, https://www.theguardian.com/law/2011/may/06/david-cameron-european-law-allergy.

11 Boyle, Frankie, 'David Cameron Used "Swarm" Instead of "Plague" in Case It Implied That God Had Sent the Migrants', *The Guardian*, 3 August 2015, https://www.theguardian.com/uk-news/commentisfree/2015/aug/03/cameron-swarm-plague-god-migrants-calais.

12 For example, the murder of Alexander Litvinenko by polonium poisoning in London in 2006.

13 'Zeid Warns Against Populists and Demagogues in Europe and US', OHCHR, 5 September 2016, https://www.ohchr.org/EN/NewsEvents/Pages/DisplayNews.aspx?NewsID=20452.

14 Sengupta, Somini, and Cumming-Bruce, Nick, 'Zeid Ra'ad al-Hussein, Top Human Rights Official, Won't Seek a Second Term', *The New York Times*, 20 December 2017, https://www.nytimes.com/2017/12/20/world/un-human-rights-al-hussein.html.

15 As former Google ethicist Tristan Harris put it in the 2020 documentary *The Social Dilemma*, 'If you're not paying for the product, you are the product.'

16 'Hackable Humans and Digital Dictators: Q&A with Yuval Noah Harari', Al Jazeera, 2018.

17 *Cambridge English Dictionary*.

18 Ibid.

19 Arendt, Hannah, *The Human Condition*, The University of Chicago Press, 1998, 2nd edn, p.322.

20 Cave, Stephen, 'There's No Such Thing as Free Will: But we're better off believing in it anyway', *The Atlantic*, June 2016, https://www.theatlantic.com/magazine/archive/2016/06/theres-no-such-thing-as-free-will/480750/.

21 Gholipour, Bahar, 'A Famous Argument Against Free Will Has Been Debunked', *The Atlantic*, September 2019, https://www.theatlantic.com/health/archive/2019/09/free-will-bereitschaftspotential/597736/.

22 See his books *Homo Deus* and *21 Lessons for the 21st Century*.

23 https://inventory.algorithmwatch.org/.

24 In its 2021 report, the digital rights campaign group Defend Digital Me explored the metaphors we use around data and their impact on the way we think about it and design policies on data protection: *The Words We Use in Data Policy: Putting People Back in the Picture*, https://defenddigitalme.org/research/words-data-policy/.

Chapter 14: Freeing Our Minds

1 Commencement address by Apple CEO Tim Cook, 16 June 2019, https://news.stanford.edu/2019/06/16/remarks-tim-cook-2019-stanford-commencement/.

2 Orwell, George, *Nineteen Eighty-Four*, Penguin Modern Classics, 2000, p.223.

3 Ibid., p.218.

4 Commencement address by Apple CEO Tim Cook, 16 June 2019,

https://news.stanford.edu/2019/06/16/remarks-tim-cook-2019-stanford-commencement/.

5 Report of the UN Special Rapporteur on the promotion and protection of freedom of opinion and expression, David Kaye, on surveillance and human rights, 28 May 2019, A/HRC/41/35, https://undocs.org/A/HRC/41/35.

6 Research report on artistic freedom of expression, UN Special Rapporteur on the promotion and protection of freedom of opinion and expression, David Kaye, A/HRC/44/49/Add.2, 24 July 2020, https://undocs.org/en/A/HRC/44/49/Add.2.

7 Fitton, Daniel, 'The Rise of Dark Web Design: How sites manipulate you into clicking', *The Conversation*, 29 September 2021, https://theconversation.com/the-rise-of-dark-web-design-how-sites-manipulate-you-into-clicking-168347.

8 *Georgel and Georgeta Stoicescu v. Romania* (application no. 9718/03), judgment of 26 July 2011.

9 Baron, Zach, 'The Conscience of Silicon Valley', *GQ*, 24 August 2020, https://www.gq.com/story/jaron-lanier-tech-oracle-profile.

10 See, for example, *Carter v. Russia*, 20914/07, 21 September 2021.

11 Kind, Carly, 'The Term "Ethical AI" Is Finally Starting to Mean Something', *VentureBeat*, 23 August 2020, https://venturebeat.com/2020/08/23/the-term-ethical-ai-is-finally-starting-to-mean-something/.

12 Hern, Alex, 'Google Threatens to Leave Australia – but its poker face is slipping', *The Guardian*, 22 January 2021, https://www.theguardian.com/technology/2021/jan/22/google-threatens-leave-australia-but-poker-face-slipping.

13 Hern, Alex, 'Facebook Says It May Quit Europe Over Ban on Sharing Data with US', *The Guardian*, 22 September 2020, https://www.theguardian.com/technology/2020/sep/22/facebook-says-it-may-quit-europe-over-ban-on-sharing-data-with-us.

14 *The Right to Privacy in the Digital Age*, A/HRC/48/31, 13 September 2021.

15 *The Age of Digital Interdependence*, report of the UN Secretary-General's High-level Panel on Digital Cooperation, 2020, https://www.un.org/en/pdfs/DigitalCooperation-report-for%20web.pdf.

16 Shaheed, Ahmed, *Freedom of Thought*, https://www.ohchr.org/Documents/Issues/Religion/A_76_380_AUV.docx.

17 Ibid.

18 Declaration by the Committee of Ministers on the manipulative capabilities of algorithmic processes (Adopted by the Committee of Ministers on 13 February 2019 at the 1337th meeting of the Ministers' Deputies), https://search.coe.int/cm/pages/result_details.aspx?ObjectId=090000168092dd4b.

19 Stokel-Walker, Chris, 'Britain Tamed Big Tech and Nobody Noticed', *Wired*, 2 September 2021, https://www.wired.co.uk/article/age-appropriate-design-code-big-tech?utm_source=pocket-newtab-global-en-GB.

20 Horne, Felix, 'Mass Arrests, "Brainwashing" Threaten Ethiopia's Reform Agenda', Human Rights Watch, 20 October 2018, https://www.hrw.org/news/2018/10/20/mass-arrests-brainwashing-threaten-ethiopias-reform-agenda.

21 WiDS podcast: https://web.archive.org/web/20201207193031/https:/

/www.widsconference.org/timnit-gebru.html.

22 Birhane, Abeba, 'Algorithmic Colonisation of Africa', *The Elephant*, 21 August 2020, https://www.theelephant.info/long-reads/2020/08/21/algorithmic-colonisation-of-africa/.

23 Wodajo's research can be found here: https://iwe.unisg.ch/en/personenverzeichnis/50cc6930-fdf3-4b51-9adb-96793e1dff76 and https://www.afronomicslaw.org/symposia.

24 Colleen Sinclair, Associate Professor of Social Psychology at Mississippi State University, provides tips on spotting and responding to misinformation here: https://theconversation.com/10-ways-to-spot-online-misinformation-132246.

25 https://applymagicsauce.com.

26 Wagenseil, Paul, 'A Group of Teens Defeated Instagram Tracking with this Clever Trick', *Tom's Guide*, 3 February 2020, https://www.tomsguide.com/news/teens-fool-instagram-tracking-shmoocon2020.

27 https://glitchcharity.co.uk/.

28 https://freedom.to/.

29 Laziuk, Estelle, 'iOS 14.5 Opt-in Rate – Daily Updates Since Launch', *Flurry*, 29 April 2021, https://www.flurry.com/blog/ios-14-5-opt-in-rate-att-restricted-app-tracking-transparency-worldwide-us-daily-latest-update/.

30 Wong, Julia Carrie, 'The Viral Selfie App ImageNet Roulette Seemed Fun – until it called me a racist slur', *The Guardian*, 18 September 2019, https://www.theguardian.com/technology/2019/sep/17/imagenet-roulette-asian-racist-slur-selfie.

31 Rea, Naomi, 'How ImageNet Roulette, an Art Project That Went Viral by Exposing Facial Recognition's Biases, Is Changing People's Minds About AI', Artnet, 23 September 2019, https://news.artnet.com/art-world/imagenet-roulette-trevor-paglen-kate-crawford-1658305.

32 www.ajl.org.

33 https://whotargets.me/en/.

34 In 2012, the United Nations Human Rights Council recognised this in a resolution on the promotion, protection and enjoyment of human rights on the internet: https://undocs.org/A/HRC/20/L.13.

35 Privacy International, Panoptykon Foundation, Open Rights Group, Bits of Freedom, Digitale Gesellschaft, digitalcourage, La Quadrature du Net and Coalizione Italiana per le Libertà e i Diritti civili are all taking part in a wider campaign that urges the ad tech industry to #StopSpyingOnUs.

INDEX